T0182130

Spatial Visualization and Professional Competence

Andrew Paquette

Spatial Visualization and Professional Competence

The Development of Proficiency Among
Digital Artists

 Springer

Andrew Paquette, PhD
CGMT
NHTV Breda University of Applied
    Sciences
Breda, Noord-Brabant, The Netherlands

ISBN 978-3-030-08213-0   ISBN 978-3-319-91289-9   (eBook)
https://doi.org/10.1007/978-3-319-91289-9

This Springer imprint is published by the registered company Springer Nature Switzerland AG
The registered company address is: Gewerbestrasse 11, 6330 Cham, Switzerland

Contents

List of Figures

List of Tables

Abstract

The teaching of digital artists has received ongoing criticism from industry sources, who feel that graduates are rarely well prepared for employment. This is a problem for students when they seek employment, for employers who must hire qualified digital artists, and for the reputation of educational institutions that provide instruction in this domain.

Students from the Netherlands' International Game Architecture and Design (IGAD) visual arts programme participated in research designed to investigate how proficiency develops in the technical and creative discipline of digital art. This study used an exploratory mixed methods design that triangulated archival data on 625 digital art students, who have attended IGAD with qualitative data collected from 20 current students, 5 digital art supervisors and 5 employed IGAD graduates. A mixed methods design was chosen so that historical performance could be compared with data collected directly from student participants, particularly on the subject of how prior experience influenced later development.

Student participants provided information relevant to their learning process, industry supervisors evaluated student work against professional standards, and employed graduates provided a perspective on the transition from student to industry practice. Data collected for the quantitative study was in the form of archival records regarding prior experience and later performance. The qualitative study utilised learning logs, progress reports, project files and interviews with all participants. Correlation and analysis of variance (ANOVA) tests were used in the quantitative phase of the study. Case study analysis was used for the qualitative phases of the study.

Based on the data gathered, visualisation of surface deformation and topology are obstacles to developing proficiency in the digital art specialty of NURBS modelling. Student digital artists developed proficiency as NURBS modellers through three specific types of visualisation skills. These allowed them to become proficient rapidly and produce work that showed the hallmarks of professional practice in the digital art.

This research adds to existing work on spatial visualisation, threshold concepts and the development of expertise by demonstrating how a type of spatial visualisation can function as a threshold obstacle to the development of proficiency and expertise. The original contribution to knowledge is that visualisation of surface deformation is shown by this research to be a threshold obstacle to developing proficiency in the digital art specialty of NURBS modelling.

Keywords Assessment · Computer graphics · Expertise · Industry
Proficiency · NURBS · Spatial visualisation · Technical education
Threshold concepts · Topology · Transfer

Chapter 1
Introduction

This is a study about the nature of proficiency in digital art as a professional practice, how it is developed in an educational setting, and how teaching practitioners assess developing proficiency. Study participants were recruited from a digital art training programme that is situated within the norms of professional practice found in the computer graphics industry, making it an appropriate subject for the research questions posed in this study (p. 8). This study is about proficiency in a specific commercial industry: what it is, and how it is developed, measured and evaluated. It is situated within a particular domain of professional and artistic practice, and within an institution, department and curriculum that prepares students for that practice.

The Computer Graphics (CG) industry employs digital artists who work with 2D and 3D imaging software to create graphic elements for special effects in feature films, video games, military simulations, and industrial visualisations. Digital artists must be proficient to fill industry positions, yet university programmes designed to educate digital artists are notorious among industry professionals for producing inadequately prepared graduates (Flaxman 2003; Livingstone and Hope 2011). Although secondary school graduates eagerly apply for admission to digital arts programmes available around the world, few of their graduates successfully enter the industry as digital artists.

My goal in making this investigation is to observe digital art students in an educational setting to learn how they develop industry-standard proficiency. If this process can be better understood, it may be possible to restructure curricula so that digital arts programmes more adequately prepare graduates for professional work in the industry. This would increase the number of employable graduates and qualified working professionals. Both universities and industries benefit from a larger pool of proficient graduates; therefore, the results of this study have implications for curricula design, learning studies, proficiency research and the local and international digital arts industry.

© Springer Nature Switzerland AG 2018
A. Paquette, *Spatial Visualization and Professional Competence*,
https://doi.org/10.1007/978-3-319-91289-9_1

1.1   Conflict Between Academic and Workplace Learning

Historically, some industries have preferred workplace learning to university education. For instance, during the Industrial Revolution, scorn for university-trained engineers was so great that independent training centres were created by the industry as substitutes for university education (Wellens 1959). This was due to a preference for 'practical' rather than 'college-trained' employees among employers (Musgrave 1966). The same reaction found in these older technical education studies is visible in the domain of digital art, where new technology has created problems for educators in higher education (McCracken 2006).

It is implicit in the context of modern competency-based standards endorsed by the UK government (Blackwell et al. 2001; Tight 1998) and accountability requirements in career and technical education set by professional associations (Castellano and Stringfield 2003; Hargraves 2000; IGDA 2008) that workplace education should fulfil unmet industry needs. This is reflected in a pair of government reports published in the UK, known as the Dearing Report and the Fryer Report, each of which supports more workplace-centric education (Blackwell et al. 2001; Tight 1998). The focus in these reports and the government initiatives that inspired them is on improving the quality of technical education by bringing students into the workplace (with internships) or by helping educators improve the quality of education in universities by providing industry-specific recommendations.

1.1.1   Digital Effects Industry Reaction to Digital Art Education Programmes

According to the U.S. Bureau of Labor Statistics (2012), employers of digital artists do not require a college degree from applicants, but they look for workers who have a good portfolio and strong technical skills. Artist demo reels provide a way to measure the success of digital art instruction. A demo reel is a collection of edited video clips that represents a digital artist's best work. Unlike in other professions, an artist's CV and educational background become relevant only if the demo reel is sufficient to demonstrate that the artist can meet industry quality standards. However, 'despite a growing market overall...hiring managers report that they must sort through hundreds of demo reels before finding a single qualified applicant' (Flaxman 2003, p.1). Based on feedback from industry sources, few digital art programmes produce graduates that meet professional standards (Ip 2012). Schools that provide inadequate instruction are described as 'get rich quick institutions' that ignore industry standards and teach software instead, resulting in 'completely unprepared' graduates (King et al. 2008, p. 1). Graduates find it difficult to find entry-level jobs because their qualifications 'fall short' of industry standards (McCracken 2006, p. 1), prompting industry experts to call for digital art programmes that include a core set of competencies (King et al. 2008).

In the UK, a review of game design and computer graphics programmes was conducted by Livingstone and Hope (2011). The review was conducted at the request of the UK Minister for Culture, Communications and Creative Industries. The results describe significant shortfalls in the way educators in the UK prepare undergraduates for careers as digital artists. The authors point out that despite a large number of available university programmes relevant to digital artists, graduates have poor job prospects due to flaws in their courses (Livingstone and Hope 2011). The problem is even more urgent because computer graphics tools and techniques migrate from entertainment-related industries to other industries that use the same technology, such as medical research, military simulation, education and product visualisation. Livingstone and Hope's conclusion that digital artists are ill-prepared for careers in the industry is consistent with the findings of McCracken (2006), who claims that 'with the reality of poor job placement, it is clear that the present model of [digital art] education is insufficient for its graduates' (p. 9).

Poor placement of digital art programme graduates in industry jobs is a well-known problem in this education sector. An example of this is provided by the rapidly growing UK industry, where artists are hired from overseas due to local skill shortages (Livingstone and Hope 2011). This is consistent with Flaxman's (2003) claim that only one out of 'hundreds' of applicants in the U.S. and abroad is qualified to work in this industry. The reason jobs remain unfilled despite willing applicants is that 'even entry-level positions have extremely high standards' (McCracken 2006, p. 8). That these jobs are left vacant despite the number of programmes graduating students in the UK every year implies that UK universities are not providing their digital arts graduates with the skills needed to be employable in the industry.

The interests of educators and students are ill-served by programmes that produce graduates who are not qualified for their target profession (Cranmer 2006). As Livingstone and Hope (2011) report, after interviewing over half of the UK's visual effects and video game industry employers, there is real dissatisfaction with the local talent pool. To improve education in the computer graphics sector, educators need to address the problems found by prospective employers. However, the approach to a solution is not consistent due to differing perspectives on the problem.

1.1.2 Conflicting Explanations for Digital Art Education Shortfalls

A study conducted in the UK analysed the curricula of 242 undergraduate game-orientated programmes and compared them with recommendations from the industry. The study found that the curricula in digital art programmes rarely coincide with industry expectations (Ip 2012). This was unexpected because digital art programmes are designed to produce work-ready graduates for industry, yet in the majority of cases do not incorporate advice from industry professionals and then produce unsatisfactory results. Why do so many digital art programmes fail to follow industry recommendations when designing their curricula?

McCracken (2006) suggests that digital art programmes should be subdivided so that 3D art and animation are not taught together as part of the same programme. He emphasises that in separating these disciplines, schools should remember that educating digital artists is as much about art as technology. In contrast, the thrust of recommendations from Livingstone and Hope (2011) is that digital art students have a deficient understanding of science, technology, engineering and math (STEM) and must therefore be encouraged to study STEM courses. This conclusion is almost the opposite of McCracken's art-centric recommendation, thus putting the two proposed remedies in conflict. If schools were to use their resources to emphasise STEM classes, those same resources cannot be applied to enhancing the art-centric classes advocated by McCracken.

The International Game Developer's Association (IGDA) published a curriculum framework for educators in 2008 to help steer university curricula in a direction more compatible with internationally-recognised industry requirements. While acknowledging that no curriculum can equally serve the needs of all industry members, it provides general guidelines for game programmers, designers and digital artists. For artists, the IGDA emphasised that teaching students visual design principles in classes such as drawing, painting and sculpture was more important than training students to use specific software applications (IGDA 2008). This emphasis on core art training instead of technology is representative of a dichotomy found when reading about education for digital artists in the literature.

According to McCracken (2006) the demands of learning digital art technology are so daunting that a four-year bachelor's programme does not provide enough time to become proficient in any given specialty, let alone provide the artistic sensibility needed to make good use of one's technical skills. On this subject he writes, 'So many courses were deemed necessary that a bachelor's student would have to attend school full-time for eight years before graduating!' (p. 9).

Ip's study (2012) of 242 game development programmes in the UK found that courses designed for visual artists only rarely matched course recommendations by IGDA or SKILLSET in the UK. For instance, in the first year of undergraduate art programmes, a maximum of 24% of taught curriculum content matched recommendations from the industry. This was particularly surprising for art programmes where art classes might be expected to be the focus on the basis of industry recommendations from the UK and abroad. The same thing was found in engineering courses where educators were

> required to reduce the total number of credits to graduation, often resulting in fewer credits available for graphics instruction. Secondly, pressure was exerted on graphics educators to include additional topics such as CAD, design, and creativity in their introductory courses. (Sorby 1999, p. 21)

Sorby (1999) and Ip's (2012) findings highlight a problem described by McCracken (2006). Any attempt to obtain a broad education as a digital artist is bound to be difficult and is unlikely to succeed because students are inevitably given too many subjects to master in depth in the time available (McCracken 2006). How then can an undergraduate digital art programme best prepare its students for careers in the various CG industries that employ digital artists around the world? A way to better understand this question is to look back at the origins of the CG industry and how early adopters of CG technology became proficient in its use.

1.1.3 Influence of the CG Industry on Education Options

The modern era of CG images in film started in approximately 1989, with the release of the film *The Abyss*, directed by James Cameron. The popularity of CG visual effects in the film and video game industries in the early 1990s created a need for skilled artists to work in the medium, but at the time (as today) the number of skilled digital artists was insufficient to supply the demand (King et al. 2008). Each technical innovation added to the possible level of sophistication and quality, thus raising expectations for digital artists and increasing the number of specialties available to learn. For example, hair and cloth simulations became separate specialties when advances in technology made this distinction possible. This makes the field of digital art progressively more fragmented and unwieldy for students and educators.

Although updated CG technology has made new things possible, it does not necessarily make them easier to do, nor does it always take the place of something else. For these reasons, CG projects become more complex and more work overall, because there are more elements to keep track of. New technology does replace old technology in many ways, thus making it hypothetically easier to accomplish tasks that were more difficult when using older software. However, the new technology tends to render the old technology and the tasks associated with it obsolete, while adding complexity that requires more work to exploit. Therefore, the outcome is higher quality and more variety in the type of effects that are possible, but no net gain in efficiency.

1.1.4 Differences Between First-and Current-Generation Digital Art Education

Artists who want to work in digital special effects must learn how to use the relevant equipment and software. For most of the 1990s, three companies made the dominant animation software in the feature film industry: Alias, Wavefront and SoftImage. All three applications ran only on UNIX computers manufactured by Silicon Graphics Incorporated (SGI). The popular SGI Indigo2 workstation was originally priced at over $100,000 when loaded with any one of these applications (Pahler et al. 1994; Seastrum et al. 1994).[1] Among less powerful PC- and Mac-based alternatives, the

---

[1] This price is converted from Japanese Yen.

most popular was Autodesk's DOS-based 3DStudio software. It was used primarily for architectural visualisation and games, and released in 1990 at a price of about $4000. These prices, even for the comparatively inexpensive 3DStudio, represented significant investments for anyone without a serious interest in the medium, particularly students, and that does not take into account the time or effort it would have taken to learn how to use the software.

Visual effects artists and animators with studio jobs had access to equipment and training at their workplaces, but others did not have this luxury. At the same time, the world's first web browser, Mosaic, had only just been launched (in 1993), and the large Internet-based support structure of user forums, developer FAQs and assistance chat lines that exists today had not yet been developed. Any person who wanted to make 3D digital art for video games or film in the early nineties had very few options beyond making a significant financial investment and then learning on his or her own or via on-the-job training at an employer that was switching from 2D to 3D animation. The need for affordable digital art education was partly answered by the first degree-granting digital art bachelor's programmes, which were introduced in the UK in 1989 and the US in 1994 (Comininos et al. 2009; Digipen 2011), but these two programmes were too few, too small and too unknown to deal with demand.

The difference between learning computer-aided design (CAD) and animation software in the nineties and today goes beyond lack of access to well-designed training materials and expensive software and hardware. Many of the people who learned digital art techniques in the nineties had at least one significant advantage not enjoyed by contemporary students. CAD users in the 1990s typically had degrees in architecture or mechanical engineering and used the technology to test the manufacturability of existing designs, as opposed to making the entire design in the software (Brown 2009). For them, CAD skills were not the basis for their employment, but one of many tools they used in their work to accomplish goals they understood from years of experience in their field.

At Industrial Light & Magic (ILM), employees trained as 2D animators or practical visual effects artists were already employed as professional artists when they were provided access to digital art software and training. At Disney, artists with decades of experience timing, posing and animating cartoon characters merely had to adapt a new tool to their existing knowledge of animation. They did not have to learn the principles of animation from scratch or pay for expensive new equipment (McCracken 2006). Early adopters of CAD and 3D animation software were learning a new tool to enhance careers that had already developed to the point of proficiency or expertise. In contrast, many contemporary students enrol in undergraduate digital art programmes as soon as they graduate from high school. When they enter a digital art programme, they have no prior experience as working professionals, nor any prior supervised training at a university.

The difference between these two generations of learners is that the first generation of digital artists had to acquire knowledge of new tools in service of existing expertise, but the current generation must acquire the knowledge and skills of an artist at the same time as they learn how to use computer-based tools. Tool knowledge may be all that is required for individuals who have well-developed art skills, but an education focussed purely on technical know-how does not suffice for students who have not yet developed the knowledge and skills that are generic to most artistic endeavours, such as drawing, colour, composition, design, story-telling and style (Ip 2012; McCracken 2006). In engineering specialties, the problem with CAD-based learning is similar; it is more difficult to teach essential elements of the design process while emphasising the use of software tools whose software-related constraints inhibit designers. For instance, CAD's role eliminates the stages of sketching and redesigning that are seen in the traditional model. If students use CAD without first working through the conceptual stages using traditional paper and pencil methods, they run the risk of deciding on an idea and spending time on creating a virtual model of something that in the end may not be viable for many reasons (Brown 2009).

This is a new problem for educators because first-generation CAD or animation software users were professional engineers, architects and animators, not software users. The importance of this should not be underestimated; the difference between the skills possessed by an animator and those of an architect is less about the tools they use than their knowledge of animation vs. architecture. To equate an artist's tool of choice, such as a given CAD application, with his or her principal skill would be like claiming that a comic book artist and a carpenter belong to the same profession because they both use pencils. CAD and animation software have many tools in common but designers and animators use them differently based on the needs of their respective professions. Domain knowledge is what separates them, and domain knowledge is not the same as tool knowledge. Based on recommendations found in the literature (IGDA 2008; McCracken 2006) a successful bachelors-level educational programme for digital art students would have to provide both domain knowledge and tool knowledge to produce proficiency.

1.2   Proficiency as a Precursor to Professional Expertise

1.2.1   Three Views of Proficiency

There are three principal views in the study of proficiency: (1) proficiency in a discipline is a required precursor to the development of expertise (Alexander 2003), (2) proficiency is synonymous with expertise (Shanteau et al. 2002) and (3) expertise can be developed rapidly in creative domains, without first developing proficiency (Simonton 2014). Definitions of proficiency and expertise are especially problematic in creative and industry contexts, such as in the digital art industry, which is the subject here. These are discussed in greater detail in Chap. 2 (p. 13)

1.2.2 Performance-Based Definitions of Proficiency and Expertise

The question of whether students can develop genuine expertise prior to entering industry becomes important only because the literature of proficiency and expertise sometimes conflates performance with expertise (Ruthsatz et al. 2014; Simonton 2012) and at other times ignores performance when broad knowledge or experience is absent (Alexander 2003; Chi et al. 1988; Dreyfus and Dreyfus 2005).

One indicator that a student project is proficient is if it is fit for use. 'Fitness for use' describes a work product that can be used in a professional context. To meet the fitness-for-use standard, work must respond to the needs of the end-user (Lessinger 1976). In the case of digital artist graduates, the end-user is their eventual employer, so it is the industry standard that governs whether work is fit-for-use. That is the standard used here, for the purpose of determining whether student work is proficient.

1.3 Research Questions Overview

The following primary research question was formulated to guide this investigation of proficiency development among visual art students enrolled at The International Game Architecture and Design (IGAD) programme at the Nationale hogeschool voor tourisme en verkeer (NHTV) University of Applied Sciences, located in the Netherlands:

1. What are the principal contributing factors to crossing the threshold between novice and proficient performance among digital art students?

The following secondary questions were designed based on research that indicated the value of validating that proficiency had been achieved, exploring spatial visualisation as a potential contributor to proficiency, and inconsistencies between two problem types in digital art that could help illustrate the relationship of spatial visualisation to the development of proficiency:

a. What criteria are used to determine student performance levels?
b. What is the relationship between spatial ability or spatial visualisation and development of proficiency among digital art students?
c. How does the NURBS problem differ from the polygon problem?

The first question, 'What are the principal contributing factors to crossing the threshold between novice and proficient performance among digital art students?' is designed to address how proficiency is developed in this domain. During the learning process, students are given information in lectures, demonstrations and critiques and they participate in workshops both in and out of class. In addition to this they do most of their project work at home. Where and how in this process does proficiency develop? Is it gradual or sudden? Why do some students develop proficiency and others do not? In all of these questions, the data this research intends to elicit is relevant to the primary question 'How is proficiency developed among digital artists?'

The second question, 'What criteria are used to determine student performance levels?' is necessary to establish whether students develop a credible level of proficiency based on definitions current in the literature. If not, it is difficult to refute criticism that students cannot develop genuine proficiency in the time span of the study.

The third question, 'What is the relationship between spatial ability or spatial visualisation and development of proficiency among digital art students?' is asked to investigate whether there is a correlation between test performance (spatial ability) and academic performance (project grades) as is suggested by the literature. In at least one study, conducted at Coventry University (Osmond et al. 2009), the only one found during this research that also used digital art students as participants, no correlation was found. Because of similarities between the Coventry and IGAD students, this question is designed to investigate whether there is a quality inherent to digital art-related tasks that explains why the test results at Coventry do not match results found elsewhere.

The fourth question, 'How does the NURBS problem differ from the polygon problem?' relates to two projects given to student participants in this study, described in more detail in the methodology chapter (p. 51). This question is asked due to the possibility that there is something about the difference between the two projects that will help determine (1) how students become proficient or (2) a method for predicting future performance in digital art-related tasks.

1.4 Conclusion

The problem of education for digital artists in the CG industry is both serious and widespread in the UK (Livingstone and Hope 2011) and elsewhere (Flaxman 2003; McCracken 2006). The goal for this research is to have a better understanding of how proficiency is developed among student digital artists. To accomplish that goal, this study seeks to observe the first transition to a proficient level of performance made by students enrolled in a digital art programme. There are examples in the literature of after-the-fact conjecture regarding where these boundaries lie (Dreyfus and Dreyfus 2005; Grabner 2014), but very little in the form of prospective research designed to observe as the transition takes place. Due to the widespread acceptance of the broad knowledge-based expertise standard, this study uses the broad knowledge standard as a starting point for the investigation. The overall thrust of this research is to improve understanding of how proficiency is developed, but it also seeks to better understand the meaning of proficiency and expertise, the role of spatial visualisation in developing proficiency as a digital artist and how spatial visualisation testing instruments affect our understanding of spatial visualisation.

1.5   Chapter Previews

In Chap. 2 (p. 7), literature relevant to this study is examined in greater depth. The terms 'expertise' and 'proficiency' are defined and the way they are understood to develop is investigated. Threshold concepts are presented as a possible explanation for rapid transitions to proficiency. An overview of this literature is presented to provide perspective on the methodology used. After this, theories related to possible connections between spatial visualisation ability and the development of proficiency are examined as potential explanations for observations made of digital art students.

Chapter 3 (p. 41) describes the methodology used in this study, a mixed-methods exploratory design with an emphasis on qualitative data. The principal body of qualitative data was collected during a nine-week class on a specialty of digital art known as 'NURBS modelling' (p. 48), during which several students became proficient. Quantitative data on between 51 and 625 students was collected from archival sources at the academy where the study was performed. These data were used to triangulate with and create context for the qualitative data. Twenty student participants were observed during the study, took questionnaires after the course was concluded, and were interviewed. In addition, five industry experts were recruited to assess selected student work against an industry standard and five employed graduates were interviewed to provide perspective on their development after graduation.

Chapters 4 (p. 81) and 5 (p. 97) present findings from the study. They are divided based on the first, quantitative, phase of the study (Chap. 4), and the following two qualitative phases (Chap. 5). These findings revealed that some students developed proficiency as NURBS modellers during the study period, whether quantitative measures predicted or reflected their performance, how experts have assessed their work relative to academic assessors and how graduates described their own progress from being students to becoming employed professionals (and sometimes experts).

Chapter 6 (p. 97) discusses the findings in the context of the literature presented in Chap. 2 (p. 7). The focus is on the development of proficiency and the role played by spatial visualisation, followed by threshold concepts and education. In this chapter, agreements and disagreements are noted, as well as any new avenues of investigation that may have been revealed by the findings. I argue that spatial visualisation plays a critical role in the development of proficiency in NURBS modelling tasks.

In Chap. 7 (p. 183), conclusions based on this research are presented. Although this research was initially conducted for the purpose of better understanding the development of proficiency among digital art students, data collected for this study is also relevant to spatial visualisation and threshold concepts. In this chapter, I discuss how NURBS modelling tasks require a different kind of spatial visualisation than is typically tested for in spatial ability tests and how this visualisation skill can perform a gatekeeper role in the development of proficiency that resembles the role played by threshold concepts.

References

Alexander PA (2003) The development of expertise: the journey from acclimation to proficiency. Educ Researcher 32(8):10–14

Blackwell A, Bowes L, Harvey L, Hesketh AJ, Knight PT (2001) Transforming work experience in higher education. Br Educ Res J 27(3):269–285

Brown P (2009) CAD: do computers aid the design process after all? Intersect 2(1):52–66

Castellano M, Stringfield S (2003) Secondary Career and Technical Education and Comprehensive School Reform: Implications for Research and Practice. Rev Educ Res 73(2):231–272

Chi MTH, Glaser R, Farr MJ (1988) The nature of expertise. Lawrence Erlbaum Associates, Publishers, Hillsdale, NJ

Comininos P, McLoughlin L, Anderson EF (2009) Educating technophile artists: experiences from a highly successful computer animation undergraduate programme. Paper presented at the SIGGRAPH ASIA'09: SIGGRAPH ASIA 2009 educators program, Yokohama, Japan

Cranmer S (2006) Enhancing graduate employability: best intentions and mixed outcomes. Stud High Educ 31(2):169–184

Digipen (2011) About page. Retrieved from https://www.digipen.edu/about/

Dreyfus HL, Dreyfus SE (2005) Peripheral vision: expertise in real world contexts. Organ Stud 26(5):779–792. https://doi.org/10.1177/0170840605053102

Flaxman T (2003) The future of computer animation education. Paper presented at the SIGGRAPH'03, San Diego

Grabner RH (2014) The role of intelligence for performance in the prototypical expertise domain of chess. Intelligence 45(0):26–33. https://doi.org/10.1016/j.intell.2013.07.023

Hargraves G (2000) The review of vocational qualifications, 1985 to 1986: an analysis of its role in the development of competence-based vocational qualifications in England and Wales. Br J Educ Stud 48(3):285–308

IGDA (2008) IGDA curriculum framework. Retrieved from https://c.ymcdn.com/sites/www.igda.org/resource/collection/0DBC56DC-B7CB-4140-BF3A-22A9E92EC63A/igda_curriculum_framework_2008.pdf

Ip B (2012) Fitting the needs of an industry: an examination of games design, development, and art courses in the UK. ACM Trans Comput Educ 12(2):1–35

King R, Weiss B, Buyyala P, Sehgal M (2008) Bridging the gap between education and professional production. Paper presented at the ACM SIGGRAPH ASIA 2008 educators programme, Singapore

Lessinger LM (1976) Quality control and quality assurance in education. J Educ finance 1(4):503–515

Livingstone I, Hope A (2011) Next generation transforming the UK into the world's leading talent hub for the video games and visual effects industries. Retrieved from http://www.nesta.org.uk/sites/default/files/next_gen.pdf

McCracken CR (2006) Issues in computer graphics education. Paper presented at the ACM SIGGRAPH 2006 educators program—international conference on computer graphics and interactive techniques, Boston

Musgrave PW (1966) Constant factors in the demand for technical education: 1860–1960. Br J Educ Stud 16(2):123–137

Osmond J, Bull K, Tovey M (2009) Threshold concepts and the transport and product design curriculum: reports of research in progress. Art, Des Commun High Educ 8(2):169–175

Pahler A, Kojima Y, Matsuzaki T (1994) PC workstations in crystallography. Nihon Kessho Gakkaishi 36(Supplement P 113):113. http://dx.doi.org/10.5940/jcrsj.36.Supplement_113

Ruthsatz J, Ruthsatz K, Stephens KR (2014) Putting practice into perspective: child prodigies as evidence of innate talent. Intelligence 45(1):60–65. https://doi.org/10.1016/j.intell.2013.08.003

Seastrum C, Cutchin J, Bennett D, Prue J, Tucker Z, DiSapio V, Frankel L, Randall R, Tsao J, Bobbitt B, Watkins RJ, Brookhart LL (1994) U.S. trade shifts in selected industries: merchandise. (2924). U.S. International Trade Commission, Washington, DC

Shanteau J, Weiss DJ, Thomas RP, Pounds JC (2002) Performance-based assessment of expertise: how to decide if someone is an expert or not. Eur J Oper Res 136(2):253–263

Simonton DK (2012) Foresight, insight, oversight, and hindsight in scientific discovery: how sighted were Galileo's telescopic sightings? Psychol Aesthetics, Creativity, Arts 6(3):243–254. https://doi.org/10.1037/a0027058243

Simonton DK (2014) Thomas Edison's creative career: the multilayered trajectory of trials, errors, failures, and triumphs. Psychol Aesthetics, Creativity, Arts 9(1):2–24

Sorby SA (1999) Developing 3-D spatial visualization skills. Eng Des Graph J 63(2):11

Tight M (1998) Education, education, education! the vision of lifelong learning in the Kennedy, Dearing and Fryer reports. Oxford Rev Educ 24(4):473–485

U.S. Bureau of Labor Statistics (Producer) (2012, 4 June 2013) Occupational outlook handbook 2012–2013 edition, multimedia artists and animators. Retrieved from http://www.bls.gov/ooh/arts-and-design/multimedia-artists-and-animators.htm

Wellens J (1959) The anti-intellectual tradition in the west. Br J Educ Stud 8(1):22–28

Chapter 2
Literature Review

2.1 Chapter Overview: The Transition to Proficiency

Definitions of proficiency and expertise are sometimes conflated, depending on the criteria used. Because proficiency and expertise studies both define levels of achievement, they are explored side-by-side for insights into skill development. This review will show that while proficiency and expertise are defined in the literature, thresholds between them are rarely discussed and causative factors in development are largely inferred from after-the-fact interview data rather than direct observation. Two themes that emerge from the literature are that spatial visualisation may be a contributing factor to the development of proficiency in many disciplines related to digital art and that threshold concepts are essential to the development of proficiency.

2.2 Conflation of Proficiency and Expertise

2.2.1 Definitions

This study is concerned with proficiency as a step toward expertise, but the two are frequently conflated. For instance, 'Research on expertise is largely founded on the idea that experts have achieved a rare proficiency' (Phillips et al. 2008, p. 297). A 'rare proficiency' is still 'proficiency' even if viewed in the context of expertise. In another paper on the development of proficiency, Alexander (2003) eliminates the distinction between proficiency and expertise by combining them as 'proficiency/expertise'.

The difference between 'proficiency' and 'expertise' is important to this study because the literature of expertise research is in many cases also the literature of proficiency. The literature is not consistent in the way these words are used, partly due to the conflation of these terms on the one hand and sharp divisions between

© Springer Nature Switzerland AG 2018
A. Paquette, *Spatial Visualization and Professional Competence*,
https://doi.org/10.1007/978-3-319-91289-9_2

them on the other. In the next sections, a brief description of the definitions found in the literature are presented, along with the definitions used here.

2.2.1.1 Proficiency

The term 'proficiency' has two principal uses: to describe a continuum of experience or a specific level of competence that may or may not rise to the level of being 'expert'.

Continuum of Experience

The continuum of experience definition of proficiency conceives of proficiency as a non-specified level of performance. According to this definition, 'proficiency' represents a scale of performance along which there are different levels. For instance, in a study of non-native English speakers adapting to American schools (Brizuela and García-Sellers 1999), proficiency is described as skill or knowledge that starts at one level of proficiency and then is raised to a higher level of proficiency. The same usage occurs in a study of learning in artificial intelligence, where it states that 'a learner's ultimate proficiency depends on its exposure to key nodes' (Epstein 1995, p. 289), and a paper on problem-solving that uses the expression 'high levels of proficiency' (Frederiksen 1984) in contrast to lower levels of proficiency, to discuss the acquisition of proficiency.

The continuum of experience perspective looks at the word 'proficiency' in much the same way one would use the term 'skill level', where the skill level can be anything from low to high.

Competence, Not Expertise

The competence-based definition of proficiency requires 'a level of proficiency that [allows subjects] to perform [their] tasks adequately and effortlessly' (Ericsson 2014 p. 82). By this definition a low level of skill is not proficient. This usage is akin to the term 'technical proficiency', meaning the technical knowledge and ability to perform specified tasks that meet a technical or professional standard, but that stops short of expertise (Helle et al. 2010). Competent proficiency is sufficient to obtain regular work, but is not equal to the standard set by the highest performers (Ericsson 2006).

Proficiency as Expertise

In a discussion of expertise, Detterman (2014) describes it as a 'high level of proficiency' (p. 2). Expertise has also been described as 'fluent proficiency' that transcends knowledge of rules and procedures (Kotzee 2012). In these examples and others, a high level of proficiency is equated with expertise.

Common Characteristics of Proficiency

Proficiency is a performance-based measure, regardless whether it is conflated with expertise. The term 'proficient' can be used to describe a level of proficiency according to specific assessment criteria. This could apply to non-professional, ordinary tasks such as facial recognition (Wong et al. 2009), or professional tasks such as typing or restaurant order-taking (Ericsson and Charness 1994). The development of proficiency as envisioned in this study is the development of skills sufficient to execute complex tasks in digital art to an acceptable professional standard.

Expertise is pertinent to this study for two reasons. Firstly, the expertise literature is a rich source of material relevant to the development of proficiency as an element of developing expertise (Dreyfus and Dreyfus 2005). Secondly, definitions of expertise often describe the practical levels of professional or technical proficiency this study seeks to understand (Sonnentag et al. 2006).

2.2.1.2 Expertise

Expertise as Quantity or Level of Experience

The term 'expertise' is found in the literature to describe a quantity or level of experience. As a quantity, 'expertise' can be conflated with 'proficiency', such as when 'perceptual expertise' is described as a non-specific level of performance in mental imagery (Sunday et al. 2017), visual expertise in medical image diagnosis (Gegenfurtner et al. 2017), musical performance (Cocchini et al. 2017) and other tasks.

The term 'expertise' is also used to describe the skill associated with the state of being an expert (Ackerman 2014a). This is a similar but more limited usage of the term, found in articles on the subject of expert performance. Although 'expertise' can be used to describe performance levels, it can also be used to designate expert status or the highest level of proficiency.

To avoid confusion, 'proficiency' is the preferred term used in this thesis to describe performance levels and 'proficient' is used to describe technical proficiency. The word 'expertise' is used to denote the performance or performance level expected of an expert and 'expert' will be reserved for describing expert status (Table 2.1).

The designation of 'expert' can be conferred or assessed in a number of different ways, giving rise to potential conflict. In the next few sections, elements of expert status and performance are briefly discussed as a way to explain conflicts found in expertise research and why they are relevant to this study on the development of proficiency.

Table 2.1 Summary of definitions used in this document

Proficiency	A measure of skill or the skill level of a proficient individual
Proficient	Having the skill to execute a professional task to a normal technical standard
Expertise	The skill or skill level of an individual identified as an expert
Expert	An individual identified as an 'expert' regardless of the basis for the identification

Table 2.2 Characteristics of expertise (Chase and Simon 1973; Holyoak 1991; Newell and Simon 1988; Shanteau et al. 2002; Sternberg and Horvath 1995)

Performance	Knowledge
Long Term Working Memory (LTWM)	Broad domain knowledge
Pattern-matching	Insight
Serial search	Meaningful data extraction
Problem-solving	Discrimination between cases

Characteristics of Expert Performance

The identification of experts is somewhat controversial because individuals who are identified as experts by one measure may not be experts according to another (Shanteau et al. 2002). Despite this, there are some expert characteristics that are generally agreed upon. First-generation expertise literature such as the work of Chase and Simon (1973) emphasise memory, pattern-matching and serial search as important to being an expert. This has been modified to include the importance of domain knowledge by Newell and Simon (1988). Second-generation research emphasises high-level problem-solving as a 'prototype' for expertise (Holyoak 1991). According to the 'expert prototype' description, the three central tendencies of experts are that experts more effectively use domain knowledge than novices, solve problems more efficiently, and are more likely to use insight to derive original solutions to novel problems (Sternberg and Horvath 1995). Some additional qualifications are the following: Experts are able to extract more meaningful information from data than novices (Chase and Simon 1973) and are able to discriminate between similar but not identical cases (Shanteau et al. 2002).

The characteristics described in the previous paragraph can be organised into two categories: performance and knowledge (Table 2.2). Performance-related characteristics require a high level of proficiency to rise to the standard of expertise, but knowledge-related characteristics require broad domain knowledge. According to the expert prototype description, expert status requires both broad knowledge and high performance.

2.3   The Contribution of Knowledge and Practice to Proficiency

2.3.1   The Broad Knowledge Standard of Expertise

In a large study funded by the U.S. Department of Education, novice physics students are found to be different from experts in knowledge alone (Chi et al. 1981). That is, experts are more likely to know the solution to a problem due to prior experience, but if prior experience is not related to the problem, they have no advantage over a novice. Beyond that, experts and novices in the study employ similarly effective search heuristics, are equally capable of identifying salient elements of problem statements and sort problems into the same or similar categories. A similar result was found in a study of computer programmers (Soloway et al. 2009), where experts were found to perform at significantly higher levels than novices when programming conventions were followed; however, violations of programming conventions caused experts to perform at about the same levels as novices. This indicates that expertise is dependent on memory of previous similar situations (broad knowledge) rather than on-the-spot problem-solving.

2.3.1.1   Experts Who Are Weak Performers

In contrast, Holyoak's (1991) meta-analysis of expertise research shows that people who have been identified as experts are not always superior performers in their field and they sometimes spend more time and effort executing their work than novices. Further, memory performance is sometimes better among novices than experts; experts do not always use forward-reasoning to solve problems or do not have superior pattern perception, nor is it clear whether it is always a factor in performance; and practice does not always improve performance at a constant rate.

All of these findings are exceptions to the first-and second-generation theoretical frameworks described in Holyoak (1991). Other researchers have also found examples where broad experience does not confer expertise (Hambrick et al. 2014; Phillips et al. 2008). As Shanteau et al. (2002) writes, 'At best, experience is an uncertain predictor of degree of expertise. At worst, experience reflects seniority—and little more' (p. 254). A study of software engineers concluded that 'it is important to differentiate between the conceptualisation of expertise as (long) experience and of expertise as high performance' (Sonnentag et al. 2006, p. 375). This is because there is no clear correlation between 'long years of' experience (broad knowledge) and high levels of performance among software designers.

2.3.1.2 Performance and Experience as They Relate to Expertise

Superior performance is supposed to be a distinguishing characteristic of experts, but not all individuals identified as experts exhibit superior proficiency, and when they do, it is not always for the same reasons. Phillips et al. (2008) argues that when 'experts' do not outperform novices, then perhaps they are not truly experts in that domain or task. Instead, they are better described as 'professionals'. This leaves open the question of whether high levels of proficiency among novices indicate that they should be classified as experts instead.

2.3.1.3 Impact of Expertise Definitions on This Study

There are three principal views of expertise: (1) broad knowledge, (2) high performance and (3) high performance enabled by broad knowledge. This study is about the development of industry-standard technical proficiency rather than expert status. However, the distinction between technical proficiency and expertise based on high performance is not always made in the literature. This is important because the literature on the development of expertise is sharply divided whether expertise can be developed without broad knowledge, but accepts that high levels of proficiency are related to expertise. The disagreements stem from research such as that of Chi et al. (1982) and Soloway et al. (2009), that find knowledge to be the defining standard of expertise. However, this may be due to the specific domains of expertise studied.

2.3.1.4 Domain-Centric Structure

Hatano and Oura (2003), among others (Ackerman 2003; Malhotra et al. 2005), describe expertise as domain-centric. This is an important characteristic because it limits the scope of expertise to the boundaries of each domain, such as chess, geology, or in this study, digital art. This means that expertise is so specific that it is not transferrable from one domain to another (Chi et al. 1988). Despite the differences between domain-specific knowledge and cognitive skills, expertise research conducted in specific domains aims to extract general theories related to cognitive skills and expertise. For instance:

> the domain of chess…is not only the first domain in which expert performance was systematically investigated — research in chess, moreover, has undoubtedly provided the vast majority of empirical findings, and, thus, most strongly contributed to today's theories and understanding of expertise. (Grabner 2014, p. 27)

If today's 'theories and understanding of expertise' are so strongly based on studies of chess, and expertise is domain-centric, the possibility arises that expertise theory related to chess-playing is not generalisable to other domains. Other studies have already determined that expertise in one domain is not transferable to another, and that experts in some disciplines are weak performers despite broad domain knowledge. Is it possible that the way expertise is developed also differs from domain to domain?

2.4 The Transition to Proficiency and Expertise

2.4.1 Three Frameworks to Explain Proficiency Development

Debate among researchers points to three primary theoretical frameworks to explain the development of proficiency. The first is based on the premise that broad knowledge is required for expertise to be present, and that it requires a slow step-wise accumulation of knowledge over a long period of time (Dreyfus and Dreyfus 1980). The second is based on the development of tacit skills through practice (Sternberg et al. 1999). The third expects that skills and knowledge essential to expertise are developed side-by-side by engaging in what is called 'deliberate practice' (Ericsson 2006).

2.4.1.1 Dreyfus Stage Model of Expertise Development

According to Dreyfus and Dreyfus (2005), the stages of expertise development break down as follows:

1. Novice: Follows rules without understanding
2. Competent: Uses experimentation to explore options
3. Proficient: Understands problems and plans solution strategy
4. Expert: Knows solution immediately due to previous experience.

Based on this definition the 'technical proficiency' standard described on p. 14 equates to 'proficient', and the difference between an expert and a proficient performer is that an expert already knows the solution to problems due to prior experience (broad knowledge). This is necessarily domain-dependent, because the expertise requires access to existing experience within the domain. According to this definition, proficiency cannot rise to the level of expertise without broad knowledge.

2.4.1.2 Tacit Knowledge and Expertise

According to Sternberg et al. (2000) there are three key features of tacit knowledge. They are:

- *Tacit knowledge generally is acquired on one's own with little support from the environment (e.g., through personal experience rather than through instruction).*
- *Tacit knowledge is viewed as procedural in nature. It is associated with particular uses in particular situations or classes of situations.*
- *Because it generally is acquired through one's own experiences, tacit knowledge has practical value to the individual (Sternberg et al. 2000, p. 107)*

Sternberg and his colleagues (1999) contend that tacit knowledge is what gives proficient performers the edge that raises their performance to an expert standard.

There is knowledge such as how a software tool functions, and then there is the skill needed to use it appropriately: tacit skill.

For example, according to Collins (2007), 'calculators do not do any calculations except when they are used by humans to calculate. The user has to decide what to calculate and how to use the answer' (p. 70). The tacit knowledge framework of expertise development looks at knowledge of a domain as separate from how the knowledge is used. Both are considered essential to expertise. Knowledge of use, particularly practical use in an industry context, is tacit knowledge, and is developed through practice in a situated environment.

The value of tacit knowledge is that because it has less environmental support and must be learned through personal experience, it is comparatively rare, thus providing an advantage to those who have acquired it (Sternberg et al. 2000). Tacit knowledge is an aspect of professional skill, but also of expertise.

2.4.1.3   Deliberate Practice Framework

Ericsson et al.'s (2007) research into expertise shows that most experts spend about 10 years engaged in what they call 'deliberate practice'. The term 'deliberate practice' refers to activities that are designed to improve performance. A key element of deliberate practice is frequent feedback designed to identify and correct errors. This is distinguished from 'play' and 'work', where performance enhancement is not the primary goal of play, but it is in work. According to Ericsson and his colleagues, deliberate practice may make the most significant contribution to eventual development of expertise than any other factor. Deliberate practice over long periods of time is a common factor in domains as disparate as piano-playing (Chaffin and Imreh 2002), decision-making (Phillips et al. 2008) and radiological diagnosis (Raufaste et al. 1998).

2.4.1.4   Consistency Among the Three Frameworks

It is possible to envision each of the expertise development frameworks as different views of the same process. Deliberate practice, as described in Ericsson (1993), could be the process by which a learner transitions from being proficient to being expert, as described in Dreyfus (Dreyfus and Dreyfus 1980). The form the deliberate practice could take, at least in part, is the acquisition of tacit knowledge in a mentored work environment, such as those described by Sternberg et al. (2000). These three frameworks taken together represent views on expertise development that are generally accepted by the research community.

2.4.1.5 Proficiency Development as It Is Viewed in This Study

Based on the previously described research, this study assumes the following:

1. Student participants of this study will, at most, develop proficiency, as described by Dreyfus. That is, they will learn to solve complex industry-standard problems at a level of technical proficiency. They will not have sufficient experience to readily recall previously worked solutions to an expert level.
2. Students will acquire tacit knowledge as a by-product of the process of engaging in the projects assigned to them in class. The specific nature of this tacit knowledge may not be obvious and likely will require some investigation to identify.
3. Students are more likely to develop the desired level of proficiency if they are given frequent meaningful feedback on their projects. That said, if technical proficiency is achieved, it will have been achieved more rapidly than is expected when (a) the performance definition of expertise and (b) the deliberate practice framework standard of approximately ten years' practice are used.

2.4.2 Deliberate Practice Undermined by Rapid Development

Some researchers have described examples where expertise appears to have developed more quickly than expected, sometimes in as little as three years or less (Simonton 2012; Sonnentag et al. 2006). The deliberate practice framework assumes a considerable amount of time devoted to deliberate practice; thus it does not explain the expertise of child chess grand masters (Howard 2009) or of individuals who quickly master entirely new fields of study, such as Galileo's many contributions to telescopic astronomy (Simonton 2012), or the work of Thomas Edison, who created many new fields of study before there was any knowledge to acquire (Simonton 2014).

Claims regarding the necessity of deliberate practice do not explain evidence that equal amounts of practice among individuals exposed to identical environmental conditions do not yield the same performance (Ackerman 2014a). This undermines the exclusive or primary role deliberate practice supposedly plays in the development of expertise, and suggests that there are other important factors involved (Wai 2014). One way to try and understand the development of proficiency is to identify the boundary between the state of not being proficient and proficiency.

2.5 Performance Boundaries and Threshold Concepts

2.5.1 Definition of a Threshold Concept

A threshold concept is a concept which is problematic to the learner, in which knowledge or methods connected to solving the problems are often irreversibly changed and the solutions must be learned to progress in one's knowledge of a given subject (Meyer and Land 2003). Other limiting criteria of threshold concepts are:

- Liminality (passage beyond an internal mental threshold)
- Transformation (a meaningful change to one's thinking)
- Integration (domain-relevant information that had been perceived as unrelated is now seen as related)
- Reconstitution (a strong change in the way the subject relates to the domain)
- Boundedness (individual concepts do not explain the full dimensions of a domain but are separately and together essential to understanding a domain)
- Discourse (knowledge of the threshold concept causes a shift in the subject's perspective that draws them closer to the perspective of established practitioners in the domain) (Baillie et al. 2013).

There is some disagreement about what constitutes a genuine threshold concept due to the generic quality of the definitions presented above. To clarify this, Myer, as reported by Quinlan et al. (2013) states that there are two 'non-negotiable features' of threshold concepts: they are always epistemologically and ontologically transformative (p. 586). Once acquired, the way a student experiences subject matter relevant to the concept is meaningfully altered.

The focus of many articles on threshold concepts is understanding what threshold concepts are in the generic sense, but 'so far, little effort has gone into exploring what this transformation actually means in different subject areas' (Scheja and Pettersson, 2010, p. 236). Many threshold concept-related methodologies encountered in the literature rely on students or teachers to identify threshold concepts in interviews or focus groups outside of a classroom context (Land et al. 2014). In one article that reviews three different methodologies, all rely on interviews with teachers and students rather than direct observation (Quinlan et al. 2013). A criticism of this approach is that 'identification in hindsight can be difficult due to the tendency for threshold concepts to be irreversible in nature' (Barradell 2013, p. 271). One way to solve this problem is to simulate it on a computer.

2.5.2 A Simulated Threshold Concept Leads to Expertise

A computer program known as Hoyle was designed to record its actions as it learned expert behaviour by playing various games (Epstein 1995). Hoyle has since learned to play 18 games as well as human experts. The complexity of the games, such as Tic-Tac-Toe, do not rise to the level of complexity found in digital art or domains studied in the expertise literature, but the experiment allows an opportunity to see how expertise is acquired by keeping a constant log of Hoyle's actions as it learns to improve its skill.

When Hoyle plays Tic-Tac-Toe, and a certain position is not encountered, Hoyle always makes an error. After the position is encountered, Hoyle plays all subsequent games of Tic-Tac-Toe perfectly. This is true regardless of when the position is encountered as Hoyle searches for solutions. This position is described as a 'key node' by Epstein (1995).

The key node required for Hoyle to play error-free Tic-Tac-Toe is not a solution, but a problem that allows Hoyle to understand a critical dynamic of the game. The key node is not knowledge but opportunity. The opportunity presented is to recognise that this specific position allows the possibility of a definite win. Once it recognises the value of the position, Hoyle alters its play strategy and plays as an expert from then on.

Epstein's (1995) study shows that exhaustive knowledge is less important to Hoyle than finding the key nodes most relevant to the games it plays. Until the key nodes are discovered it plays like a novice, but after the key nodes are reached it plays like an expert. This is regardless of how many nodes have been encountered at that point. If it finds the key nodes immediately, its play immediately becomes that of an expert. If it has to search the entire problem space before it encounters the key nodes, then its transition to expert play is delayed. Once the key node is encountered and its relationship to the game is understood, Hoyle never reverts to non-expert play. The change to game strategy is sudden and irreversible. This meets Meyer's (Quinlan et al. 2013) non-negotiable features of threshold concepts, that they are epistemologically and ontologically transformative.

The two qualities of being counter-intuitive and irreversible are associated with threshold concepts. This example, though grounded in the study of artificial intelligence, contains all of the elements of human problem-solving. If problem space navigation plays a role in human problem-solving as it does for the Hoyle program, it could explain the rapid development of expertise. This means that although it normally takes many years of deliberate practice to develop expertise, it can be accomplished more rapidly if the route to a key node is shorter (Fig. 2.1).

It should be noted that the Hoyle example is of an AI routine becoming an 'expert' in a task that is not connected to a profession, nor is it considered difficult, despite error-free play after encountering the key node. This is an example of expertise because it is error-free, but the complexity of the task is low enough to cast doubt on whether it is an appropriate example. What Hoyle demonstrates is a mechanism by which knowledge of a small fraction of an available problem space can substitute for broad knowledge because it confers understanding of the entire domain.

If key nodes are responsible for the development of expertise, what would they look like in practice?

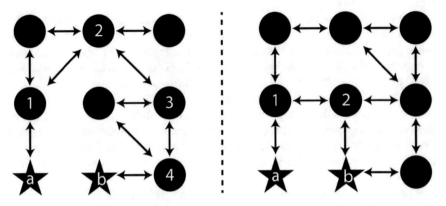

Fig. 2.1 Key node navigation in problem space, where arrows illustrate possible routes between key node 'a' and key node 'b'

2.5.3 Transition to Proficiency Sudden Among Telegraph Operators

A classic 19th century study of learning among telegraph operators (Bryan and Harter 1897) finds that (1) many student operators give up ('between 60 and 75%') before attaining proficiency due to the difficulty of the profession and (2) those who transition to becoming experts have been observed to do so suddenly. This last point is worth quoting because it suggests a cognitive change rather than simple acquisition of knowledge, 'According to all who have experience in the matter…Suddenly, within a few days, the change comes, and the senseless clatter becomes intelligible speech' (Bryan and Harter 1897, p. 53). This description creates the impression of a sudden realization or change, rather than the gradual accumulation of knowledge expected in expertise development. The study is silent on the cause of the change, but other research has attempted to understand rapid development as influenced by talent.

2.5.4 Talent as an Explanation for Rapid Development

The word 'talented' is used to describe exceptional individuals who are experts in one or more domains as a way to explain their often precocious mastery of a skill (Ruthsatz et al. 2014). The word 'talent' is narrowed further by Ruthsatz, et al. to mean 'innate talent' on the basis that it is inherent and cannot be created or developed, though innate talent can allow development of other skills. The sudden acquisition of skill by telegraph operators in Bryan and Harter's (1897) study might be the product of talent, but it resembles more closely the acquisition of a key node, as described by Epstein (1995).

2.5.5 Threshold Boundaries Between Proficiency and Expertise

The theoretical underpinning of threshold concepts is that learners transition from one level of knowledge to another by acquiring a threshold concept that bridges the two levels (Land et al. 2014). Implicit in this is that there is a threshold to be crossed and that the threshold represents a boundary between the state of understanding and not understanding. In a study of first-year dental students, the transition from directed to self-regulated learning is described as a process that takes place over the course of an academic year (Bowman 2017). This is in contrast to the 'few days' mentioned for the transition to proficiency among telegraph operators. Both studies make implied references to the existence of a boundary and approximately when it may have been encountered by students, but neither attempts to explicitly observe the transition or what makes it possible.

On the subject of transition between knowledge boundaries, Kneebone (2009) writes, 'In the case of mastering a skill, it becomes impossible for a learner to put themselves fully back in the position they occupied while still learning' (p. 956). This view is not uncommon, and illustrates one of the limitations of methodologies used in the study of threshold concepts. They depend on after-the-fact interviews with study participants, rather than direct observation (Quinlan et al. 2013).

The literature of threshold concepts provides the possibility of an answer to the question, 'how can some learners make sudden and rapid transitions to proficiency and expertise?' However, it does not provide much information regarding specific causes of such transitions. Instead, the literature provides indicators to look for among students who have encountered a threshold concept: resistance, frustration, and lack of progress despite consistent effort. This can help identify when a student encounters a threshold concept, but says nothing about the threshold concept itself or how it was overcome. Interviews conducted after the fact are sufficient to identify the threshold concept, but how it was overcome is more difficult to assess using retrospective reports.

Some studies described in the expertise literature propose that certain cognitive abilities, such as verbal or spatial ability correlate with potential performance among learners (Ackerman 2014b; Cocchini et al. 2017; Hambrick et al. 2014). The implication is that if a cognitive ability such as spatial visualisation does correlate with improved performance, that it may also contribute to that performance, and thus to any proficiency that develops. A condition is that the cognitive skill is appropriate for the domain or task in question. Among the cognitive skills described in these studies, spatial visualisation, also called 'spatial reasoning' and 'spatial ability' was most closely related to the type of work done by digital art students.

2.6 The Contribution of Spatial Visualisation to Proficiency

2.6.1 Reflective Thinking in Design

The type of problems encountered in digital art tend to change significantly with the creation of new technology (Peng et al. 2014). Similarly, designers are frequently faced with new problems that cannot be addressed with knowledge gleaned from textbooks or prior practice (Hong and Choi 2011). Faced with new problems, how are designers, particularly experts, expected to solve them? Studies of the development of expertise in designers emphasise the importance of 'reflective thinking' because it is essential to solving design problems (p. 691). With reflective thinking, designers are able to iterate potential solutions rapidly, analyse their qualities and accept or reject those aspects of each iteration that best suit their project brief (Atman et al. 2007). In this way, 'the design process opens up possibilities for surprise that can trigger new ways of seeing things' (Schön 1992, p. 131).

The difference between seeing and understanding is illustrated in a study by Gamble (2001). In the study, instructors can tell from looking at student craftspeople's finished products whether their drawing skills meet the right standard. The instructor's observations are of work on the shop floor where only tools such as a cross-cutting saw or a lathe are in use and no drawings are present. Instructors are able to do this because student behaviour while working with tools reflects how they have learned to visualise or 'see' proportion (Gamble 2001). It is for this reason that CG industry professionals recommend against digital art curricula that focus on software training rather than on practical examples of craft (such as drawing) (Ip 2012).

We have seen in this section how the theme of proficiency development leads from tacit knowledge to visualisation. Sternberg et al. (2000) write about successful senior managers who rely on 'intuitive' (tacit) reactions to problems rather than formulaic (explicit) problem-solving methods. Ferguson (1992) writes that 'visual thinking is necessary' for engineers because information related to engineering is conveyed using a visual language (pp. 41–42). Henderson (1999) describes the process of design work as heavily influenced by visualisation of solutions, as represented by engineering sketches that form the basis for communication among designers. For creative professionals, Simonton (2014) emphasises the importance of risk-taking during the design process, something that is evocative of bridging the gap between what is known (the problem) and unknown (the solution) through visualisation of a potential solution. Throughout the literature of expertise, tacit knowledge and design learning there are references to visualisation or related concepts being critical to the success of students and professionals. Because these references are frequent and prominent, in the next section the literature of spatial visualisation is investigated to better understand the role of visualisation in learning.

2.6.2 The Tower of Hanoi Problem

One well-established test of cognitive skill learning is the Tower of Hanoi problem. It consists of a board, three pegs and a stack of disks of varying sizes. The disks are positioned on one peg and then study participants are asked to move the entire stack to another peg following a set of rules: only one disk can be moved at a time; a disk can only be moved if it is the uppermost disk on a stack; and no disk may be placed on top of a smaller disk. This problem allows separate cognitive abilities to be measured independently, such as planning, problem-solving, inhibition, self-regulation and monitoring (Vakil and Heled 2016).

The Tower of Hanoi problem has a few isomorphs, in which the scenario is represented differently to participants but the underlying task is the same. Kotovsky et al. (1985) describes isomorphs as problem variants whose problem space is identical to the original problem because they have the same structure (or topology). However, changes to the cover story of these problems dramatically increase the amount of time human study participants take to solve them. This is in contrast to artificial intelligence, whose performance does not change, regardless of cover story variant. This appears to be because human subjects have associations with data that interfere with treating each option equally. It is worth understanding this because it provides insight into the kind of problems faced by digital artists.

In the normal version of the Tower of Hanoi problem, participants of the Kotovsky et al. (1985) study are able to solve it in an average of 1.83 min. The isomorphically identical 'Monster Move'[1] problem, in which participants are told a story about monsters of varying sizes holding globes of different sizes and asked to rearrange the globes according to a set of rules so that each monster is holding a globe proportionate to its own size, takes 13.95 min on average to solve. A variant called 'Monster Change'[2] took 29.39 min on average to solve. For each variation of the problem the majority of the difference in time to solution can be accounted for by (1) learning the rules or limitations of the problem and (2) the degree of resemblance to real world knowledge within the rules.

In a related study that supports this explanation (Clément and Richard 1997), isomorphs are created for the Monster Move and Monster Change problems. The study shows that the original forms of the puzzles have implicit rules that affect their difficulty, namely that test participants tend to assume that the Move and Change problems require logical moves and growth. When this limitation is removed by making the rules more explicit, the puzzles are solved more quickly. The disparity between the original Tower of Hanoi problem and the two 'Monster' versions of the problem remains, indicating again that the way participants visualise the different problems plays a significant role in problem difficulty. These results are anticipated by Wason and Shapiro (1971), who show that performance on logic problems given to study participants dramatically improves if the problem is presented in a concrete form that is easily visualised.

---

[1] See Appendix 5 (p. 216) for example.
[2] See Appendix 5 (p. 216) for example.

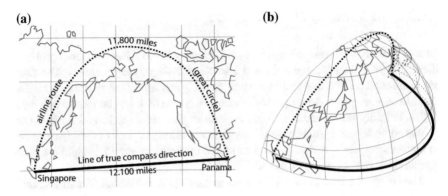

Fig. 2.2 2D (**a**) and 3D (**b**) projections to show optimal airline route, based on Anderson and Leinhardt (2002)

The effort of learning the rules of a problem while maintaining a visualisation of the steps necessary to solve it is similar to problems encountered by digital artists, who must translate observations into a form that can be understood by their software. To make matters more challenging, the large size of the problem space and the difficulty of visualising the effect of unfamiliar rules combine to create complex and challenging tasks for digital artists as they develop proficiency.

2.6.3   Visualisation in Problem-Solving

In a study of expert and novice cartographers,[3] differences in problem solution strategy illustrate differences in visualisation abilities (Anderson and Leinhardt 2002). Here is an example of how one of the advanced novices in the study solves a flight path problem by using spatial visualisation skills (Fig. 2.2):

> He imagined that he was drilling a straight line into the earth between the two locations and then saw how the line would be curved on the earth's surface. He then imagined he was peeling back the skin of the earth to see how the line would bend when it was stretched on a flat surface (pp. 304).

The ability demonstrated in this example to create a mental visualisation of the problem and its solution is categorised as 'spatial visualisation'. Spatial visualisation has been measured since the earliest intelligence tests in the United States (Terman 1916). It is relevant to the problems digital artists must solve, which require the creation and manipulation of computer-generated models representing objects in three-dimensional space.

---

[3]The 'novices' in this case are teachers and students. The 'experts' are described as either 'experts' or 'advanced novices'.

2.6.4 Testing Spatial Visualisation Ability

Mental rotation tests are designed to test spatial visualisation ability using isometric or perspective drawings of 3D objects, rather than the flattened 2D patterns used in the spatial visualisation tests described by Salthouse et al. (1990) (Fig. 2.3). This is because mental rotation tests have been found to be more reliable indicators of performance in disciplines that require 'a strong visuoperceptual sense to grasp the dynamics and structures of objects in 3D space…' than other types of spatial ability tests (Maeda and Yoon 2013).

In mental rotation tests, isometric drawings of a 3D object are provided in addition to a rotated or mirrored view of the same object in the company of other similar objects. Subjects are asked to pick out the matching object from the decoys by mentally rotating the original object and comparing it with the options provided. The Mental Rotations Test (MRT) and the Vandenberg Mental Rotations Test (Vandenberg and Kuse 1978) are both examples of this type of test. More recently, the Purdue Visualization of Rotations Test (PVRT) has been used to test for the ability to re-orient a three-dimensional object by mental rotation (Branoff 2000). Figure 2.4 is an example question from a mental rotation test.

The PVRT is one of the more common mental rotation tests found in the literature. Results from this test consistently correlate with performance in various academic disciplines (Alias et al. 2002; Branoff 2000; Titus and Horsman 2009). Taken together, studies that utilise the Purdue test indicate that the test is valid and reliable. Of interest to this study is whether mental rotation tests can predict performance among digital artists. If they can, it would imply a relationship between spatial visualisation and problem-solving skills relevant to developing expertise as digital artists. If this proved to be the case, it could explain why curricula that focus on learning technology rather than developing cognitive skills such as mental visualisation is less successful in the eyes of CG industry representatives.

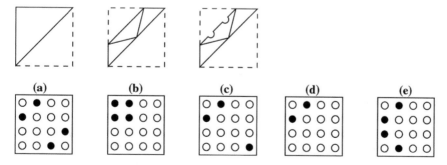

Fig. 2.3 In this hole punch pattern test, subjects must determine which of the options correctly depicts the arrangement of holes punched in the folded paper at the top

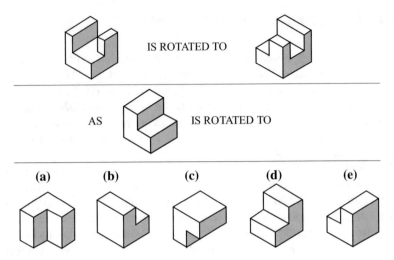

Fig. 2.4 In this mental rotation test, test-takers must determine how the first object is rotated, then apply the same rotation to a different object (Bodner and Guay 1997)

A study conducted in the Coventry University automotive design programme used the PVRT to predict performance among first year transportation design majors. Their students are digital artists and use the same tools and techniques as students in this study. For this reason, it is interesting that of all the spatial visualisation papers reviewed, the Coventry University study is the only one that does not show a significant correlation between PVRT scores and academic performance (Osmond et al. 2009). In a similar example, the Perceptual Ability Test (a spatial visualisation test used in schools of dentistry) does not correlate with G.P.A., but does correlate with some pre-clinical operative skills (Hegarty et al. 2009). These results presented a question for this study, because the literature of spatial visualisation research strongly supports the hypothesis that because spatial visualisation test scores correlate with general performance in related domains such as mechanical engineering and architecture, that there would not be significant exceptions within those domains.

2.6.5 Mental Rotation and Experience

An explanation for the lack of correlation between academic performance and PVRT test results at Coventry University may be provided by a study that uses the paper-folding test as a measure of spatial ability. In that study, subjects self-report their level of experience prior to attending an advanced course in laparoscopic surgery. That value is then compared to their spatial visualisation test scores. The results show that correlations between test scores and performance degrade with experience. Correlations are strongest with less-experienced surgeons and diminish to near nonsignificance with the most-experienced surgeons. The conclusion of the study is that experience mediates the use of spatial visualisation because it is not required after a problem has been solved and become rote (Keehner et al. 2004). This conclusion supports that of Bodner and Guay (1997), who find that the PVRT is predictive in cases of 'true problem solving' and 'novel problems'. This presents a problem because the skills learned at Coventry appear to be novel in the experience of the student cohorts at the time the tests are taken. However, this neglects the possibility that mental rotation itself has become routine for these students.

Playing video games leads to rapid improvement of spatial ability as measured by mental rotation tests (Terlicki and Newcombe 2005). The use of CAD tools such as Google Sketch-Up have a similar effect (Kurtulus and Uygan 2010). Students at Coventry use CAD software on a daily basis, thus creating the potential for significant gains in spatial visualisation ability.

It is possible that students at Coventry University have developed above-average mental rotation skills through the use of CAD software and video games. This suggests that students improve their spatial ability to such a level that mental rotation test scores no longer correlate with performance on other digital art tasks. If true, it indicates that the 'novel problem solving' described in Bodner and Guay (1997) applies to mental rotation-related problems, but that the type of spatial visualisation problem encountered by transportation design students at Coventry University is meaningfully different.

The next section addresses how CAD software can improve mental rotation test scores without improving ability in NURBS modelling.

2.6.6   Mental Rotation and Spatial Visualisation

Mental rotation tests are designed to measure spatial ability based on one's ability to mentally rotate an object's form or to change the viewing angle of a static object. If perspective is understood, the result of changing either camera angle or the rotation of an object relative to a camera will result in exactly the same image every time. However, not all spatial problems are as simple as rotation. For instance, one of the problems faced by garment pattern designers is to efficiently divide a three-dimensional object; a garment, into separate shapes that can be cut out of a flat section of fabric to create a pattern (Yang et al. 2011). Unlike rotation, which can be programmed into software based on known rules, the kind of structural analysis required of garment pattern designers cannot easily be automated. Attempts have been made, but versions that have found their way into commercially available software generally require considerable hand-editing to achieve optimal results.

2.6.7   Topological Awareness and Cognitive Search

Garment pattern design is an example of a topological problem, or one that involves the way parts are interrelated or arranged; in this case, the pattern designer must be aware of how each pattern piece will connect to the rest to form the finished garment. In architectural design, a connection between design visualisation and topology is also evident in the work of Frank Lloyd Wright, who has used the same topological structure for houses that have radically different geometry (Akin and Moustapha 2004). Topology can be an effective design tool for architects, who first infer a workable topological relationship between the site and the structure they intend to build, then a sub-topology for the structure itself that becomes the basis for its major axes and structure.

The value of a topological understanding of structure is that it strips a representation of distracting details and reduces it to its structural minimum. This allows the structure to be analysed in its purest form, as nodes and connections. An example of this is a London Underground map, which provides a graphic depiction of stations, their names and their positions relative to each other. These maps also show which Underground lines are connected at junctions to allow transfers between trains. What an Underground map does not show are accurate positions of stations relative to a map of London, the distances between stations or the shape of the path between stations. These maps represent the 'topological awareness' of the map maker, or the understanding of how the elements of the Underground system relate to each other. They allow anyone who views them to gain this topological awareness as well.

Topological awareness is only found as a subject in papers on network computing (Santoro 1984; Xi and Liu 2009) and even then, the total number of topological awareness-related articles found for the review is very small: only eight over a period of several decades. In network computing, 'topological awareness' is used to develop faster routing of data. The way topological awareness affects order-processing speed in computing tasks resembles human cognitive search processes (Fraigniaud et al. 2004) such as those thought to be indicators of expertise.

When a computer network has only partial topological awareness it lacks connection information between members of a group and may not be able to deliver information to certain entities on a network (Fraigniaud et al. 2004). This is similar to the kind of reasoning difficulties encountered by students engaged in problem-solving when they do not understand its structure (Eriksson et al. 2012; Haag et al. 2006). Some problems in digital art are almost entirely topology-based, because a solution requires understanding of how spatial elements connect to each other. The reason for this is described in more detail in the Methodology chapter on p. 49.

So far, this chapter has argued that problem-solving in art and design can rely on mental visualisation, but that mental rotation tests have not predicted academic results among transportation majors at Coventry University. One possible explanation for this is that topological awareness is more relevant to the work of automotive designers than mental rotation. In any case, the disparity between mental rotation test results and student performance in the Coventry University study indicates a potential gap in the literature of spatial visualisation that may be specific to the domain of digital art.

2.6.8 Spatial Visualisation Tests Compromised

This literature review shows that spatial visualisation is widely accepted as a contributing factor that leads to or predicts proficiency in many domains. However, it also shows that the literature of spatial visualisation is dependent on the type of tests used to gauge performance. These tests, I will argue, may be compromised when used in the domain of digital art because CAD tools and the playing of video games have the effect of training participants in the specific type of spatial visualisation used in the most popular tests, mental rotation. The effect is to mask other skills thought to be connected to spatial visualisation, like problem-solving ability, while concentrating only on this one aspect that is easily trained.

2.7 Conclusion

The original purpose of this research was to learn how proficiency is developed among students enrolled in a digital art programme. This question was interesting because complaints from industry suggest that an educational solution could provide relief from the current skills shortage. Further research suggested that the development of technical proficiency might hinge on the acquisition of threshold concepts or spatial visualisation skill. If threshold concepts were critical to the development of proficiency, methodologies used elsewhere would not be able to capture the boundary between non-proficiency and proficiency. This suggested a study design that attempts to directly observe students as they develop proficiency.

In the sections that follow, the impact of the literature review on this study is described in more detail, followed by the research questions.

2.7.1 CG Literature not Written for Digital Artists

The field of digital art is relatively new and institutions of higher education with degree-granting programmes in the field are even newer. Most of the literature in the field is written by programmers on subjects related to graphics programming. Digital artists are end-users of CG software but are rarely represented in peer-reviewed literature. Despite this, there are some papers that address issues of concern to visual artists, but these represent a minority of papers published in the field.

The development of expertise among digital artists is treated in the literature as a problem to be solved through education, but representatives of the digital art industry have expressed that most education programs designed to accomplish this goal produce inadequate results. The recommendations found in the literature about how to solve this problem are typically based on consultation with industry representatives rather than as the product of a study, meaning that the suggestions have not been tested and the validity of the suggestions is unclear. There are papers that report results from different universities (Anderson and Peters 2009; Comininos et al. 2009) but these are not numerous and leave wide gaps between them in the material covered. This study adds to that material by contributing data that is directly relevant to improving the quality of education in a domain that is currently strongly criticised by the industry they serve (Ip 2012).

2.7.2 Gaps in the Literature

2.7.2.1 Transition to Proficiency/Expertise Not Observed in the Literature

There are two principal gaps in the literature that this research addresses. The first is that many papers suggest that it should not be possible to observe the transition from novice status to technical proficiency. The second gap is found in the literature of spatial visualisation, where an over-reliance on mental rotation tests presents the possibility that some forms of spatial visualisation are overlooked.

The reason given in some papers for the difficulties of observing the transition to expert performance is that they assume the necessity of developing either broad knowledge of a field or spending approximately 10 years in deliberate practice (Ericsson 1993) before expertise can emerge. If either of these conditions is required for expertise to develop, and technical proficiency is equated with expertise, then this study can only hope to watch as students begin their studies, but would end before they develop technical proficiency.

Based on previous student performance at IGAD there is a credible possibility that the transition from novice to proficient performance will be observed. A possible explanation for why it has been observed at IGAD but not in research of expertise in other domains is that it is a less complex task than it appears to be or there is something about the discipline of digital art that differentiates its requirements for proficiency and expertise.

2.7.2.2 Over-Reliance on Mental Rotation Tests in Literature

The literature of spatial visualisation research suggests that spatial visualisation tests are able to predict performance in a number of fields, some of which are related to digital art, such as mechanical engineering and architecture. However, when students who use CAD software are tested, the results do not reliably correlate with later performance. It appears possible that the relationship between spatial visualisation and performance in digital art is different from other domains where spatial visualisation is not augmented by computer simulations, such as CAD software and video games provide. This makes it possible to isolate new factors relevant to developing expertise in digital art by ruling out mental rotation and looking for something else. If successful, this research could provide the basis for new types of spatial visualisation tests that do not replicate a CAD application's normal 3D interface.

2.7.2.3 Topological Awareness and Visualisation in Digital Art

Related to spatial visualisation is the subject of topological awareness. Topological awareness in NURBS modelling refers to a student's ability to visualise multiple topologies, or subdivision patterns, to solve shape-related problems inherent to the NURBS modelling task. This subject is discussed in more detail on p. 45, but the importance of topological awareness can be stated simply here. Topological awareness is an awareness of how things are connected to each other. The better one's understanding of those connections is, the more flexible one's solutions to shape problems can be. This type of visualisation ability is not found in the literature of computer graphics, education, or expertise, though it is found in articles on network computing (Fraigniaud et al. 2004) and one article was found on the subject of spatial visualisation that mentioned topology (McLeay and Piggins 1996). Because the project made by Coventry University students depends on the visualisation of topology, there is the possibility that this aspect of the project explains why spatial visualisation tests are inconclusive. The possibility of a connection between visualisation of topology and the development of spatial visualisation skills useful to digital artists presents an opportunity to contribute to the literature of spatial visualisation.

This study aims to combine existing expertise theory with spatial visualisation to create a better understanding of learning as it relates to the development of proficiency among digital artists. This addresses a gap in the literature regarding the discipline of digital art and the possible connection between spatial visualisation, proficiency and expertise.

2.8 Contributions to the Literature

The literature reveals gaps in a few areas that can be addressed in this study, namely direct observation of how proficiency is developed, the capture of the transition between novice and proficient performance, the possible importance of threshold concepts and spatial visualisation to developing expertise and a unifying theoretical framework to explain the observations.

Next, in the methodology chapter, I describe how the research questions were addressed.

References

Ackerman PL (2003) Cognitive ability and non-ability trait determinants of expertise. Educ Researcher 32(8):15–20

Ackerman PL (2014a) Nonsense, common sense, and science of expert performance: talent and individual differences. Intelligence 45:6–17. https://doi.org/10.1016/j.intell.2013.04.009

Ackerman PL (2014b) Facts are stubborn things. Intelligence 45:104–106. https://doi.org/10.1016/j.intell.2014.01.002

Akin O, Moustapha H (2004) Strategic use of representation in architectural massing. Des Stud 25(1):31–50

Alexander PA (2003) The development of expertise: the journey from acclimation to proficiency. Educ Researcher 32(8):10–14

Alias M, Gray D, Black TR (2002) Attitudes towards sketching and drawing and the relationship with spatial visualisation ability in engineering students. Int. Educ J 3(3):165–175

Anderson KC, Leinhardt G (2002) Maps as representations: expert novice comparison of projection understanding. Cogn Instr 20(3):283–321

Anderson EF, Peters CE (2009) On the provision of a comprehensive computer graphics education in the context of computer games: an activity-led instruction approach. Paper presented at the Eurographics 2009, Munich, Germany. http://coventry.academia.edu/EikeFalkAnderson/Papers/117485/On_the_Provision_of_a_Comprehensive_Computer_Graphics_Education_in_the_Context_of_Computer_Games_An_Activity-Led_Instruction_Approach

Atman CJ, Adams RS, Cardella ME, Turns J, Mosborg S, Saleem J (2007) Engineering design processes: a comparison of students and expert practitioners. J Eng Educ 96(4):359–379. https://doi.org/10.1002/j.2168-9830.2007.tb00945.x

Baillie C, Bowden JA, Meyer JHF (2013) Threshold capabilities: threshold concepts and knowledge capability linked through variation theory. High Educ 65(2):227–246. https://doi.org/10.1007/s10734-012-9540-5

Barradell S (2013) The identification of threshold concepts: a review of theoretical complexities and methodological challenges. High Educ 65(2):265–276. https://doi.org/10.1007/s10734-012-9542-3

Bodner GM, Guay RB (1997) The purdue visualization of rotations test. Chem Educ 2(4):1–14

Bowman M (2017) The transition to self-regulated learning for first-year dental students: threshold concepts. Eur J Dent Educ 21(3):142–150. https://doi.org/10.1111/eje.12193

Branoff TJ (2000) Spatial visualization measurement: a modification of the purdue spatial visualization test—visualization of rotations. Eng Des Graph J 64(2):14–22

Brizuela BM, García-Sellers MJ (1999) School adaptation: a triangular process. Am Educ Res J 36(2):345–370

Bryan WL, Harter N (1897) Studies in the physiology and psychology of the telegraphic language. Psychol Rev 4(1):27–53. https://doi.org/10.1037/h0073806

Chaffin R, Imreh G (2002) Practicing perfection: piano performance as expert memory. Psychol Sci 13(4):342–349. https://doi.org/10.1111/1467-9280.00462

Chase WG, Simon HA (1973) Perception in chess. Cogn Psychol 4(1):55–81

Chi MTH, Glaser R, Rees E (1981) Expertise in problem solving. Lawrence Erlbaum Associates, Hillsdale, NJ

Chi MTH, Glaser R, Rees E (1982) Expertise in problem solving. In: Sternberg RJ (ed) Advances in the psychology of human intelligence, vol 1. Lawrence Erlbaum and Associates, Hillsdale, NJ

Chi MTH, Glaser R, Farr MJ (1988) The nature of expertise. Lawrence Erlbaum Associates, Publishers, Hillsdale, NJ

Clément E, Richard J-F (1997) Knowledge of domain effects in problem representation: the case of Tower of Hanoi isomorphs. Think Reason 3(2):133–157

Cocchini G, Filardi MS, Crhonkova M, Halpern AR (2017) Musical expertise has minimal impact on dual task performance. Memory 25(5):677–685. https://doi.org/10.1080/09658211.2016.1205628

Collins H (2007) Peripheral vision: bicycling on the moon: collective tacit knowledge and somatic-limit tacit knowledge. Organ Stud 28(2):257–262. https://doi.org/10.1177/0170840606073759

Comininos P, McLoughlin L, Anderson EF (2009) Educating technophile artists: experiences from a highly successful computer animation undergraduate programme. Paper presented at the SIGGRAPH ASIA'09: SIGGRAPH ASIA 2009 Educators Program, Yokohama, Japan

Detterman DK (2014) Introduction to the intelligence special issue on the development of expertise: is ability necessary? Intelligence 45:1–5. https://doi.org/10.1016/j.intell.2014.02.004

Dreyfus SE, Dreyfus HL (1980) A five-stage model of the mental activities involved in directed skill acquisition. Retrieved from

Dreyfus HL, Dreyfus SE (2005) Peripheral vision: expertise in real world contexts. Organ Stud 26(5):779–792. https://doi.org/10.1177/0170840605053102

Epstein SL (1995) Learning in the right places. J Learn Sci 4(3):281–319

Ericsson KA (1993) The role of deliberate practice in the acquisition of expert performance. Psychol Rev 100(3):363–406

Ericsson KA (2006) The influence of experience and deliberate practice on the development of superior expert performance. In: Ericsson KA (ed) Cambridge handbook of expertise and expert performance. Cambridge University Press, Cambridge, UK, pp 685–706

Ericsson KA (2014) Why expert performance is special and cannot be extrapolated from studies of performance in the general population: a response to criticisms. Intelligence 45(1):81–103. https://doi.org/10.1016/j.intell.2013.12.001

Ericsson KA, Charness N (1994) Expert performance its structure and acquisition. Am Psychol 49(8):725–747

Ericsson KA, Prietula MJ, Cokely ET (2007) The making of an expert. Harvard Business Review, 1–7 July–Aug

Eriksson B, Dasarathy G, Barford P, Nowak R (2012) Efficient network tomography for internet topology discovery. IEEE/ACM Trans Networking 20(3):931–943

Ferguson ES (1992) Engineering and the mind's eye. MIT Press, Cambridge

Fraigniaud P, Gavoille C, Paul C (2004) Eclecticism shrinks even small worlds. Proc 23rd Annu ACM Symp Principles Distrib Comput 18(4):279–291. https://doi.org/10.1007/s00446-005-0137-4

Frederiksen N (1984) Implications of cognitive theory for instruction in problem solving. Rev Educ Res 54(3):363–407

Gamble J (2001) Modelling the invisible: the pedagogy of craft apprenticeship. Stud Continuing Educ 23(2):185–200

Gegenfurtner A, Kok E, van Geel K, de Bruin A, Jarodzka H, Szulewski A, van Merriënboer JJG (2017) The challenges of studying visual expertise in medical image diagnosis. Med Educ 51(1):97–104. https://doi.org/10.1111/medu.13205

Grabner RH (2014) The role of intelligence for performance in the prototypical expertise domain of chess. Intelligence 45:26–33. https://doi.org/10.1016/j.intell.2013.07.023

Haag M, Komerska R, Bartos R, Agu E, Chappell SG (2006) Status packet deprecation and storefor-ward routing in AUSNet. Paper presented at the 1st ACM international workshop on underwater networks, Los Angeles

Hambrick DZ, Oswald FL, Altmann EM, Meinz EJ, Gobet F, Campitelli G (2014) Deliberate practice: is that all it takes to become an expert? Intelligence 45:34–45. https://doi.org/10.1016/j.intell.2013.04.001

Hegarty M, Keehner M, Khooshabeh P, Montello DR (2009) How spatial abilities enhance, and are enhanced by, dental education. Learn Individ Differ 19(1):61–70

Helle L, Nivala M, Kronqvist P, Ericsson KA, Lehtinen E (2010) Do prior knowledge, personality and visual perceptual ability predict student performance in microscopic pathology? Med Educ 44:621–629

Henderson K (1999) On line and on paper. MIT Press, Cambridge

Holyoak KJ (1991) Symbolic connectionism: toward third-generation theories of expertise. In: Ericsson KA, Smith EJ (eds) Toward a general theory of expertise. Cambridge University Press, Cambridge

Hong Y-C, Choi I (2011) Three dimensions of reflective thinking in solving design problems: a conceptual model. Educ Tech Res Dev 59(5):687–710

Howard RW (2009) Individual differences in expertise development over decades in a complex intellectual domain. Mem Cogn 37(2):194–209. https://doi.org/10.3758/MC.37.2.194

Ip B (2012) Fitting the needs of an industry: an examination of games design, development, and art courses in the UK. ACM Trans Comput Educ 12(2):1–35

Jan Meyer HF, Land R (2003) Threshold concepts and troublesome knowledge: linkages to ways of thinking and practising within the disciplines. In: Rust C (ed) Improving student learning—ten years on. Oxford, Oxford

Keehner MM, Tendick F, Meng MV, Anwar HP, Hegarty M, Stoller ML, Quan-Yang D (2004) Spatial ability, experience, and skill in laparoscopic surgery. Am J Surg 188(1):71–75

Kneebone R (2009) Perspective: simulation and transformational change: the paradox of expertise. Acad Med 84(7):954–957

Kotovsky K, Hayes JR, Simon HA (1985) Why are some problems hard? evidence from Tower of Hanoi. Cogn Psychol 17(2):248–294

Kotzee B (2012) Expertise, fluency and social realism about professional knowledge. J Educ Work 27(2):161–178. https://doi.org/10.1080/13639080.2012.738291

Kurtulus A, Uygan C (2010) The effects of Google sketchup based geometry activities and projects on spatial visualization ability of student mathematics teachers. Procedia—Soc Behav Sci 9:384–389. https://doi.org/10.1016/j.sbspro.2010.12.169

Land R, Rattray J, Vivian P (2014) Learning in the liminal space: a semiotic approach to threshold concepts. High Educ 67(2):199–217

Maeda Y, Yoon SYY (2013) A meta-analysis on gender differences in mental rotation ability measured by the purdue spatial visualization tests. Educational Psychology Review 25(1):69–94. https://doi.org/10.1007/s10648-012-9215-x

Malhotra V, Lee MD, Khurana A (2005) Domain experts influence decision quality: towards a robust method for their identification. J Petrol Sci Eng 57(1–2):181–194

McLeay H, Piggins D (1996) The mental manipulation of 2-D representations of knots as deformable structures. Educ Stud Math 30(4):399–414

Newell A, Simon HA (1988) The theory of human problem-solving. In: Collins A, Smith EE (eds) Readings in cognitive science a perspective from psychology and artificial intelligence. Morgan Kaufmann Publishers Inc, Burlington, MA

Osmond J, Bull K, Tovey M (2009) Threshold concepts and the transport and product design curriculum: reports of research in progress. Art, Des Commun High Educ 8(2):169–175

Peng X, McGary P, Ozturk E, Yalvac B, Johnson M, Valverde LM (2014) Analyzing adaptive expertise and contextual exercise in computer-aided design. Comput. Aided Des Appl 11(5):597–607

Phillips JK, Klein G, Sieck WR (2008) Expertise in judgment and decision making: a case for training intuitive decision skills. In: Koehler DJ, Harvey N (eds) Blackwell handbook of judgment and decision making. Blackwell Publishing Ltd, Malden, MA, USA

Quinlan KM, Male S, Baillie C, Stamboulis A (2013) Methodological challenges in researching threshold concepts: a comparative analysis of three projects. High Educ 66(5):585–601

Raufaste E, Eyrolle H, Mariné C (1998) Pertinence generation in radiological diagnosis: spreading activation and the nature of expertise. Cogn Sci 22(4):517–546. https://doi.org/10.1016/S0364-0213(99)80048-2

Ruthsatz J, Ruthsatz K, Stephens KR (2014) Putting practice into perspective: child prodigies as evidence of innate talent. Intelligence 45(1):60–65. https://doi.org/10.1016/j.intell.2013.08.003

Salthouse TA, Babcock RL, Skovronek E, Mitchell DR, Palmon R (1990) Age and experience effects in spatial visualization. Dev Psychol 26(1):128–136

Santoro N (1984) Sense of direction, topological awareness and communication complexity. ACM SIGACT News 16(2):50–56

Scheja M, Pettersson K (2010) Transformation and contextualisation: conceptualising students' conceptual understandings of threshold concepts in calculus. High Educ 59(2):221–241. https://doi.org/10.1007/s10734-009-9244-7

Schön DA (1992) The theory of inquiry: Dewey's legacy to education. Curriculum Inq 22(2):119–139. https://doi.org/10.2307/1180029

Shanteau J, Weiss DJ, Thomas RP, Pounds JC (2002) Performance-based assessment of expertise: how to decide if someone is an expert or not. Eur J Oper Res 136(2):253–263

Simonton DK (2012) Foresight, insight, oversight, and hindsight in Scientific discovery: how sighted were Galileo's telescopic sightings? Psychol Aesthetics, Creativity, Arts 6(3):243–254. https://doi.org/10.1037/a0027058243

Simonton DK (2014) Thomas Edison's creative career: the multilayered trajectory of trials, errors, failures, and triumphs. Psychol Aesthetics, Creativity, Arts 9(1):2–24

Soloway E, Adelson B, Ehrlich K (2009) Knowledge and processes in the comprehension of computer programs. In: Chi MTH, Glaser R, Farr MJ (eds) The nature of expertise, vol 1. Lawrence Erlbaum Associates Inc, Hillsdale, NJ, pp 129–152

Sonnentag S, Niessen C, Volmer J (2006) Expertise in software design. In: Ericsson KA, Charness N, Feltovich PJ, Hoffman RR (eds) The Cambridge handbook of expertise and expert performance. Cambridge University Press, Cambridge, UK, p 918

Sternberg RJ, Horvath JA (1995) A prototype view of expert teaching. Educ Researcher 24(6):9–17

Sternberg RJ et al. (1999) Tacit Knowledge in the Workplace (0602785A). Retrieved from Alexandria, VA

Sternberg RJ, Forsythe GB, Hedlund J, Horvath JA, Wagner RK, Williams WM, Snook SA, Gigorenko EL (2000) Practical intelligence in everyday life. Cambridge University Press, Cambridge, UK

Sunday M, McGugin RW, Gauthier I (2017) Domain-specific reports of visual imagery vividness are not related to perceptual expertise. Behav Res Methods 49(2):733–738. https://doi.org/10.3758/s13428-016-0730-4

Terlicki MS, Newcombe NS (2005) How important is the digital divide? the relation of computer and videogame usage to gender differences in mental rotation ability. Sex Roles 53(5):433–441

Terman LM (1916) The binet scale and the diagnosis of feeble-mindedness. J Am Inst Crim Law Criminol 7(4):530–543

Titus S, Horsman E (2009) Characterizing and improving spatial visualization skills. J Geosci Educ 57(4):242–254

Vandenberg SG, Kuse AR (1978) Mental rotations, a group test of three-dimensional spatial visualization. Percept Mot Skills 47(2):599–604

Vakil E, Heled E (2016) The effect of constant versus varied training on transfer in a cognitive skill learning task: the case of the Tower of Hanoi puzzle. Learn Individ Differ 47:207–214. https://doi.org/10.1016/j.lindif.2016.02.009

Wai J (2014) Experts are born, then made: combining prospective and retrospective longitudinal data shows that cognitive ability matters. Intelligence 45:74–80. https://doi.org/10.1016/j.intell.2013.08.009

Wason PC, Shapiro D (1971) Natural and contrived experience in a reasoning problem. Q J Exp Psychol 23(1):63–71

Wong AC-N, Palmeri TJ, Gauthier I (2009) Conditions for facelike expertise with objects: becoming a ziggerin expert–but which type? Psychol Sci 20(9)

Xi F, Liu Z (2009) Small world topology-aware geographic routing in wireless sensor networks. Paper presented at the 2009 international conference on communications and mobile computing, Kunming, China

Yang Y, Zou F, Li Z, Ji X, Chen M (2011) Development of a prototype Pattern based on the 3D surface flattening method for MTM garment production. Fibres Text East Eur 19(5):107–111

Chapter 3
Methodology

3.1 Overview

This study used an exploratory mixed methods research design to investigate and explain the development of proficiency among visual art students enrolled in a game development course. The focus of the investigation was on NURBS modelling, a specialty subject in computer graphics that has a reputation for difficulty (see p. 45). The study was split into three phases: pre-observation, observation and post-observation. The pre-observation phase was a quantitative study that used archival records to explore the relationship of prior experience to development. The observation and post-observation phases of the study were primarily qualitative. They were designed to extract data relevant to the development of proficiency as it happened in class. The type of data collected was in the form of digital artefacts (student projects), interviews and learning logs. Quantitative data was analysed using ANOVA and correlation tests. Qualitative data was analysed using a case study method. Quantitative and qualitative data were then triangulated to enhance understanding and increase confidence in the data.

3.2 Mixed Methods Methodology

To answer the research questions developed for this investigation, the methodology had to make it possible to (1) observe whether proficiency was developed, (2) explain factors related to how proficiency was developed, (3) determine whether and how spatial visualisation contributed to the development of proficiency and (4) assess the difference between the problem type and difficulty of the polygon and NURBS projects, respectively (p. 45). These four goals led to the use of an exploratory mixed methods strategy. Exploratory mixed methods design emphasizes a targeted search for knowledge based on general expectations, to leave room for the development of

© Springer Nature Switzerland AG 2018
A. Paquette, *Spatial Visualization and Professional Competence*,
https://doi.org/10.1007/978-3-319-91289-9_3

theory (Creswell and Plano-Clark 2011). In this case, it was known that previous groups of students had developed proficiency. How they developed the proficiency was unknown, and that became the central theme of exploration in this study.

The use of mixed methods was more controversial than it is today (Johnson and Onwuegbuzie 2004). Despite wider acceptance at the time this is written it is worth briefly discussing the more frequently cited arguments against the use of mixed methods. The core argument is that quantitative and qualitative methods are onto-logically and epistemologically incompatible, and thus, should not be mixed (Alise and Teddlie 2010; Creswell and Plano-Clark 2011; Howe 1988). However, although this might be strictly true in the sense that an objective stance cannot simultane-ously be subjective, in practice the division is less clear. This is because quantitative and qualitative methodologies can contain similar underlying assumptions. As Howe explains, (1988) 'one gets to the point of employing statistical tests only by first mak-ing numerous judgments about what counts as a valid measure' (p. 12). At the same time, supposedly qualitative data can be treated quantitatively, such as by counting them.

Quantitative purists maintain that quantitative methods are strictly objective, and qualitative methods are not (Johnson and Onwuegbuzie 2004). Therefore, combining the two cannot increase objectivity. To counter claims that mixed methods increase objectivity, Bergman (2011) writes that, 'the method effect introduced by the QL component is not cancelled out by the introduction of a QN component because the latter introduces its own method effect' (p. 274). This criticism is relevant to studies where the use of mixed methods is intended purely to increase objectivity. In this study the purpose of using each method is designed to accomplish different goals: the validation of prior experience as a factor in development (quantitative), and an exploration of other contributing factors (qualitative).

Qualitative purists maintain that reality cannot be understood without taking into account multiple views, as constructed by those who perceive them, each of which may be different (Johnson and Onwuegbuzie 2004). Such a stance explicitly denies the legitimacy of quantitative measures, which purport to represent an objective reality, free from subjective inference. My view is more constructivist than positivist, in that I accept the premise that reality may be impossible to understand in an absolute way, such as by measuring 'learning' quantitatively, but I do accept the value of quantitative data as something that can enhance understanding. I agree with Creswell (2011) that the key to using qualitative data well is that it is *critical* with the views of participants subjected to rational scrutiny' (p. 277). Quantitative data is similar, in the sense that it can be used productively if one understands its limited purpose and is critical of its meaning during analysis.

A quantitative approach can use a survey to ask students how they viewed the learn-ing experience, but the transition to proficiency is a complex subject. It is resistant to such measures due to the potential for misunderstandings related to the way questions are interpreted (Foddy 1993). Qualitative approaches, such as the interviews under-taken in this study, allow a dialogue to ensure that answers more accurately reflect the views of the speaker. Similarly, although students can say whether they believe prior experience did or did not aid their progress, quantitative data can help validate answers by making correlative analyses of final grades with measures related to prior experience. This is consistent with the pragmatist paradigm, which endeavours to utilise the methods most likely to 'make a difference, as well as connecting abstract issues on the epistemological level to the methodological level' (Shannon-Baker 2016, p. 325).

Criticisms are not limited to mixed methods studies. In an example of a problematic type of monomethod study, Schindler and Burkholder (2016) write of training transfer studies, where a quantitative approach is able to determine whether supervisor support predicts training transfer, but cannot explain how supervisor support influences training transfer. For this reason, mixed methods were recommended. This is analogous to the present study, where one goal is to determine whether a specific performance standard has been achieved, and another is to understand how it was accomplished. Comparison of grades and spatial visualisation test scores with interview data can shed light on whether students with certain pre-existing experience consistently perform differently from students in other groups.

My research stance is that of a pragmatist, also called a 'what works' paradigm. This is because, as Johnson and Onwuegbuzie (2004) write 'obviously, the conduct of fully objective and value-free research is a myth, even though the regulatory ideal of objectivity can be a useful one' (p. 16). Pragmatism is a compatibilist paradigm that explicitly endorses mixed methods as a good research strategy due to the mutually reinforcing strengths of quantitative and qualitative methods (Alise and Teddlie 2010).

In this study, quantitative data were used to measure prior experience and skills. This was then compared to later performance at IGAD to determine what, if any, influence pre-existing knowledge or abilities had on performance. Qualitative measures were used to investigate visual thinking, the use of spatial visualisation, and development of proficiency (through interviews with students and professionals). The results of both strands of the study were then integrated for triangulation. 'Triangulation' is the process of using quantitative data to validate qualitative data, and vice versa. If used well, triangulation in mixed methods studies is known to have strengthened the overall validity of findings (Raimondo and Newcomer 2017), and will have 'complementary strengths and non-overlapping weaknesses' (Johnson and Onwuegbuzie 2004, p. 18).

Triangulation of data is particularly important here because this study is exploring cognitive processes that are inherently subjective. Quantitative data enhances understanding of qualitative data that might otherwise rely too much on claims by students, and qualitative data provides a better understanding of the process of development and factors contributing to the quantitative results. On their own, a purely quantitative or qualitative study would have been unsatisfying; therefore, a mixed methodology was called for.

3.3 Case Study

To study expertise in chess players, representative tasks are analysed instead of full games (Chase and Simon 1973; de Groot 1972). In chess, a representative task is typically a critical mid-game position upon which the end game depends. How players react to these positions has proven to be an accurate reflection of their measured playing ability. If chosen well, representative tasks allow research questions to be answered more efficiently than if a broader range of data had been collected. For laboratory research in particular, it is considered essential by some to use representative tasks as a way to limit the number of variables without sacrificing the value of data collected (Ericsson and Ward 2007).

For the field of digital art, it is difficult to say that any one task, such as modelling, texturing, lighting, rendering, animation or visual effects, is more representative of expertise in digital art than any other. The tasks are too different to allow such a determination. However, at IGAD, the first examples of professional quality work tend to be produced in the first year NURBS modelling class, MD2. In addition, it is one of the few subjects that students have no prior experience with. To follow the example of de Groot (1972), Chase and Simon (1973), and Ericsson and Ward (2007), the MD2 class was chosen as representative of the development of proficiency as a digital artist. It was selected because it is the first example of proficient work in a complex task produced by IGAD students. To track development of proficiency, the MD2 class was observed over seven weeks of classes, followed by two weeks of independent study by students, for a total of nine weeks.

All students were given the same task in the same conditions regardless of their level of ability or experience. This allowed data regarding persons not presumed to be proficient to be collected at a time when their NURBS modelling experience was equal with other students'. Doing this controlled for individual differences in later performance.

Although the intent of this study is similar to that espoused in 'classic' grounded theory, as Glaser's version of grounded theory is called (Lapan et al. 2012). It will not be used here due to its incompatibility with mixed methods, and a tighter focus in the present study than is typically envisioned in grounded theory (Glaser 2007). Instead, traditional case study is used to guide data collection and analysis. By doing so, the study can be situated in the context of historical performance among previous IGAD students and utilise mixed methods to observe current ones (Charmaz 2017). This study design is consistent with others where 'statistical analysis [is used] to identify patterns and deviant cases, and case studies to point out omitted variables and/or explore causal mechanisms' (Harrits 2011).

To have a better understanding of the problems faced by students, the next three sections present a detailed overview of modelling projects at IGAD, the NURBS project and a brief discussion of NURBS (pp. 45–51). These details are provided to better appreciate aspects of the project that could have an impact on how NURBS modelling skills are learned and implications for the acquisition of proficiency.

3.4 Observation Frame: The MD2 NURBS Modelling Class

3.4.1 Modelling Projects at IGAD

The type of projects assigned to professional digital artists varies depending on their specialty, but the most common tasks belong to one of four groups: modelling, texturing, animation and rendering. The specifics vary depending on the purpose, and there are many sub-groups within each of these primary categories. However, most are dependent on modelling as a starting point for other tasks. A 'model' in CG is a virtual definition of a 3D object. For example, an animation of a character requires a definition of the shape of that character. That is the model.

To make a model, an artist can use any one of several types of 'geometry'. In CG, the word 'geometry' refers to the descriptive method used to define 3D structure. Two of the most common types of geometry are 'polygons' and Non-Uniform Rational Bezier Splines (NURBS). A polygonal object is composed of a series of connected straight lines. A geodesic dome is an example of how a polygonal hemisphere would look if built from polygons. A NURBS object is defined by mathematically accurate curves, which allows NURBS objects to be perfectly smooth at any resolution. A NURBS hemisphere is not faceted like a polygonal sphere, but smooth (Fig. 3.1). After a model is built, it is assigned material properties, colour and texture. It may then be animated, lit and turned into a final image.

IGAD students must build three modelling projects in their first year. Each was designed to function primarily as a visualisation exercise. Grades from these projects were used in phase one of this study as measures of performance. The three projects were:

- Folding Carton (polygons)
- Illusion (polygons)
- Vehicle (NURBS).

These projects are similar to the kind of projects assigned to digital artists in industry. There are, however, some crucial differences. For instance, in the folding

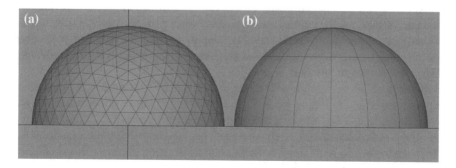

Fig. 3.1 Comparison polygons (**a**) and NURBS (**b**)

carton project, students must fold a digital representation of a folding carton into its final shape by rotating vertices instead of transforming them directly into their final position. This is not always the most efficient method to build these objects, but it requires that students frequently use and re-use a small number of common tools. This allows them to quickly familiarise themselves with the interface. In addition, seeing a 2D object: the unfolded carton, folded into a 3D object enhances their ability to visualise 3D shape transformations.

For the Illusion project (Fig. 3.2), students are asked to build a 3D model based on a drawing that contains impossible connections. Objects that appear to be connected in the drawing cannot be connected in 3D space, so students must figure out how to construct the model so that its separate parts appear connected when viewed from a certain angle. Students are not allowed to skew their model to make it fit the drawing they are working from. In an industry project, if the goal were to make a static render from one viewpoint, this would not matter as much and might not be a restriction. This and other constraints are focussed on learning goals as opposed to imitation of industry projects. For instance, the alignment illusion embedded in the illusion project forces students to manipulate the focal length of the camera, an action that demonstrates how important lens length is to the final appearance of a scene. In a professional context a supervisor might be more flexible regarding this constraint. As long as the end product looks good, there is no cause for complaint. Because exactitude is required from the students, they must experiment a great deal, thus learning the concept more thoroughly. To execute the Illusion project well, most students also find it necessary to make preliminary drawn sketches on paper of possible solutions, thus providing an opportunity to learn another practical skill, drawing, in an appropriate practical context.

The NURBS vehicle project is meant to challenge student visualisation and problem-solving ability. Like the two projects just described, it has some requirements that do not reflect industry norms to emphasise learning goals embedded in the project. For instance, students are only allowed to build cars that are designed with CAD tools because the curves are more complex than clay modelling methods used in the automotive design industry prior to the CAD era of design. In an entertainment project, this would not be a limitation.

Before this research was formally contemplated, students were asked which classes they felt had the strongest impact on them. In response, several reported that the NURBS modelling class was pivotal in their development as digital artists. Although it is considered an advanced technique, it is taught in the first year of the visual art curriculum to give IGAD students more time to practice NURBS modelling. The class it is taught within is 'Modelling 2' (MD2).

Statements by successful students regarding the NURBS project indicated that it possessed a quality that they considered essential to their development as artists. The project cannot be used as a way to predict performance of incoming students because it is first encountered only after students have been accepted for admission, but it can be used to learn whether there is something about the class that is relevant to general proficiency in digital art.

Fig. 3.2 Illusion sketch provided to students (courtesy of and © 2012 Simen Stroek) and final rendered image by study participant

Students also mentioned the Carton project as important to their development, but because it is too simple to reflect a normal project from industry, it could not be used as a realistic test of student proficiency as modellers. In contrast, based on the quality and complexity of student NURBS projects, it seems at least possible that some students develop technical proficiency as NURBS modellers during the MD2 class or within the first three quarters of the first year (Fig. 3.3).

Fig. 3.3 An example of a NURBS vehicle made by a first-year student

Only one to five students a year achieve what teachers feel is industry-level proficiency, but for any student to hand in a project of that quality in the first year is impressive. This is particularly true in the context of their level of experience at the time they take the class. Unlike first-generation CAD users and animators, first-year IGAD students have no working experience, no experience with NURBS prior to the class and most have only about five months of general CG experience at IGAD.

3.4.2 The MD2 NURBS Project

Students of the MD2 class were asked to build a 3D model of an existing automobile in a computer graphics application known as Maya 2013, using NURBS geometry.[1] NURBS are one of several methods for representing the structure of three-dimensional objects in a computer. This type of representation is used in the industrial design field to design complex curved surfaces such as those found in automobiles (Besl 1998; Krause et al. 2003). In games, polygons are used instead.

One difference between NURBS and polygons is that NURBS geometry can be smooth to an infinite level of detail, but polygons cannot. This is because polygons are collections of points connected by straight lines, but NURBS are defined by curves that pass through specified points (Fig. 3.4). Practically speaking, this means that product designers must use NURBS to ensure that their designs can be manufactured

---

[1] The full instruction sheet given to students can be found in Sect. 8.2 (p. 205).

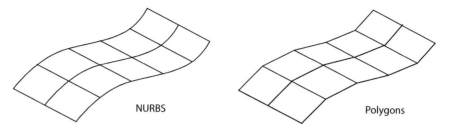

NURBS

Polygons

Fig. 3.4 NURBS geometry is based on mathematically defined curves. This allows for smooth, unfaceted representations of curved shapes

as real-world objects. If polygons were used, the manufactured objects would have faceted rather than smooth surfaces because polygonal geometry is made of linked straight-line segments.

The core problem in the NURBS project is how to take an existing complex curved surface: the body of an automobile, and determine how to represent it accurately using NURBS patches. A NURBS patch, also called a 'surface', depending on context, is the basic unit used to describe the structure of NURBS objects. To be professionally competent, a finished file must have an efficient layout and be a likeness of the target vehicle (Fig. 3.5). Students are not expected to replicate the patch layout used by the vehicle's original designers because (a) the original layout is not available for comparison and (b) it would be almost impossible to accurately determine the patch layout based on an existing manufactured vehicle alone.

3.4.3 What Are NURBS?

NURBS allow surface structure to be represented by mathematically accurate curves. Industry jargon describes a 'legal' patch, or 'surface', as one that follows the single rule of NURBS geometry: It must have four sides. An 'illegal' surface cannot be

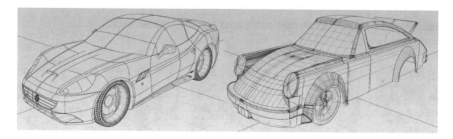

Fig. 3.5 These wireframe renders highlight the patch layout of each vehicle. The layout on left is well-organised and has correct tangency and good detail. The model on the right has inappropriate weighting of detail, discontinuity across surfaces and distortion

made because the software is incapable of representing such a surface. This means
that triangular shapes must be subdivided into three four-sided patches or cut out of
a four-sided shape to satisfy the four-sided rule (Fig. 3.6).

The most challenging aspect of working with NURBS surfaces is designing a patch
layout where patches seamlessly blend together (Besl 1998) (Fig. 3.7). NURBS are
known by industry professionals to be difficult to work with due to this limitation
(Gao et al. 2006; Müller et al. 2006). Successfully breaking down the bodywork
of an automobile into a complex group of surfaces requires practice, planning and
persistence. This is the challenge students must face in the MD2 class. To get around
the limitations of NURBS geometry, subdivision surfaces were invented (Catmull
and Clark 1978), which allow NURBS and polygons to work together for easier
manipulation. However, despite the success of subdivision surfaces for entertainment
applications, NURBS remain the standard for industrial design because of their ability
to represent shapes accurately.

The two most important qualities of the finished NURBS model made for the
MD2 class are tangency and likeness. 'Tangency', in this context, is a quality that
defines any two or more surfaces that seamlessly blend together. To achieve this, the
direction of tangents at boundaries must be the same on both sides of the boundary.
This is easily achieved for planar surfaces, but can be very complex for arbitrary
curved shapes such as those found in vehicles. The term 'likeness' refers to the
fidelity of the NURBS model to the source object. That is, any deviation from the
shape of the source vehicle reduces the quality of the likeness. An example of this is
if the curve of the bonnet is too flat, too bowed or distorted.

Tangency and likeness are evaluated as product components are made. If any
component fails the tangency or likeness test, it must be rebuilt (Fig. 3.8). After all

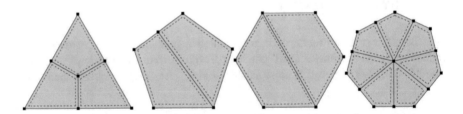

Fig. 3.6 Non-four-sided shapes subdivided into groups of four-sided patches

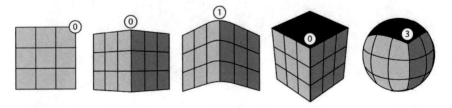

Fig. 3.7 Tangency is required to establish curvature continuity across adjacent NURBS patches.
Numbers represent the number of tangent surfaces at the labelled corner

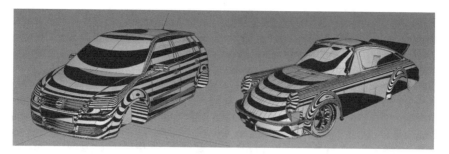

Fig. 3.8 'Zebra stripe' pattern on NURBS model emphasises surface flow problems. In this example by student participants there are no serious flow problems in the vehicle at left, but on the right, there is evidence of severe problems, such as in the windshield

of the components have been tested by the student and passed through to the end of the pipeline, a finished vehicle model is submitted to a teacher for grading. In practice, most student projects contain some tangency and likeness errors, but in each of the previous five years in which this project has been a part of the IGAD curriculum, between one and five projects have been free of serious errors.

In summary, the NURBS project asks students to reverse-engineer the body of an existing contemporary automobile. Their model is to be built using NURBS patches, which impose limitations on how structure is represented. The models should be a good likeness of the target vehicle.

3.5   Participant Selection

Student participants were enrolled at The International Game Architecture and Design (IGAD) programme at the Nationale Hogeschool voor Tourisme en Verkeer (NHTV) University of Applied Sciences, located in the Netherlands. NHTV is located in the south of the Netherlands and has about 7700 students in total. The IGAD programme was chosen because it is well-known in the Netherlands and elsewhere for its ability to produce graduates who are qualified for employment in the computer graphics industry. As a lecturer at IGAD, I have easy access to classes there, making it a practical as well as an appropriate choice of location.

The goal of this research is to understand how proficiency developed in the academic and professional careers of IGAD students by observing current students as they undergo similar training and experiences. This is practitioner research because the lead investigator (the author) was also a teacher of the student participants, but it is not action research because there was no observe-intervene-observe-report methodology involved (Virkki-Hatakka et al. 2013). The goal was not to change what happens to determine what effect that change might have on student learning, but to witness what happens naturally as a way to better understand it.

The emphasis of this study is prospective (development as it happens) and involved undergraduate students who had not yet demonstrated their potential as digital artists. Participants in this study were divided into three classifications: students, industry, and employed graduates. A fourth category is archival student data provided by NHTV. Each of these participant groups provided a different perspective on the research questions. Students generated data relevant to the learning process and provided project files that could be compared to self-reported data. Industry participants fulfilled two functions: to assess student work against industry standards and to provide feedback on how the work of professional digital artists is assessed. Employed graduates are graduates of the IGAD programme who were employed as digital artists in industry after their graduation. These participants offered their perspective on the transition from student to professional work and standards. Archival data was used to establish pre-existing experience and to compare with later performance, as measured by grades and course credit accumulations.

There were 20 student participants, 5 industry participants and 5 employed graduate participants (Table 3.1). Archival data was available for 625 IGAD students (inclusive of study participants). The student participants comprised 24% of the 83 students enrolled in the MD2 class for the 2012–2013 academic year. All students were invited to participate in the initial call for participation; none were rejected. Due to 4 dropouts from the 20 original members of the student group, students who had not initially volunteered as participants were allowed to participate in the study at the conclusion of the MD2 class.

Industry participants were invited based on recommendations from IGAD lecturers or my own contacts, with the goal of finding at least five participants with supervisor-level industry experience out of the invitations that were sent. Employed graduates were selected in the same way: a number of email invitations were sent to all graduates known to be employed in good standing and all graduates who volunteered were accepted.

The number of students who enrolled for the study was the minimum hoped for. It was desirable for the initial group to be as large as possible to enhance the probability that the study group would include students who would perform well on the NURBS project. Only one of the eight students who received 'professional'-level grades in the MD2 class was originally enrolled in the study. The remaining seven students who had met this standard were solicited to participate in the study at the conclusion of the class. Two of these students accepted the invitation. Because they entered at the conclusion of the class they did not have learning logs or spatial visualisation test scores. Apart from that, they were able to provide the same data at the same time as all other students. A fourth student from a previous year allowed his project to be used so

Table 3.1 Study participant categories

Participant type	Students	Industry	Employed graduates	Archival (inclusive)
n=	20	5	5	625

that professional participants would have four files to review. This compromise was made for the purpose of increasing the validity of industry assessments by providing more examples to assess. It also allowed a project graded by a different lecturer to be compared with grades given during the study to establish that grading criteria were consistent.

Professionals from companies in several different countries were invited. Those who accepted were from the United States, the Netherlands and Belgium. None of the industry participants worked at the same company. Four of the companies were game development studios and the fifth was a supplier of 3D models and motion capture data to a variety of industries that included game development, feature films, the U.S. military and medical visualisation. All of the professionals had a minimum of 10 years of industry experience. All had experience as supervisors of other digital artists in modelling tasks. These participants were considered experts on the subject of assessing the work of junior artists on the basis of their years of experience doing exactly that in industry as supervisors of digital artists. In consideration of the small number of industry participants, it is possible they do not represent the industry as a whole. Their diversity related to nationality, place of employment and studio specialty, recommends the position that the more their results are in agreement, the more probable it is that their assessments represent industry norms. This is another reason why all participants were asked to review the same files, so that inter-rater reliability could be compared.

The five employed graduates worked in the following countries at the time of their interviews: the Netherlands, Belgium, the United Kingdom and Canada. Two of the employed graduates worked at the same company, but not in the same department and each had different responsibilities. Each of the employed graduates had between one and three years' industry experience at the time of the interviews. They worked in the following specialties: character modelling (games), visual effects (games), procedural modelling (games), visual effects/compositing (feature film) and technical direction (games). None of the employed graduates was required to use NURBS modelling to carry out their work responsibilities, but some used the method when they felt it was appropriate.

Students were interviewed at the NHTV campus during normal school hours. Industry participants and employed graduates were interviewed in person if they were located in the Netherlands. More distant participants were interviewed online using the Skype video conferencing software. To view student work for assessment, it was loaded onto the principal investigator's computer, then the screen was shared via Skype for distant industry participants. Local industry participants were allowed to open and manipulate anonymised student files on the principal investigator's laptop computer.

3.6   Three Phases of Data Collection

3.6.1   Overview Phase Descriptions

This study is organised into three phases, one of which is quantitative. The quantitative and qualitative studies are described separately, because the majority of data collected for each was collected at different times. Each of the phases are presented below.

3.6.2   Data Collection

Data collected for this study came from four sources: archival data (NHTV), first year students, employed graduates and industry participants (Table 3.2). All participants participated in interviews. Industry participants also assessed student projects. Students kept learning logs, filled out a questionnaire, turned in weekly progress files for their project and took the PVRT spatial visualisation test. Archival data was available for 625 students, inclusive of study participants.

Not all students have records corresponding to all data types. This is because some dropped out before taking the MD2 class, some weren't present when spatial visualisation tests were given and some intake ranks were unavailable. The range of usable records is therefore between 51 and 625, depending on which combination of records was used. The data can be sorted into four groups: (1) intake assessment, (2) spatial visualisation tests, (3) later performance and (4) demographics.

Table 3.2 Data types and their sources

Archival data	Students (n = 20)	Employed graduates (n = 5)	Industry (n = 5)
School type (n = 625)	Questionnaire	Interviews	MD2 Grades
Carton grades (n = 568)	Learning logs	–	Interviews
MD1 grades (n = 593)	MD2 project	–	–
MD2 grades (n = 474)	Weekly progress	–	–
PVRT (n = 111)	Interviews	–	–
RMFBT (n = 66)	PVRT	–	–
End-view (n = 52)	–	–	–
DAT (n = 51)	–	–	–
Intake rank (n = 227)	–	–	–
Credits (n = 241)	–	–	–

3.6.3   Data Type Flow Chart

The central focus of the methodology used in this study was to observe the NURBS modelling class, known as 'MD2' at IGAD, to learn how students develop NURBS modelling proficiency. Data were collected before, during and after the class to gain insight into the learning process and factors that contributed to making the transition from novice to proficient performance. The way quantitative and qualitative data are integrated is illustrated in Fig. 3.9.

As the diagram shows, the primary division of data types was between quantitative data relevant to prior experience and qualitative data relevant to the student experience of developing proficiency. The principal question asked of the quantitative data was whether student performance can be predicted on the basis of prior performance. If the answer was yes, then prior experience would have been added to the significant factors leading to proficiency. If not, then interviews would have been modified to explore why. What actually happened was that the answer was yes and no, depending on the type of experience and the type of performance it was compared to.

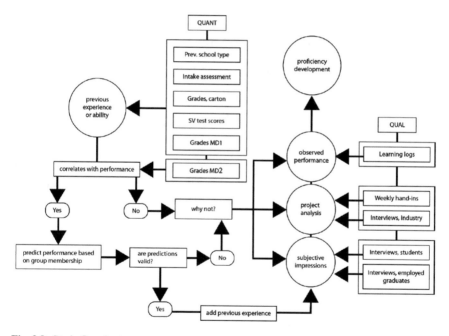

Fig. 3.9 Study flowchart

3.6.4   Quantitative Phase, Phase One

3.6.4.1   Prior Experience and Rapid Development

Rapid development of expertise has not been adequately or conclusively demonstrated, as Ericsson (2014) argues. One of the main arguments against it is that prior
training and experience has not been taken into consideration. To determine when
training, and therefore deliberate practice, began for the IGAD students being studied, archival data was analysed using analysis of variance (ANOVA) and correlation
tests. The raw data was comprised of student intake portfolio assignment evalua-
tions, previous school types, intake rankings, project grades, credit accumulations
and spatial visualisation test scores.

The goal was to discover characteristics prevalent among novices, in contrast to
experts, which could influence their later development into proficient performers
as a prerequisite to becoming experts. By identifying what traits novices possessed
prior to the beginning of training, it became possible to collect data relevant to
competing theories that portray the development of expertise as the result of talent,
intelligence, inherited traits or deliberate practice. This is important because of the
potential for prior experience to explain later development (Ericsson 2014). If student
performance was predictable on the basis of prior experience, the result would support
the deliberate practice framework of expertise development. If prior experience was
not predictive, then other explanations would have to be considered.

3.6.4.2   Quantitative Data Measures Previous Experience

All but one of the quantitative data types are related to experience prior to attending
IGAD, or experience prior to taking the NURBS class. The last category is grades
for the NURBS modelling class itself (MD2). This data is from archival sources for
non-participants or is generated during the study for student participants. This is the
key quantitative performance metric used for statistical comparisons. It is also used
to verify proficiency, so that interview statements can be understood in the context
of actual performance, rather than a student's subjective perception of it.

3.6.4.3   Archival Data

The number of student participants ($n = 20$) in this study was too small to perform
any statistical tests. However, IGAD routinely collects various types of anonymised
student data, which were made available for this study. The number of datasets
responsive to questions in this study was sufficient to establish statistical significance
(between 51 and 625 subjects, depending on the data type). The data were used to
establish context for qualitative data gathered from student participants. Specifically,
they allowed statistical tests that compared previous school types, PVRT scores,

RMFBT scores, intake assessment rankings, assessment scores and grades on the Carton, Illusion and NURBS projects (described starting on p. 45). These comparisons allowed some conclusions to be drawn regarding the impact of prior experience, previous school type, spatial visualisation and performance in other IGAD classes.

3.6.4.4 SV Testing

Spatial visualisation tests have been used as part of college admissions processes, training in domains thought to demand strong spatial visualisation skills, and hiring decisions (Hegarty et al. 2009; Likert and Quasha 1994; Samsudin et al. 2011). The prevalent use of these tests, and the reasons for using them: testing spatial abilities thought to indicate aptitude in certain tasks, recommend that they be taken into account in this study. This is because the domain of digital art includes some of the same tasks, such as orthographic drawing and projection, that are associated with proficiency in domains that depend on spatial visualisation skill (Samsudin et al. 2011). This is despite finding no references to the use of spatial visualisation tests in the CG industry, possibly due to the ubiquitous use of demo reels.

3.6.4.5 PVRT Chosen to Test SV

The principal instruments used to measure spatial visualisation skills are paper and pencil tests (Salthouse et al. 1990). There is considerable variety within the hundreds of available tests, but they fall into a smaller number of groups, such as: maze (route-finding), embedded figures, visual memory, paper formboard, figural rotation, block rotation, paper folding, surface development, perspective and mental rotation (Eliot and Smith 1983). This study will use the most common test associated with 3D spatial visualisation, the Purdue Visualisation of Rotations Test (PVRT) (Bodner and Guay 1997; Peters et al. 1995). One benefit of this test is that it is the same test used in the Coventry study (Osmond et al. 2009), thus allowing a direct comparison of results. The reason this test was used is to find out why the test scores did not correlate with performance in the Coventry study and the early tests at IGAD.

3.6.4.6 MD2 Projects and Grades

Student projects were graded after the MD2 course was complete. The co-teacher for the class graded the work of study participants and I graded non-participants to prevent grading bias. This followed the example of other researcher participants who have utilized two or more teachers to balance potential bias (Dymond et al. 2006).

Four MD2 projects by students who earned a grade of 8 or higher were selected for review by industry participants. The purpose of the industry interviews was to identify whether any student projects were proficient by industry standards and to define proficiency in the context of the industry standard they were familiar with. Interviews with industry participants were limited to one hour each. To avoid inefficient use of industry participants' available time while maximising the potential that proficient quality projects would be found, only the highest-scoring projects were delivered to them.

It would have been possible to review more projects if each industry participant had been given different project files, but that would not have allowed comparisons of results for inter-rater reliability. It also would have involved reviewing projects that could not meet a professional standard because they were severely incomplete or contained serious errors, as was true of many of the files given a grade lower than 8. The purpose of this review was to determine whether any of the project files met a professional standard. Therefore, only the best projects, which had the highest chances of being deemed professional quality, were selected for industry assessment.

3.6.5 Qualitative Phases, Phase Two and Three

3.6.5.1 Complex Tasks Versus Simple Tasks

Early examples of development studies rely on student volunteers, who are given a simple task to learn, like typing or navigating an unfamiliar environment, over a short period of time (Ericsson and Polson 1988). The studies investigated the acquisition of simple skills only, hence the short durations of the tasks. This is fundamentally different from more modern studies, which focus on expertise in domains, the knowledge relevant to the domain and skill developed over time with practice (Ericsson 2014).

The present study combines elements of methodologies used in early and more recent studies by observing student participants as they learn complex tasks relevant to developing proficiency. A difference is that students cannot be observed for the full period in which they are engaged on the project. They will be observed in the classroom (about 32 h), but will be required to do much of their work outside the classroom (an expected average of 10 h a week, or 70 h). To track the unobserved work, this study relied on interviews, questionnaires, weekly hand-ins and learning logs produced by students.

3.6.5.2 Retrospective Studies of Expertise

For the deliberate practice framework, wherein the development of expertise is thought to be the product of many years of deliberate practice, methodologies require the identification of existing experts, and then structuring interviews to elicit the history of their development (Ericsson 2014). A fault with this type of methodology is highlighted by Hambrick et al. (2014), who point out that reliance on self-reports, particularly regarding events from decades earlier, is inherently unreliable without some way to independently verify the accounts. To address this fault, this study sought to observe proficiency as it developed rather than ask experts to recall the process after it had occurred.

Thus, unlike other studies, none of the participants have been verified to be experts or proficient prior to the beginning of the study. This is quite different from studies using the expert/novice paradigm, which compare groups of experts with groups of novices. The expert/novice approach allows comparisons to be made about median IQ values, the amount of deliberate practice and other factors thought to be germane to being an expert but not a novice (Grabner 2014). In those studies, experts and novices are analysed as two separate groups. By contrast, there are no experts (or proficient performers) at the start of the study to compare novices to, but by the end of the study some of the novices may have become technically proficient.

3.6.5.3 Overview Phase 2 and 3

Quantitative data from the first phase of the study were used to identify areas of interest, such as spatial visualisation ability and performance on a related but different task (see p. 51), which were then checked in the second and third phases as students progressed through the NURBS modelling task. The latter two qualitative phases of this study, observation and post-observation, were designed to observe as students develop skills in a complex task (NURBS modelling), hopefully become proficient, and then explore factors that led to the transition from non-proficient to proficient status. The data used in these phases of the study utilised observation of performance and self-report via learning logs, weekly progress reports, pre-interview questionnaires and interviews as recommended in an article on experiment designs used to research expertise (Farrington-Darby and Wilson 2006).

3.6.5.4 Qualitative Data Overview

Students were asked to maintain learning logs during the course of the MD2 project and hand in progress on their projects every week. This was used to track their development and problems encountered during the learning process. They were then asked to submit final projects for assessment, resulting in the grade that would determine their overall performance in the class. When the class concluded, they were asked to fill in a questionnaire and participate in an hour-long interview to record their thoughts on the learning process. All industry participants filled out a questionnaire to establish their background in computer graphics and then took part in an hour-long interview to assess the work of student participants. Employed graduates took part in an hour-long interview only, to provide perspective on their transition from academic to industry standards.

3.6.5.5 Phase 2 Methods (Data Collection)

Learning logs and weekly work hand-ins were used to track student progress. Learning logs were in the form of an Excel template file given to each student, with instructions how to make weekly entries. Work hand-ins were Maya format files containing current progress on the NURBS project.

3.6.5.6 Phase 3 Methods (Data Collection)

Phase 3 began with a pre-interview questionnaire designed to help prepare interview questions for students, followed by recorded interviews to elicit information about the students' learning processes. Industry participants filled out a short questionnaire to establish their credentials as supervisors with appropriate knowledge and experience. After filling out the questionnaire, they were interviewed to receive their opinions on whether the student projects shown to them met a professional standard. Employed graduates did not fill out a questionnaire, but were interviewed to gain insight into their transition from novice student to employed professional.

Student questionnaires focused on five categories of information: (1) demographics (age, gender, local/international status), (2) potential non-school related impediments to performance (length of commute to school, part-time job, housing situation), (3) prior experience (previous school type, drawing, self-taught, type of previous experience, amount of previous experience), (4) attitude toward NURBS class (see Sect. 8.3, p. 211) and (5) progress during NURBS class (see Sect. 8.3, p. 211) to evaluate possible factors influencing performance.

Answers to these questions were used as a starting point for semi-structured student interviews. For instance, the following question was asked in the interview to understand why a student provided the answer given on the questionnaire: 'It looks like you said that MD2 did enhance your problem-solving skills. What do you mean by that?' The student was then asked follow-up questions to flesh out the meaning of his answer. Depending on the answers given, the interview could take a new direction, or continue to follow the template laid out by questionnaire answers. The goal was to gain insight into the learning process from the student's perspective.

3.6.5.7 MD2 Industry Assessment Interviews

After selection, the four NURBS projects were shown to industry participants for review in open-ended interview sessions. Each industry participant was interviewed separately and each viewed the same four files. Each participant had one hour to review all four files and make comments and judgment of them to determine whether they met an industry standard.

All projects were carefully reviewed to track learning and development, but of those, only the four files with the highest grades were shown to industry participants to determine whether proficiency had been achieved.

3.6.6   Data Collection Conclusion

Data collected for all three phases of this study were sufficient to establish perfor-mance norms and prior experience (archival data), details of progress as it happened (learning logs and weekly hand-ins), credible assessments of student proficiency (industry assessments) and reflections on the learning process (student and employed graduate interviews). Archival data was available in sufficient numbers to perform statistical tests (described in the next section). Qualitative data contained enough depth to develop an understanding of the learning process from the student point of view.

3.7   Analysis

3.7.1   Analysis of Quantitative Data

3.7.1.1   To Establish Prior Experience

The archival data are able to confidently establish the type of prior education students had prior to attending IGAD, spatial visualisation ability as measured by mental rotation tests and performance in class as measured by grades and earned credits. The data are also able to provide information relevant to prior knowledge of subjects relevant to digital art, though these data require some interpretation. The data were analysed using correlational and ANOVA analysis tools. This is similar to other studies in education, where test scores are compared to later performance, such as a study on the relationship of English as a second language test scores and later academic performance (Lee and Greene 2007).

3.7.1.2   Spatial Visualisation Tests

Analysis of quantitative data was performed to answer a number of questions, some that emerged from the data and others inspired by the original research questions. Most of these were either analysis of variance (ANOVA) tests to compare homo-geneity of groups, or more commonly, Kruskal-Wallis H tests to understand whether grades differed based on prior educational level or initial intake assessment scores. At a general level, the goal was to determine if any known factor pre-disposed students to perform at a higher level than others, or to develop more quickly.

Prior to collecting data, the groups of greatest interest were: type of previous school attended, ranking at intake assessment and spatial visualisation test scores. The other major comparison measure of interest was polygon project versus NURBS project grades. These were made into groups that were then compared to every appro-priate quantitative measure to determine whether there was a statistically significant difference in the way students scored on these projects based on other group categories they belonged to. For example, were VWO students (the highest level in the Dutch system) more likely to earn high grades than MBO students (the lowest level)? If so, this would indicate that either the VWO education or selection into a VWO programme somehow improved performance on digital art tasks and could be the basis for further research.

Spatial visualisation tests were also compared to various groupings of students and project grades for the purpose of establishing whether spatial visualisation, as tested for in mental rotation tests, is relevant to performance in polygon or NURBS modelling. If the answer is the same for both, whether positive or negative, it indicates homogeneity on that factor. If the results differ, then it may be inferred that there is a difference in the way spatial visualisation is used on the two projects that might be helpful in understanding the relationship of spatial visualisation to digital art.

3.7.1.3 Exception to Statistical Validity

It is important to note that there are two distinct groups of similar data in this study and they are used differently. These two groups are defined as related to the students whose data appears in the archival data (n = 51 to n = 625) and students enrolled in this study as participants (n = 20). The figure of 625 archival records is inclusive of the 20 student participants. The archival data was used only for statistical comparisons and analysis. Data from the group of 20 student participants, including 'counted' data, such as the number of students who come from various school types, or who fall into other categories, are not used to establish statistical validity because the sample size is too small. Instead, when mentioned, such data is only intended to show how the student participant group deviates from or conforms to the much larger archival data group.

The goals of using these data are to establish:

- previous educational experience
- prior understanding of topic (digital art, general art and academic aptitude)
- prior predictions of performance by teachers
- spatial visualisation performance
- the relationship of these factors to performance.

In this case, the goal is not to end the study after checking for correlations between prior experience and later development, but to use that information to develop a working portrait of IGAD students as a group, to better understand data gathered during the qualitative phase. In this way, complementary strengths of the different phases of the study are designed to produce a better result than either type of data alone.

3.7.1.4 Quantitative Correlation to Generate Qualitative Questions

If correlations are found between a certain type of prior experience and specific performance levels, the student participants who have that type of experience may be expected to perform at the same levels. If they do not, asking questions to investigate why not becomes useful to further develop theory and to better understand findings from the quantitative phase of the study. Likewise, if student participants are deemed to have achieved proficiency through the quantitative measure of grades, questioning why may provide insight into other factors influencing their success.

This approach is consistent with Johnson and Onwuegbuzie (2004), who point out that corroboration across methods yields higher confidence, and disagreements raise questions that increase knowledge on the topic (p. 19).

3.7.1.5 Professional and Academic Grading

At IGAD, a grade of 6 out of a maximum score of 10 is academically sufficient to pass the class. A grade of 8 or higher corresponds to what is considered by teachers to be a professional level of proficiency. Files that receive a grade of 8 or above should be fit for use in an industry context based on the standard used by IGAD teachers.

The IGAD grading scale is not a smooth gradient. The difference between a grade of 7, or 'good academic standard' and an 8, an 'acceptable professional standard', is much greater than the difference between a 6 and a 7 or an 8 and a 9 because each grade pair belongs to a different standard: academic versus professional. Students can pass the class without developing proficiency, but their ultimate goal is to be proficient so that they may be successful candidates for industry positions. This grading standard is intended to provide feedback to students that is relevant to their goal of becoming proficient.

Unlike the academic standard, all passing grades given by industry participants in the 6 to 10 range are 'proficient'. This is because a failing grade, understood in the Netherlands to be a 5 or less on a 10-point scale, denotes a project that cannot be used in a professional context and therefore is not fit for use. To ensure that academic and industry grades had equivalent meanings, the industry grades were scaled so that a 6 on the industry scale was an 8 on the academic scale (Table 3.3).

3.7.1.6 Academic Assessment

The academic grading method for the MD2 project was designed to be as objective as possible. The result was scoring that emphasised technical defects (see Sect. 8.3 for details, p. 209). All projects that were turned in for grading started with a grade of 10. From there, up to a maximum of three points were added or subtracted in each of four categories: level of completion, likeness, tangency and technical errors. Raw grades could exceed 10 or be less than 0 due to bonuses given or a high number of errors. The final grade was capped at 10 and had a minimum value of 1 (Table 3.4).

Table 3.3 Industry grades scaled to fit professional range of academic grades

	Industry (original)	Industry (adjusted)	Academic (fractional grades not given at IGAD)
Not fit-for-use	<6	<8	<8
Acceptable	6	8	8
Average	7	8.5	NA
Good	8	9	9
Very good	9	9.5	NA
Excellent	10	10	10

Table 3.4 Example NURBS vehicle grading

File number	Delivery score	Completion score	Likeness score	Tangency score	Technical score	Raw vehicle grade
1	0	–	–	–	–	0
2	10	0	−1	−1	−1	7
3	10	0	1	1	−2	10

In practice, most students earned a grade of 6 or 7, with grades tapering off to either extreme.

Grades were accompanied by notes to explain grades to students. The goal of providing these notes, as well as grading criteria, was to demonstrate to students that all grades were based on objective criteria (Table 3.5).

The criteria selected for grade deductions were chosen on the basis of what teachers at IGAD perceived to be highest-priority problem categories for industry clients. The strategy behind this grading method was to eliminate complaints from students about unclear grading criteria. This was particularly important because of the university's rule that students with less than 54 credits are expelled. Classes that use more subjective grading methods can have grades overturned if the university's testing committee believes the assessment criteria are unclear or arbitrary.

Table 3.5 Example feedback for NURBS project

File number	Feedback
1	Model not delivered
2	Model delivered. No missing parts. Likeness is average. Moderate tangency errors. One type of technical error found. Good first impression. Windshield should not be flat. Tangency errors in A-pillar area. Transforms on hood
3	Model delivered. No missing parts. Likeness is excellent. No tangency errors. Two types of technical errors found. Excellent first impression. No appropriate sub-groups, such as doors, nor are there logical names for some objects

Students have two years to earn the 60 credits available from the first year, provided that 54 or more of those credits are earned in the first year. Once they have the full 60 credits, they cannot be expelled even if they subsequently do not turn up for a single class, sit for any exams or hand in any assignments. The Dutch Ministry of Education punishes universities economically for retaining students beyond four years, thus creating a financial incentive to expel students in the first year if possible. It also creates a corresponding incentive to graduate students who have earned their first-year credits, within four years.

What this means is that the primary goal of the grade from the lecturer's perspective: to provide an objective measure of quality as constructive feedback to students, is affected by factors unrelated to industry concerns or student needs. In industry, there would be no need to favour objective over subjective assessment methods for fear of a complaint by an employee.

The specific criteria chosen for the NURBS project were also influenced by the need for efficient grading. Knowledge tests in the form of written exams were not given because the tests can be time-consuming to grade, do not provide a demonstration of skill and their results are redundant with performance demonstrated in the final project. The four performance criteria: completeness, technical errors, tangency and likeness represent categories of interest to industry that can be checked quickly, accurately and yield objective feedback that is easily understood by students.

3.7.1.7 Validating Proficient Performance

This study intended to capture the development of proficiency among university students enrolled in a digital art programme. More specifically, this study sought to isolate when the transition to proficiency occurred, and by doing so, to provide a means of observing contributing factors.

Anonymised MD2 projects were given to industry participants to grade by their standards for professional use. The projects were graded in my presence. The output from this interaction was a grade for the project and a semi-structured interview that was coded in NVIVO 10. This interview type was chosen to give participants an opportunity to provide their own insights within their narrative, while providing answers to a set of questions that would allow comparisons between participants.

After providing a grade, industry participants were asked to verify that they understood that a grade of 6 or higher could only be used if they were confident that the project met a professional standard. They were then asked to validate that they were comfortable with the grade. Once validated by industry participants, grades were considered authoritative regarding student performance as NURBS modellers. The grade given by industry participants was then compared to grades given in class to determine if there were any significant disagreements.

3.7.1.8   Grades Used as Performance Measure

At the end of the academic year, MD1 and MD2 grades were entered into an IBM SPSS Statistics file that included PVRT results, questionnaire answers and end-of-year course credit accumulations for student participants and archival data on students from previous years. These data were compared with actual performance on the NURBS project to see if they were predictive. Next, grades were compared with demographic data to determine if there was a reasonable indication of a relationship between any of these items and student performance as measured by grades and credits. Lastly, project grades were used as a basis for comparison with grades given by industry participants.

3.7.2   Analysis of Qualitative Data

Data was coded into categories related to questionnaire items (prior experience, learning experience, quality of learning, etc.). Coded items were sorted several more times, to find commonalities among participants, as well as differences, and how their statements related to the research questions.

3.7.2.1   Learning Logs

Students were asked to keep learning logs to record their progress during the MD2 course. These logs consisted of an Excel file given to each student at the beginning of the course, with prepared data fields for them to enter their progress on a weekly basis and any comments they might have. The file contained three columns for each of the first eight weeks of the class: 'problems', 'successes' and 'comments'. The ninth week was omitted because it was reserved for exams. The purpose of these logs was to provide insight into the type of problems students encountered, how they overcame them, when they overcame them and to provide students an opportunity to provide any additional insights they may have had as they progressed through the MD2 course. This usage of learning logs is in keeping with other research, where learning logs are used to record student thinking (Hirsto et al. 2013) and student learning behaviour (Dow et al. 2014).

   It was initially hoped that the learning logs would capture important moments in each student's progress during the MD2 project. In particular, it was hoped that if any students became proficient on the project, important events in their learning history would be memorialised in their logs. In practice, many students' English skills or diligence were not up to the task of maintaining the logs. Only two students filled them in every week and five others made only sporadic entries. The remaining 13 students did not hand in their logs or they were empty. The logs that were turned in proved to be helpful despite the poor response. However, the study was originally designed to utilise the learning logs as the basis for the student interviews conducted at the conclusion of the project. With such a small number turned in and most only fragmentary, it was decided to base interview questions on the student questionnaire instead because it was completed by all student participants. This decision was made before the questionnaire was distributed, thus allowing time to adjust questions.

3.7.2.2 Progress Files

To answer questions about weekly progress, instead of relying on the partial or missing learning logs, weekly progress files were used. The idea for using these is not grounded in the literature, but was a necessity for tracking student progress in the absence of learning logs or other data that would show week-by-week progress. Although these files did not contain data on the students' thinking process, they were adequate for tracking their progress and could be analysed to determine what types of problems students encountered on the project. For instance, a file might contain a vehicle made entirely of what is called 'boundary' patches. These are patches based on curves that represent the final shape of the vehicle. Typical of such files is that there are cusps, an error, along every boundary. A file like this shows that the student does not understand how to visualise a working order of construction, topology, or basic shapes needed to make a cusp-free model.

Progress files represented weekly vehicle project progress. Images of each file were assembled into a PDF file for easy comparison of each student's work on a week-by-week basis. If all students had handed in a new file every week, there would have been 120 progress reports. Instead, there were 102 total progress files turned in and 18 that were missed. When asked about missing files, students wrote that they had made no progress during those weeks because they had shifted their focus to deal with deadlines in other classes. For all weeks when progress had been made, they submitted a progress file, thus making a complete record of weeks spent engaged on the project.

3.7.2.3 Student Pre-interview Questionnaire

The student questionnaire was posted online after students received their grades for the MD2 class. It was organised into three sections. The first asked demographic questions such as: 'What is your age?', 'What is your gender?' and 'How long is your commute to school?' to gather information on factors that might have influenced performance.

For instance, the age question is connected to the issue of prior experience and the rapid development of proficiency, the idea being that the younger the student, the less exposure he or she has had to the material. The question about commute time addresses a concern raised by many students over the years, namely, that long commutes (over four hours a day in some cases) interfered substantially with their studies. All of these questions were fact-oriented questions for the purpose of recording background information to be used in interviews.

The second section of the questionnaire asked students to provide answers to questions about the MD2 class as measured on a 5-point Likert scale, in order to gain insight into students' subjective states during the project. A problem with Likert scale questions is that they can be interpreted in various ways by respondents who weight the values differently (Foddy 1993), but this study deals with that weakness by using the answers as part of the interview. For instance, if a student answers '3' on a 5-point Likert scale question that asks 'Did the MD2 class challenge you to solve problems on your own?', the student would be asked the following in the interview: 'Why did you answer the question that way?' This would then be followed up as appropriate with more questions, such as, 'Did you intend your answer to be interpreted as neutral?' 'Does this mean that you weren't challenged because you didn't notice any problems to solve?' 'Were you not challenged because you didn't complete the project?' and so on.

The last portion of the questionnaire invited students to answer open questions in their own words and then offer any other comments that they felt had a bearing on the study. The purpose of providing students open questions at the end of the study was to provide a counter-balance to the possibility that they did not interpret earlier questions the same way (Foddy 1993). It also made it possible for students to write in concerns or original insights related to the MD2 project that were not raised by questions in the questionnaire. For the full set of questions, please see Sect. 8.3 (p. 209).

Questions about age, previous education and previous experience in traditional or digital art were designed to establish whether each student was a beginner or novice prior to starting the NURBS class. Questions about residence type, nationality, whether they held part-time jobs and commute times were designed to elicit whether there were any significant extracurricular obstacles to their progress in class. In the past, students had complained that long commute times, family-related concerns, or other external factors affected their study at IGAD. If this proved to be the case for any of the students in this study, these questions were intended to capture them as mitigating circumstances that might have a bearing on the analysis of their learning trajectory.

Many of the Likert scale questions were meant to elicit subjective responses to the cognitive difficulty of the project, a subject that later proved difficult to put into words by students with weaker English language skills. Some questions from this group were: 'Did the MD2 class challenge you to solve problems on your own?', 'Were your mental visualisation skills challenged during MD2?' and 'Did the MD2 class enhance your problem-solving skills?' These were paired with questions regarding their satisfaction with the class, for the purpose of comparing satisfaction with performance and perceived difficulty.

Students were questioned closely in interviews about the trajectory of their learning and cognitive processes during the MD2 class. Specifically, they were asked to comment on the following:

- Whether they noticed a transition from novice to proficient skill levels in their own work, and if so, when it happened and what caused it.
- Aspects of the project that gave them the most difficulty.

- Cognitive processes during problem-solving activity.
- The role of mental visualisation in their own work: whether they noticed if they employed it, in what way and what the results were.

Students were then asked, in an open text box, to describe what they liked the least and the most about the class and then to write in anything they wished regarding the class in a third box. The purpose of the last group of open-ended questions was to provide students an opportunity to describe things they may not otherwise have had an opportunity to mention. It was hoped that these questions would provide novel observations as a way to counter any expectations or biases that might have been present in other questions. As it turned out, one of the answers to an open-ended question had a strong effect on the study by focussing more attention on threshold concepts during interviews than was originally planned.

3.7.2.4 Industry Questionnaire

Industry participants filled out a questionnaire prior to their interviews. The purpose of the questionnaire was to establish their credentials by asking how long they had worked in the computer graphics industry, whether they had supervisor or managerial level expertise and what branch of the industry they had worked in (video games, feature films, simulation, or other). They were also asked questions to elicit their general opinion of the effectiveness of computer graphics education in the higher-education sector. Unlike the student questionnaires, questionnaires filled out by industry participants did not serve as structure for their interviews. Their purpose was to establish validity of their assessments of what meets an industry standard and to gain insight into professional opinions of the results of computer graphics education.

3.7.2.5 Interviews

Student participants who were members of the original group of enrolees and two that were added at the end of the MD2 project, were interviewed in the week following the conclusion of the MD2 project. Two other students were invited in the following year on the basis of their performance, but they were interviewed about a month after the conclusion of their class. For all of the original participants, questionnaire answers were entered into a database on an iPad during the interview, which was recorded by two different devices (an iPad and a separate mini-recorder) with the student's knowledge and consent. The digital recordings were then transcribed into MSWord files by an independent transcription service located in the UK.

The interviews were semi-structured as suggested in Sternberg et al. (2000) to ensure that certain topics would be covered and to elicit tacit knowledge. This method was chosen to address concerns that if the structure of the interviews were too rigid, students would be less forthcoming with potentially valuable insights, while if interviews had been open-ended, important topics might be skipped. The interviews lasted approximately an hour each and took place at an official school building during school hours.

Interview questions were not homogenous because successive interviews had a tendency to impact later ones by highlighting or introducing ideas not explicitly covered in the questionnaires. Despite this, they were thematically consistent because all questions were designed to elicit information pertinent to how each student developed (or failed to develop) proficiency during the MD2 class. As the interviews developed a clearer picture of themes relevant to the research questions, the interviews became more focussed.

None of the current or former IGAD student participants spoke English as a first language. This proved to be a problem to varying degrees with most participants. In some cases, it was not that prominent, such as with Maike,[2] whose English was nearly fluent, but caused serious difficulties with others, who were unable to responsively discuss the types of abstract cognitive subjects raised in the interviews. For example, in his interview, Martin described the problem in this way: 'I have to translate English to Dutch to understand [your question], to translate again [my answer], so…while I'm translating I forget your question, then I form an answer but I don't know the question anymore.'

On some questions, students with weak responsive English understood the questions well enough to agree or disagree with leading questions but could not answer without the leading information. Although this seemed adequate at the time of the interview, almost all such exchanges were discarded to prevent leading questions from becoming a source of bias. In the few instances they were used, they are identified by phrasing of the following form: 'X student agreed that…'

Student interviews were conducted prior to interviews with industry participants. This was so that material from the student interviews could be used to guide the dialogue during the interviews with industry participants.

Industry participants were asked to grade and rank student projects during their interviews and to describe their thinking as they assessed the work. They were also asked about their own learning experiences prior to working in industry and about any thoughts they might have on how they developed expertise in the field. The principal goal of these interviews was to establish whether industry participants agreed that some students produced professional-quality work and the reasons behind their assessment.

Industry participants were asked to think aloud as they assessed student work, but all had a tendency to forget to do this. They were prompted to a point, but thinking aloud seemed to interfere with their effort to study student projects, so they were also asked questions as they assessed projects.

This study did not originally contemplate collecting data from employed IGAD graduates. However, several questions raised during the student interviews were best answered by adding employed graduates to the study. These questions had to do with the transition to expertise and reflections on academic versus professional tasks. Current students were ill-equipped to compare school to a workplace environment,

---

[2]All participant names used in this document are pseudonyms.

just as industry participants recruited for the study had too many years of intervening experience between their days in school (if they had a formal education) and their present status as industry professionals to be able to reliably comment on the fine details of their education. An advantage the recent IGAD graduates had is that they had all taken the MD2 class and could place it in the context of their later development as professionals.

Interviews with employed graduates were semi-structured, but with more open-ended questions than in student interviews. This was done to allow for the story-telling method (Sternberg et al. 2000) of gathering information related to their own progress as digital artists. Like all other interviews, these were limited to an hour each.

Employed graduates were interviewed about how they developed expertise. This question became important during the study as student participants frequently differentiated between proficiency and expertise. This disagreed with some definitions of expertise that appear to be synonymous with proficiency (Gentner 1988), but agreed with others who consider them different but related (Alexander 2003). Employed graduates were chosen to answer this question because they had both the professional credentials to understand what expertise is and recent experience as IGAD students that would aid any attempt to gauge when this transition occurred for them.

3.7.2.6 Coding

Answers to the interview questions were coded in the nVivo 10 qualitative data organisation and analysis program. Interviews were broken down into three major categories based on the original research questions: proficiency development, industry feedback and learning. Within these categories, sub-categories were created based on themes that emerged during thematic analysis of interview data.

Using nVivo, significant themes were explored to identify areas of agreement and disagreement among student participants, such as the importance of spatial visualisation or tool knowledge to development. Interviews were also checked for instances of agreement and disagreement with quantitative data, such as a low MD2 grade given to a student who stated that he had been successful in the MD2 class. The purpose of both of these comparisons was to establish the validity of interview data. Answers that meaningfully engaged the research questions were deemed to have 'answered' them, even if no single answer was definitive on its own.

After establishing validity of the data, it was coded into categories of interest relative to the research questions. This data was then investigated for consistency in information and themes relevant to the questions. This was then broken down further based on cross-referencing with quantitative data to determine whether it supported student statements or any of the overall themes that emerged.

3.7.3 Triangulation

3.7.3.1 Methods

One of the motivations for using mixed methods was to allow triangulation of qualitative data to increase confidence in its validity. Interview data with industry participants would have been sufficient to determine whether students were proficient, but
by also grading their performance, it became possible to make a quantitative analysis
of agreement between academic and industry-provided grades.

Some of the data collected were in the form of student self-reports. These were
used because the students were either the most convenient or the only source for
information such as their subjective reactions to the learning process. The approach
taken here allowed the collection of data on subjective mental states and activities,
from which an explanation of performance results could be reasoned. The drawback
is that these states could not be measured directly. If participants were unable to
recall or recalled incorrectly their progress from one cognitive state to another (from
naïveté to awareness), it would not be easily disproved through the textual analysis
tools available.

To avoid some of the problems associated with self-reports (Ericsson 2006), independent objective sources were used when possible for confirmation. This was most
crucial to determine the (a) start of training, (b) timing of transition to proficiency and
(c) explanation of transition to proficiency. Each of these items was checked independently by reviewing intake assessment documents and weekly project updates
to triangulate the data, in keeping with practitioner research norms (Dymond et al.
2006).

3.7.3.2 QUAN Data Common to Participants and Archival Data

There are six categories of quantitative data and five categories of qualitative data
collected for this study (see Fig. 3.9, p. 55). The quantitative data are relevant to
previous classes of visual art student at IGAD, as well as current students and student
participants. Because this material is common to both groups, it can be used to
generate predictions regarding current students, who have not yet started the NURBS
modelling course.

Qualitative data collected from student participants can be used to explain some
quantitative results. For instance, if the archival data shows that students from HAVO
schools (a type of Dutch school, see p. 82 for more), perform better than other
students, then it may be expected that a HAVO student among the student participants
will also perform at a higher level than other students. Whether this happened or not,
the reasons can be explored in the qualitative interviews, as a way to determine if
an important factor was left out of the quantitative tests, if the student is unusual, or
why the hypothesis is confirmed (if that was the case).

3.7.3.3 Four Perspectives on Development

Interviews with industry experts and employed graduates from IGAD were used to compare with data collected from students, to further enhance understanding of performance development. In this way, four perspectives were utilised: the teacher (grades and archive data), students (interviews, learning logs and hand-ins), industry experts (interviews) and employed graduates (interviews). The data collected from these sources are complementary and do not overlap, because each is segregated by their role (teacher, student, expert, graduate). Teachers have information on how the projects are constructed and graded, students can talk about their experiences learning for the first time, industry experts allow grading by industry standards rather than academic standards and employed graduates provide insight into the transition between performance in school to proficiency in industry.

3.8 Strengths and Limitations

3.8.1 Trustworthiness and Validity

The participants in this study are a convenience sample, so generalisability may be limited to digital art students of the type involved in this study (Cor 2016). To know if the results generalise beyond this population, more studies would be needed in other schools and disciplines. This study is concerned with an art form that is at least partially technology-dependent. The conclusions of this study point to a non-technology dependency for developing proficiency, but whether this remains a dependency after new technology is introduced is unknown. Follow-up studies could investigate this question. Findings from this study indicate the importance of spatial visualisation to digital artists. However, it is not clear whether that finding will generalise beyond NURBS modelling tasks. To know for certain, further studies would have to be conducted in other digital art specialties, such as animation, rendering and visual effects.

3.8.1.1 Phase One (Quantitative) Measures

Intake assessment materials provided by students were assessed by teachers at IGAD. Although scoring among teachers is consistent and they are experienced professionals in the domain of digital art, it is possible that assessments are not an accurate reflection of students' prior experience. This is not a serious concern however, because there is secondary evidence in the form of self-reported experience during assessment interviews, grades from their previous education and the type of school previously attended. Taken together, it is unlikely that intake assessment scores inaccurately reflect actual prior experience among students to a statistically significant degree.

The sample size of 625 students is large enough to be valid for generalising results to incoming classes (n = 60) with high confidence, and to general populations of digital art students in the Netherlands. In addition, they are an accurate reflection of how students are assessed at IGAD. Studies in other countries and schools would be needed to determine whether findings from this study generalise further.

The spatial visualisation tests used in this study are widely used in many domains. All are considered valid instruments for statistical purposes (Bodner and Guay 1997; Eliot and Smith 1983; Hegarty et al. 2009; Likert and Quasha 1994). Spatial visualisation tests were given to IGAD students in 2011 and 2012. Because of the small number of students accepted into the program (between 60 and 90 per year) and the smaller number who remain after each block, the number of tests available for statistical comparisons are less than ideal. Depending on the test, the n value is between 51 and 111. The tests are meant to predict results among incoming classes, currently limited to 60 students each. With a 6% margin of error and a 95% confidence level, 50 respondents are sufficient for validity. For the larger sample of 111 students who took the PVRT test, it is more than sufficient for results with a target population of 60, a 1% margin of error and a 99% confidence level. These sample sizes are not large enough to generalise beyond incoming IGAD visual art classes, but are robust enough to identify characteristics of learning at IGAD that could be used to inspire studies elsewhere, with larger samples, to find out if, or how far, the results generalise.

The remaining quantitative data exist in sufficient numbers (n = 241–625) to be valid for incoming classes at IGAD and larger groups of digital art students.

3.8.1.2   Phases Two and Three (Qualitative) Measures

A questionnaire was given to students prior to their interviews. Answers from the questionnaire were used to guide questions during interviews. The questionnaire was not used for any kind of statistical analysis, nor were answers accepted at face value. Instead, answers were explored during interviews and those answers became the core data for evaluation. In the few places quantitative information from the questionnaires is presented, it is not intended to represent statistical validity, but to show whether student participants are similar to the profile of the larger sample (n = 625) of student data that is used for statistical tests.

Student participants are self-selected. As shown in the findings chapter (p. 82), this resulted in a larger percentage of former MBO students (see p. 82 for an explanation of Dutch school types) than are found in the general population at IGAD. This could have resulted in bias for a large-scale quantitative study, but in this case, student participants provided qualitative data for case study analysis, where the goal was to follow the progress of as many students as possible in the hopes of capturing at least one student transition to proficiency during the class. In that context, all student data is valid as it pertains to each student's experience, and its value for identification of potential factors critical to the development of proficiency. Further studies would have to be conducted to verify that these factors have the expected result elsewhere.

Industry participants, like student participants, are self-selected from among the dozens of professionals who received invitations to participate. That said, they represent diverse types of digital art consumers, companies and countries. All have appropriate experience and industry credentials. These participants are meant to represent industry standards. To the degree that their ratings agreed, the ratings were considered legitimate representations of industry norms.

Employed graduates were included to provide their perspective on their learning process. Data obtained from these participants was valid for their own experience and was intended to be used as insight into the results obtained from other participants. It is not intended to be taken as generally authoritative. Further study would be needed to determine if their answers generalise beyond their own experience.

3.8.2 Limitations

The character of NURBS modelling allows this study to capture the development of proficiency within a narrow time frame in a complex discipline known by experts to be difficult to master. It also allows development to be followed along a spectrum of novice to proficient performance because many of the student participants had no prior CG experience, including half of the students who developed proficiency. In addition to this, the study allows for a test of transfer of relevant skills by observing students with a variety of backgrounds as they develop proficiency in a new skill.

As a qualitative study, this research depended on student feedback for insight into their learning process. Discussing cognition with young students can be expected to be challenging in any circumstance, but it was particularly so in this study because the cohort of student participants was made up entirely of non-native English speakers. Most understood English without difficulty, but a few found it difficult to answer responsively to questions about learning and cognition. When asked simpler questions, particularly yes or no questions, the students found it much easier to communicate, but this resulted in some interviews containing leading questions. With very few exceptions, these types of answers were excluded from analysis, but when they were included, they were supported with secondary evidence such as learning logs, weekly progress files, or grades.

A potential problem with this study design was that there was no guarantee that any students would develop proficiency. If that had happened, the transition to proficiency would not have been observed, nor could contributing factors have been identified. However, in the past, at least one student at IGAD had always made the transition from naïve to proficient performance during the MD2 class, which suggested it would also happen during this study. If it had not, then student work, learning logs, interviews and other data could still have been analysed to determine why none of the students became proficient during the class. However, by the end of the study, multiple students were found to have become proficient during the course.

The number of students in the study who transitioned to proficient performance is too small to establish any kind of statistical validity. Despite this, the research is capable of identifying possibilities and exceptions that would not have been revealed otherwise and this does not require large numbers (Ackerman 2014). Those possibilities can then be explored later with more focussed studies and larger groups of participants as suggested by Ericsson and Williams (2007).

This study is focussed on the development of proficiency among digital artists, but touches on other topics: expertise, threshold concepts, spatial visualization, cognitive processes, curriculum design and higher education. Any of these topics are worthy of independent investigation, but in the context of this study, they were secondary to the primary aim: to understand how student digital artists develop proficiency. As such, this study does not include investigative tools that would have allowed a deeper investigation of the subjects just mentioned. The study is designed to be open to possibilities to allow for an exploration of student progress as they develop rather than try to pin down causes beforehand, thus limiting the scope of possible discovery.

3.9   Bias

This study of expertise development took place at the university I am employed by, with students I teach. This introduces the potential for researcher bias because I am familiar with the design of the project that is the subject of this study and may have a tendency to see only what the project is designed to accomplish. There is also a risk that grading criteria developed for the project would influence whether student work was assessed to have met a proficient standard. To counter this, some forms of data checking were used to minimise the potential for bias to distort the results (Dymond et al. 2006).

The MD2 class is taught by me and a co-teacher. I deliver all of the lectures to a group of 83 students (in the year this study took place). The students are then split into three classes and those classes are instructed by me and the co-teacher. In addition, students have three voluntary study periods each week. These are supervised by the co-teacher of the class. The co-teacher is a control for any bias I might have in the sense that he teaches in his own way, graded the student participants based on criteria mutually agreed to over past years and is not directly involved in this study. I did not grade the work of any student participants for this study. However, I did grade retake projects by student participants who submitted retakes of the project and by two participants from a later year. Another control was provided by industry participants who graded a sample of projects from the MD2 class. In this way, student results were checked by multiple persons both within and outside of the academy. The assessment measures can be found in Sect. 8.2 (p. 205).

3.10 Ethical Compliance

This study complies with the British Guidelines for Ethical Research, 2011 edition ('Ethical guidelines' 2011). The primary concern was for privacy. To ensure that their identities were protected, all participants were assigned study identification numbers. These became the only source of identification for material generated by them. All files were renamed to reflect their study ID codes. Once the data were entered, the master list with their names was destroyed. In addition to this, pseudonyms were made for every participant and entered into a database for use in all published material. Moreover, study ID codes have not been used in any published material, thus eliminating the possibility of linking the Study ID codes with pseudonyms or real names. All audio files were kept on my home computer for the duration of this research project.

All participants were informed of the nature of the research, their rights as participants and what would be expected of them. Additionally, participants were informed that they could withdraw from the project at any time without explanation and without repercussions. Four students and one industry participant subsequently withdrew from the study but were replaced by other volunteers.

Archival data collected from IGAD archives had all identifying details removed. However, those cases were not used to review any single student, but to compare groups that met certain criteria. Pseudonyms were not generated for those students because none were referenced by name or as individuals.

3.11 Conclusion

The guiding methodology for this study was a mixed-methods exploratory design with an emphasis on observation of progress as it happens. Data were collected in the form of archival IGAD data; spatial ability test scores; weekly progress reports from students; project deliverables; questionnaires from student and industry participants; interviews with students, employed graduates and industry participants; and project grades from teachers and industry participants. These data were used to establish when students first engaged in the active practice of art-related skills, if they transitioned to proficient performance during the MD2 class, when the transition occurred and what factors were relevant to making the transition from novice to industry-standard proficient performance.

This study attempted to capture the development of proficiency in situ, while other methodologies utilise retrospective analysis of fully realised experts (Grabner 2014). Retrospective analysis of expert development is performed in other studies to address the assumption that it would take too long to witness the transition from novice to expert performance within the time frame of a study (Ericsson 2009; Ericsson and Charness 1994). However, if a large knowledge base is unnecessary, as suggested by Ruthsatz et al. (2014), Simonton (2012), Ackerman (2014) and Howard (2009), or the time frame needed for expertise development can be compressed, then it should be possible to find a domain where proficiency or expertise can be learned within a reasonable period of time.

This type of study, where observations of practice, performance and development are made as they happen, has been recently called for by expertise researchers (Ericsson and Williams 2007). The NURBS class allowed such an opportunity and it was utilised to do what Ericsson and Williams (2007) recommend. According to them, a methodologically ideal study would have the following elements: a large random sample, an arbitrary domain of expertise and an observational methodology designed to witness who develops expertise and who does not. Each of those elements are present to some degree in the present study:

- The student participant sample is sufficient for a qualitative study. This is augmented with archival data that is sufficient for quantitative analysis and can be used to establish context for data collected from student participants.
- The choice of NURBS modelling was not arbitrary, but for this purpose it may as well have been. Ericsson's (2007) use of the word 'arbitrary' in 'arbitrary domain of expertise' appears to be for the purpose of finding a task where students are unlikely to have any previous experience (true for all IGAD students regarding NURBS) and no special interest. Most IGAD students do not want to learn NURBS or are curious about NURBS only because of its reputation for difficulty.
- Students are followed for nine weeks to see who develops expertise and who does not. This may not seem like a very long period for a longitudinal study, but in the past, this has been enough time to witness the transition from novice to proficient performance in this discipline. Ericsson's (2007) recommendation of longitudinal studies is simply for the purpose of being able to observe as students develop expertise, a goal that should be achievable with the present design for observing the development of proficiency, a lower standard than expertise.

In the next two chapters, findings based on data collected for this study are presented.

References

Ackerman PL (2014) Nonsense, common sense, and science of expert performance: talent and individual differences. Intelligence 45:6–17. https://doi.org/10.1016/j.intell.2013.04.009

Alexander PA (2003) The development of expertise: the journey from acclimation to proficiency. Educ Researcher 32(8):10–14

Alise MA, Teddlie C (2010) A Continuation of the Paradigm Wars? Prevalence Rates of Methodological Approaches Across the Social/Behavioral Sciences. J Mixed Methods Res 4(2):103–126. https://doi.org/10.1177/1558689809360805

Bergman MM (2011) The good, the bad, and the ugly in mixed methods research and design. J Mixed Methods Res 5(4):271–275. https://doi.org/10.1177/1558689811433236

Besl P (1998) Hybrid modeling for manufacturing using NURBS, polygons, and 3D scanner data. In: Proceedings of the 1998 IEEE International Symposium on Circuits and Systems, 31 May–3 June 1998. ISCAS '98

Bodner GM, Guay RB (1997) The Purdue visualization of rotations test. Chem Educ 2(4):1–14

Catmull E, Clark J (1978) Recursively generated Bspline surfaces on arbitrary topological meshes. Comput Aided Des 10(6):350–355. https://doi.org/10.1016/0010-4485(78)060350-06

Charmaz K (2017) The power of constructivist grounded theory for critical inquiry. Qual Inq 23(1):34–45. https://doi.org/10.1177/1077800416657105

Chase WG, Simon HA (1973) Perception in chess. Cogn Psychol 4(1):55–81

Cor MK (2016) Trust me, it is valid: research validity in pharmacy education research. Curr Pharm Teach Learn 8(3):391–400. https://doi.org/10.1016/j.cptl.2016.02.014

Creswell JW (2011) Controversies in mixed methods research. In: Denzin NK, Lincoln YS (eds) The Sage handbook of qualitative research. Sage, Thousand Oaks, pp 269–283

Creswell JW, Plano-Clark VL (2011) Designing and conducting mixed methods research, 2nd edn. Sage, Thousand Oaks

de Groot AD (1972) Thought and choice in chess. Amsterdam University Press, Amsterdam

Dow C-R, Li Y-H, Huang L-H, Hsuan P (2014) Development of activity generation and behavior observation systems for distance learning. Comput Appl Eng Educ 22(1):52–62. https://doi.org/10.1002/cae.20528

Dymond SK, Renzaglia A, Rosenstein A, Chun EJ, Banks RA, Niswander V, Gilson CL (2006) Using a participatory action research approach to create a universally designed inclusive high school science course: a case study. Res Pract Persons Severe Disabil 31(4):293–308. https://doi.org/10.1177/154079690603100403

Eliot J, Smith IM (1983) An international directory of spatial tests. The NFER-Nelson Publishing Company Ltd., Windsor

Ericsson KA (2006) Protocol analysis and expert thought: concurrent verbalizations of thinking during experts' performance on representative tasks. In: Ericsson KA (ed) Cambridge handbook of expertise and expert performance. Cambridge University Press, Cambridge, pp 223–242

Ericsson KA (2009) Enhancing the development of professional performance: implications from the study of deliberate practice. In: Ericsson KA (ed) The development of professional expertise: toward measurement of expert performance and design of optimal learning environments. Cambridge University Press, New York, pp 405–431

Ericsson KA (2014) Why expert performance is special and cannot be extrapolated from studies of performance in the general population: a response to criticisms. Intelligence 45(1):81–103. https://doi.org/10.1016/j.intell.2013.12.001

Ericsson KA, Charness N (1994) Expert performance its structure and acquisition. Am Psychol 49(8):725–747

Ericsson KA, Polson PG (1988) A cognitive analysis of exceptional memory for restaurant orders. In: Chi MTH, Glaser R, Farr MJ (eds) The nature of expertise, vol 1. Lawrence Erlbaum Associates Inc., Hillsdale, pp 23–70

Ericsson KA, Ward P (2007) Capturing the naturally occurring superior performance of experts in the laboratory toward a science of expert and exceptional performance. Curr Dir Psychol Sci 16(6):346–350

Ericsson KA, Williams AM (2007) Capturing naturally occurring superior performance in the laboratory: translational research on expert performance. J Exp Psychol: Appl 13(3):115–123

Farrington-Darby T, Wilson JR (2006) The nature of expertise: a review. Appl Ergon 37(1):17–32. https://doi.org/10.1016/j.apergo.2005.09.001

Foddy W (1993) Constructing questions for interviews and questionnaires theory and practice in social research. Cambridge University Press, Cambridge

Gao K, Park H, Rockwood A, Sowar D (2006) Attribute based interfaces for geometric modeling. Paper presented at the Sandbox Symposium 2006, Boston, Massachusetts

Gentner DR (1988) Expertise in typewriting. In: Chi MTH, Glaser R, Farr MJ (eds) The nature of expertise, vol 1, 1st edn. Lawrence Erlbaum Associates Inc., Hillsdale, pp 1–21

Glaser BG (2007) Remodeling grounded theory. Hist Soc Res, Supplement 19(19):47–68

Grabner RH (2014) The role of intelligence for performance in the prototypical expertise domain of chess. Intelligence 45:26–33. https://doi.org/10.1016/j.intell.2013.07.023

Hambrick DZ, Altmann EM, Oswald FL, Meinz EJ, Gobet F, Campitelli G (2014) Accounting for expert performance: the devil is in the details. Intelligence 45:112–114. https://doi.org/10.1016/j.intell.2014.01.007

Harrits GS (2011) More than method?: a discussion of paradigm differences within mixed methods research. J Mixed Methods Res 5(2):150–166. https://doi.org/10.1177/1558689811402506

Hegarty M, Keehner M, Khooshabeh P, Montello DR (2009) How spatial abilities enhance, and are enhanced by, dental education. Learn Individ Differ 19(1):61–70

Hirsto L, Lampinen M, Syrjäkari M (2013) Learning outcomes of university lecturers from a process-oriented university pedagogical course. Trames 21(1):347–365. https://doi.org/10.3176/tr.2013.4.03

Howard RW (2009) Individual differences in expertise development over decades in a complex intellectual domain. Mem Cogn 37(2):194–209. https://doi.org/10.3758/MC.37.2.194

Howe KR (1988) Against the quantitative-qualitative incompatibility thesis or dogmas die hard. Educ Researcher 17(8):10–16. https://doi.org/10.3102/0013189x017008010

Johnson RB, Onwuegbuzie AJ (2004) Mixed methods research: a research paradigm whose time has come. Educ Researcher 33(7):14–26

Krause FL, Fischer A, Gross N, Barhak J (2003) Reconstruction of freeform objects with arbitrary topology using neural networks and subdivision techniques. CIRP Ann Manuf Technol 52(1):125–128. https://doi.org/10.1016/s0007-8506(07)60547-2

Lapan SD, Quartaroli MT, Reimer FJ (eds) (2012) Qualitative research: an introduction to methods and designs, 1st edn. Wiley, San Francisco

Lee Y-J, Greene J (2007) The predictive validity of an ESL placement test: a mixed methods approach. J Mixed Methods Res 1(4):366–389. https://doi.org/10.1177/1558689807306148

Likert R, Quasha WH (eds) (1994) Revised Minnesota paper form board test manual, 2nd edn

Müller K, Reusche L, Fellner D (2006) Extended subdivision surfaces: building a bridge between NURBS and Catmull-Clark surfaces. ACM Trans Graph 25(2):268–292. https://doi.org/10.1145/1138450.1138455

Osmond J, Bull K, Tovey M (2009) Threshold concepts and the transport and product design curriculum: reports of research in progress. Art Des Commun High Educ 8(2):169–175

Peters M, Laeng B, Latham K, Jackson M, Zaiyouna R, Richardson C (1995) A redrawn Vandenberg and Kuse mental rotations test—different versions and factors that affect performance. Brain Cogn 28(1):39–58

Raimondo E, Newcomer KE (2017) Mixed-methods inquiry in public administration: the interaction of theory, methodology, and praxis. Rev Public Pers Adm 37(2):183–201. https://doi.org/10.1177/0734371x17697247

Ruthsatz J, Ruthsatz K, Stephens KR (2014) Putting practice into perspective: child prodigies as evidence of innate talent. Intelligence 45(1):60–65. https://doi.org/10.1016/j.intell.2013.08.003

Salthouse TA, Babcock RL, Skovronek E, Mitchell DR, Palmon R (1990) Age and experience effects in spatial visualization. Dev Psychol 26(1):128–136

Samsudin KR, Hanif A, Samad A (2011) Training in mental rotation and spatial visualization and its impact on orthographic drawing performance. Educ Technol Soc 14(1):8

Schindler LA, Burkholder GJ (2016) A mixed methods examination of the influence of dimensions of support on training transfer. J Mixed Methods Res 10(3):292–310. https://doi.org/10.1177/1558689814557132

Shannon-Baker P (2016) Making paradigms meaningful in mixed methods research. J Mixed Methods Res 10(4):319–334. https://doi.org/10.1177/1558689815575861

Simonton DK (2012) Foresight, insight, oversight, and hindsight in scientific discovery: how sighted were Galileo's telescopic sightings? Psychol Aesthetics Creativity Arts 6(3):243–254. https://doi.org/10.1037/a0027058243

Sternberg RJ, Forsythe GB, Hedlund J, Horvath JA, Wagner RK, Williams WM, Grigorenko EL (2000) Practical intelligence in everyday life. Cambridge University Press, Cambridge

Virkki-Hatakka T, Tuunila R, Nurkka N (2013) Development of chemical engineering course methods using action research: case study. Eur J Eng Educ 38(5):469–484. https://doi.org/10.1080/03043797.2013.811471

Chapter 4
Quantitative Findings

Data collected for this study are organised based on whether they are from the quantitative or qualitative portions of the study. Quantitative data are presented first, in this chapter, because they represent the known history of performance and assessment at IGAD leading up to the qualitative portion of the study, which is presented in the next chapter.

The focus of the present chapter is to present archival data pertaining to the performance of students in previous years and performance of student participants in this study prior to the nine-week observation period. This material is pertinent to the primary research question, 'What are the principal contributing factors to crossing the proficiency skill threshold among digital art students?' by presenting potential contributing factors and a context for them in the form of archival data regarding student performance from previous years. Archival data can also be used to help answer the third question, 'What is the relationship between spatial ability or spatial visualisation and development of proficiency among digital art students?' by providing the results of spatial visualisation tests in the context of past performance.

All statistical analyses presented in this chapter are based on datasets provided by NHTV. Depending on the test used, or the question answered, the number of subjects ranges from a low of 51 to a high of 625. Comparisons to student study participants $(n = 20)$ are not presented for the purpose of establishing statistical validity, but to situate them in the context of IGAD norms as established by the larger number of data points available in the archival data.

4.1 Previous Experience

The literature of expertise development makes reference to the importance of determining when skill development begins because unknown prior experience can create the false impression of rapid development (Ericsson 2014). For the sake of understanding how proficiency is developed among student participants, it is useful to be

© Springer Nature Switzerland AG 2018
A. Paquette, *Spatial Visualization and Professional Competence*,
https://doi.org/10.1007/978-3-319-91289-9_4

aware of any pre-existing skills that may contribute to later development of proficiency. Data relevant to this subject were collected during intake assessment procedures and subsequent grades earned after enrolling at IGAD.

4.2   School Type

All prospective IGAD students were asked to identify what type of school they
previously attended when they applied for admission to IGAD. This was done because
each type of school in the Dutch system is meaningfully different from the others.
To understand the relationship of prior education to some of the findings presented
here, it is necessary to explain a few aspects of the Dutch educational system.

In the Netherlands, schools attempt to segregate students based on ability and
interests, to better serve them and to make higher education institutions from the
Netherlands function more efficiently. There are three independent tracks that students may follow beginning in secondary school and continuing into higher education. Each track can be described as more advanced and difficult than the previous
one. This is illustrated by math exam scores from secondary school leaving exams
in each of the three tracks. As the level increases, the pass rate decreases (Table 4.1)
(Resnick et al. 1995).

In the Dutch university hierarchy, a *middelbaar beroepsonderwijs* (MBO) school
is the bottom tier of a three-tier higher education system. An MBO is the only type
of university that a *voorbereidend middelbaar beroepsonderwijs* (VBO) or *middelbaar algemeen voortgezet onderwijs* (MAVO) high school student is qualified for
upon graduation. An MBO offers an associate's degree, in contrast to the bachelor's degrees offered by *hoger beroepsonderwijs* (HBO) applied arts universities and
wetenschappelijk onderwijs (WO) universities. If a VBO/MAVO student wants to
attend a higher-level institution, they must first earn an MBO degree. This qualifies
them for an HBO course like IGAD, but not a WO course. To attend a WO degree
granting university, students must first earn a *voorbereidend wetenschappelijk onderwijs* (VWO) or HBO degree (see Table 4.2) (Brown et al. 1999).

Table 4.1 Pass rates of Dutch school leaving exams (Resnick et al. 1995) Note that 'Math A' and
'Math B' are not the same from track to track

VWO (highest level secondary school)	Math A	62%
	Math B	52%
HAVO (middle level secondary school)	Math A	68%
	Math B	60%
VBO/MAVO (lowest level secondary school)	Math A	58%
	Math B	80%

Table 4.2 Qualifications required for Dutch higher education institutions

Secondary diploma	VBO/MAVO	HAVO	VWO/GYM/LYC
Qualified to enrol for	MBO associate	HBO bachelor	WO bachelor
		MBO associate	HBO bachelor
			MBO associate
Higher education degree	MBO associate	HBO bachelor	WO bachelor
Qualified to enrol for	HBO bachelor	HBO master	HBO master
		WO bachelor	WO master
		MBO associate	HBO bachelor

A WO is designed to educate research scientists and professionals in research-orientated disciplines such as medicine, science and law. HBOs are applied arts universities that are designed to educate professionals in fields that demand high standards of practice, but are less dependent on scientific research. MBO colleges specialise in management, clerical occupations and exploration of subjects that prepare students for a higher degree at an HBO.

Although it is possible for a student from any tier in the hierarchy to attend any other tier, the lower one starts, the more expensive it becomes. This is because the government pays for the first four to five years of education depending on the year started and other factors. After that, tuition is either no longer paid to the educational institution, paid in part as a reduced fee, or the student is responsible for tuition.[1] Each successive degree as one works up the higher education hierarchy adds years to the total study time, thus increasing its cost in time and money. This also means that students who have attended MBO institutions prior to enrolling at IGAD are older than HAVO students who enter directly after high school.

All qualifying Dutch secondary school types were represented within the student participant cohort at IGAD. Although IGAD is an HBO designed to receive graduates of HAVO schools, the majority of student participants come from the lower level MBO schools. Compared to overall enrolment for the years 2006–2013, the proportion of students from an MBO education were over-represented in this study (Table 4.3). Over the years 2006–2013, 25.4% of the 625 students enrolled at IGAD were from MBO institutions, but 45.0% of student participants in this study (n = 9) were former MBO students. This means that a higher percentage of student participants had experience of higher education, supervised drawing and CG techniques than are found on average at IGAD.

---

[1]This describes the current limit, which became more restrictive in 2011. This varies from school to school, but is governed by the Dutch Ministry of Education.

Table 4.3 Distribution of participants by previous education compared

	Study participants	Study participants percent	2006–2013 IGAD VA students	2006–2013 IGAD VA students percent
MBO	9	45.0	162	25.4
HAVO	7	35.0	264	41.4
VWO/GYM/LYC	1	5.0	101	15.9
Foreign	2	10.0	76	11.9
HBO	0	0.00	5	0.8
Over 21	1	5.0	17	2.7
Total	20	100.0	625	100.0

4.2.1 CG Experience

On the questionnaire given to student participants, they were asked how much experience they had with computer graphics prior to applying for admission to IGAD. Most students belonged to one of two groups: former MBO students, all but one of whom had two or more years of experience with 3D-modelling software at their MBO-level school ($n = 9$); and students from other types of schools ($n = 11$), all but one of whom had no previous CG experience (Table 4.4). It should be noted that the 'CG experience' referred to is with polygon modelling tools alone, not NURBS modelling. This is because NURBS modelling is not taught at the MBO schools previously attended by these students, but polygon modelling is. This was confirmed in interviews with student participants, none of whom had used NURBS prior to the MD2 class.

Table 4.4 CG experience prior to enrolling at IGAD

Previous study type			Frequency	Percent
MBO	Prior exp	No	1	11.1
		Yes	8	88.9
		Total	9	100.0
HAVO	Prior exp	No	6	85.7
		Yes	1	14.3
		Total	7	100.0
VWO	Prior exp	No	1	100.0
Foreign	Prior exp	No	2	100.0
Over 21	Prior exp	No	1	100.0

4.3 Intake Assessment

After submitting applications containing their previous academic history to IGAD, prospective students were asked to make three drawings as part of their application materials: a self-portrait, an architectural subject and a vehicle (Sect. 8.1, p. 203). Each was to be drawn from life. The term 'drawn from life' is an art term that describes a work that is based on observations of a three-dimensional subject rather than based on a photograph, drawing, or made without reference. Students were given the option of making a 3D model of a vehicle of their choice to demonstrate their CG modelling ability. Together, these items were referred to as their 'submission'. Each item was graded by two assessors on a scale of 0–2, where a 0 represented inexperienced work and a 2 denoted a high level of quality. Each assessor's scores were added together for a final score and then these two scores were averaged (Table 4.5). Students were then given one point if they received above average math grades in their previous education and another point if their previous school was a VWO or foreign equivalent.

Students were assigned to 'intake groups' labelled A, B, C and D based on their submission scores. The A group comprised students who had scores in the 5–10 range and were considered the most desirable candidates. Scores of 4–4.75 were assigned to the B group, 2–3.75 to the C group and 0–1.75 to the D group.

To investigate whether prior education influenced initial assessment performance, a chi-square test for association was conducted between previous study type and intake assessment group membership. All expected cell frequencies were greater than five. There was no statistically significant association between previous study type and intake assessment group membership, $\chi2(1) = 16.005$, $p = .067$ (n = 227). The lack of agreement between these variables indicates that the criteria used by IGAD assessors to evaluate student submissions did not capture or overlooked experience from prior school type. This could be explained by the intake assignment emphasis on drawing (three assignments) over CG skills (one optional assignment).

The extreme simplicity of CG assignments created by applicants who had prior experience was below the complexity of the Illusion project (see p. 45) given in the first block to IGAD students (Fig. 4.1). The scores given 3D models shown in Fig. 4.1 are based on the following: the score of 0 is for the toy train model, which lacks detail and texture. The score of 1 was given to the model of the ball on string with a wooden bell because, though the model itself is simple, it has texture maps (wood grain and painted stripes). The highest score of 2 was given to the character model on the basis of complexity, because it is made of many compound curved shapes.

Table 4.5 Example submission scoring method

	Self-portrait	Vehicle	Architecture	3D model	Math score	Previous study	Score
Assessor 1	2	2	1	NA	0	0	5
Assessor 2	1	1	1	NA	0	0	3
Average	1.5	1.5	1	0	0	0	4

Fig. 4.1 Student 3D submissions, with scores in upper left corner

In contrast, there was a wider range of quality and complexity in drawing assignments than in the CG assignments. The work of two applicants clearly demonstrated considerable practice. The remaining drawings by students who had prior drawing experience were only slightly more accomplished than work by students who had no prior drawing experience (Fig. 4.2).

Of the 225 students for whom intake assessment values are available, 76 earned a score of 5 or higher (33.8%). Of those, 23 students (30.3%) had attended an MBO institution prior to IGAD. Those students are presumed to have experience with polygon modelling and supervised drawing because both courses are found in most of the art-related programmes previously attended by IGAD students, such as at the Graphisch Lyceum Rotterdam, or the Hogeschool voor de Kunsten Utrecht. The remaining 69.7% of students who scored a 5 or higher on their intake assessment ($n = 53$) had no prior experience of higher education and had no formal 3D training or university level supervised drawing instruction.

There were four measures available at the beginning of Block A to determine whether students had experience relevant to their studies at IGAD: school type, prior experience, submission assignments and intake group membership. A comparison of these variables to earned grades for first block projects is described in the next section as a way to determine whether prior experience influenced subsequent performance.

Fig. 4.2 Student drawing submissions from each score group, with scores in upper right corner

4.4 First Block Grades

In the first block of the year, Block A, students were asked to complete the Carton project described in the Methodology chapter (p. 45). This project has the highest fail rate of any project given to IGAD students in the first year. In the six years leading up to this study, the number of students who failed ranges between a high of 85.9% (n = 67) in 2012 and a low of 51.3% (n = 39) in 2009 (Table 4.6).

Of the 148 students who passed between 2006 and 2012, only 45 had prior CG experience at an MBO (30.4%) (Table 4.7).

Archival data from IGAD shows that if Carton results are compared to previous education type, within each group, MBO students pass more often (28.1%, n = 45) than HAVO (21.2%, n = 56), VWO/LYC/GYM (21.8%, n = 22), Foreign (23.7%, n = 18) and students aged 21 and over (over 21) (25.0%, n = 4). Among student participants of this study, HBO students had a higher pass rate than MBO students (42.9%, n = 3) but their numbers are too small to be reliable in this comparison nor are they relevant to the subject population studied here (n = 625), where HBO student participants were uncommon (0.8%, n = 5).

After completing the Carton project, students were given seven weeks to complete the MD1 Illusion project described in Chap. 3 (p. 45). For clarity, MD1 final

Table 4.6 Carton project grades 2007–2012

Year			Frequency	Percent	Cumulative percent
	Missing	System	31	100.0	
2007	Valid	Fail	69	78.4	78.4
		Pass	19	21.6	100.0
		Total	88	100.0	
2008	Valid	Fail	45	66.2	66.2
		Pass	23	33.8	100.0
		Total	68	100.0	
2009	Valid	Fail	39	51.3	51.3
		Pass	37	48.7	100.0
		Total	76	100.0	
2010	Valid	Fail	70	76.9	76.9
		Pass	21	23.1	100.0
		Total	91	100.0	
2011	Valid	Fail	52	60.5	60.5
		Pass	34	39.5	100.0
		Total	86	100.0	
2012	Valid	Fail	67	85.9	85.9
		Pass	11	14.1	100.0
		Total	78	100.0	

Table 4.7 Students who earned a passing grade on the Carton project, grouped by previous education

		Frequency	Percent	Valid percent	Cumulative percent
Valid	Foreign	18	12.2	12.2	12.2
	HAVO	56	37.8	37.8	50.0
	HBO	3	2.0	2.0	52.0
	MBO	45	30.4	30.4	82.4
	Over 21	4	2.7	2.7	85.1
	VWO/GYM/LYC	22	14.9	14.9	100.0
	Total	148	100.0	100.0	

grades (Carton and Illusion projects combined) from the years 2008 to 2013 were coded as 'original' (first opportunity), 'retake' (second and all subsequent opportunities) and 'MD1MAX', the highest grade of the retake and original grade groups. The MD1MAX scores were used in several statistical tests because they better represented student ability than MD1original or MD1retake values, both of which included many projects that were not handed in or were incomplete. The number of student participants and students from 2008 to 2013 who failed all attempts, passed a retake, or passed on the original submission are provided in Table 4.8. This comparison shows that student participants of this study outperformed the average across all years by 26.3% on the original delivery. It also shows that the overall failure rate for the six-year period covered, 2008–2013, is 30.3% ($n = 482$).

A Kruskal-Wallis test was conducted to determine if there were differences in MD1MAX scores between the four intake groups. Distributions of MD1MAX scores were similar for all groups, as assessed by visual inspection of a boxplot. MD1MAX scores were statistically significantly different between the different intake groups, $X2(3) = 14.146, p = .003$. Subsequently, pairwise comparisons were performed using Dunn's (1964) procedure with a Bonferroni correction for multiple comparisons. Adjusted p-values are presented. This post hoc analysis revealed statistically significant differences in MD1MAX scores between the C (mean rank $= 93.07$) and

Table 4.8 MD1 pass category (The Illusion project wasn't given at IGAD in the years 2006–2007)

	Frequency participants	Percent	Frequency all students 2008–2013	Percent
Fail both attempts	1	5.0	146	30.3
Fail original, pass retake	3	15.0	77	16.0
Pass original	16	80.0	259	53.7
Total	20	100.0	482	100.0

A (mean rank = 135.28) intake groups (p = .009) and D (mean rank = 98.75) and A groups (mean rank = 135.28) (p = .029), but not between any other group combination. This showed that the A group is different from the C and D groups to a statistically significant degree but that remaining groups are not significantly different. Therefore, intake assessment scores can distinguish between students who are likely to earn the highest and lowest scores in MD1, but cannot distinguish between students who will earn median passing scores from those who fail.

MD1MAX values were next compared to previous education groups to determine whether there was a relationship between grades earned in the MD1 class and previous experience as represented by type of previous education. There were outliers in the data, as assessed by inspection of a boxplot. Because there were outliers, the Kruskal-Wallis H test was run instead of a one-way ANOVA to determine if there were differences in MD1MAX scores between six groups in their type of previous education: 'MBO' (n = 162), 'HAVO' (n = 264), 'VWO/GYM/LYC' (n = 101), 'Foreign' (n = 76), 'Over 21' (n = 17) and HBO (n = 5).

Distributions of MD1MAX scores were not similar for all groups, as assessed by visual inspection of a boxplot. MD1MAX scores were statistically significantly different between the different types of previous education, $X2(5) = 17.666$, p = .003. Subsequently, pairwise comparisons were performed using Dunn's (1964) procedure with a Bonferroni correction for multiple comparisons. Adjusted p-values are presented. This post hoc analysis revealed statistically significant differences in MD1MAX scores between the HAVO (mean rank = 283.03) and MBO (mean rank = 353.35) (p = .001) groups, but not between any other group combination. The difference between these groups favoured students with an MBO education (mean = 6.44, n = 162), who earned on average 0.91 of a grade point higher than HAVO students (mean 5.49, n = 264) (Table 4.9). These results show a relationship between previous experience and subsequent performance on polygon modelling tasks.

The distribution of outliers showed that they represent grades of 0 and 1. At IGAD, if a student does not submit a final project for grading or does not take a final exam, instead of receiving a grade, the notation 'GK' is supposed to be made in their record. 'GK' stands for 'Geen Keuze', translated as 'missed opportunity' in English. This rule was not well-known or enforced at IGAD until about 2010. For this reason, lecturers were inconsistent about awarding a grade of 0 or 1 to students who did not hand in a final project. A '0' always means that no project was delivered, but due to

Table 4.9 MD1MAX means

	Mean	Std. deviation	N
MBO	6.48	2.43	162
HAVO	5.53	2.55	264
VWO/GYM/LYC	6.15	2.31	101
Foreign	6.13	2.73	76
Over 21	5.53	2.63	17
HBO	5.20	3.56	5

inconsistency among teachers, '1' was sometimes given when a project is not turned in or for plagiarism. In the data used here, only one file received a 1 for plagiarism and all the rest were for files that were not turned in. Due to the possibility that scores in this range biased test results, another Kruskal-Wallis test was run with grades of 0 and 1 excluded (n = 563).

Distributions of MD1MAX scores were not similar for all groups, as assessed by visual inspection of a boxplot. MD1MAX scores were statistically significantly different among the different types of previous education, $X2(5) = 17.732, p = .003$. Subsequently, pairwise comparisons were performed using Dunn's (1964) procedure with a Bonferroni correction for multiple comparisons. Adjusted p-values are presented. This post hoc analysis revealed statistically significant differences in MD1MAX scores between the HAVO (mean rank = 281.12) and MBO (mean rank = 336.39) ($p = .027$) groups and between HAVO (mean rank = 281.12) and Foreign (mean rank = 357.04), but not between any other group combination. In this test, MBO students (mean = 6.48, n = 162) had a 0.95 grade point advantage over HAVO students (mean = 5.53, n = 264). Foreign students (mean = 6.13, n = 76) had a 0.60 grade point advantage over HAVO students.

This result is not meaningfully different from the previous test, but when the same two tests were run with MD2MAX grades instead of MD1MAX grades, the results were different (see pp. 94–95). This is examined in more detail in the discussion chapter (p. 157).

4.5   Spatial Ability Test

IGAD students were given the PVRT after the Illusion project was concluded, but prior to the block in which the NURBS project was taught. The decision to use the PVRT was made after five tests, including the PVRT, were given to students in the previous year and compared. The tests were the PVRT, Revised Minnesota Form Board Test version AA, Revised Minnesota Form Board Test version BB, hole punch test (Dental Aptitude Test) and end-view test. Of this group, given to between 51 and 66 students, the only one that showed promise was the PVRT, which correlated with MD1 grades (n = 40, $p = .001$). The version of the PVRT used had a maximum possible score of 20. The mean score of IGAD students is 16.68 (n = 111). This mean score is higher than all Purdue University undergraduate groups whose test results were reported by Bodner and Guay (1997) and the Coventry University results among transportation design majors (Osmond and Turner 2007) (Table 4.10).

An unpaired t-test was run to compare the IGAD mean to each of the Purdue means and the Coventry mean (Table 4.11).

There was a significant difference between IGAD PVRT scores and Purdue 1 PVRT scores (m = 13.84, SD = 3.84): t(5.922), df = 1464, $p = <.0001$; IGAD PVRT scores and Purdue 2 PVRT scores (m = 13.96, SD = 3.80): t(5.6542), df = 1839, $p = <.0001$; IGAD PVRT scores and Purdue 3 PVRT scores (m = 14.16, SD = 3.78): t(3.5153), df = 349, $p = <.0005$; IGAD PVRT scores and Purdue 4

Table 4.10 IGAD PVRT scores compared to Purdue results (Bodner and Guay 1997, p. 11)

Population	n	Mean	Standard deviation
IGAD visual art students (2010–2012)	111	16.68	2.936
Transportation design majors (Coventry University)	105	13.43	Not reported
General chemistry course of science/engineering majors (Purdue 1)	1273	13.84	3.84
General chemistry course of science/engineering majors (Purdue 2)	1648	13.96	3.8
Sophomore organic course for biology/pre-med majors (Purdue 3)	158	14.16	3.78
General chemistry course of agriculture/health science majors (Purdue 4)	757	12.49	4.08
General chemistry course of agriculture/health science majors (Purdue 5)	850	11.66	3.96
Sophomore organic course for agriculture/health science majors (Purdue 6)	127	12.35	4.02

Table 4.11 Unpaired t-test comparison of IGAD PVRT scores with Purdue and Coventry results (Bodner and Guay 1997; Osmond et al. 2009; Osmond and Turner 2008)

	IGAD mean	Mean, other schools	SD	t	df	p
IGAD mean compared to Purdue 1 mean	16.68	13.84	3.84	5.922	1464	<.0001
IGAD mean compared to Purdue 2 mean	16.68	13.96	3.8	5.6542	1839	<.0001
IGAD mean compared to Purdue 3 mean	16.68	14.16	3.78	3.5153	349	<.0005
IGAD mean compared to Purdue 4 mean	16.68	12.49	4.08	9.5564	948	<.0001
IGAD mean compared to Purdue 5 mean	16.68	11.66	3.96	12.5403	1041	<.0001
IGAD mean compared to Purdue 6 mean	16.68	12.35	4.02	7.2724	318	<.0001
IGAD mean compared Coventry mean	16.68	13.43	4.05	4.5697	296	<.0001

PVRT scores (m = 12.49, SD = 4.08): t(9.5564), df = 948, p = <.0001; IGAD PVRT scores and Purdue 5 PVRT scores (m = 11.66, SD = 3.96): t(12.5403), df = 1041, p = <.0001; and IGAD PVRT scores and Purdue 6 PVRT scores (m = 12.35, SD = 4.02); t(7.2724), df = 318, p = <.0001. IGAD PVRT scores were also compared to Coventry University's PVRT scores. There was a statistically significant difference between IGAD PVRT scores and Coventry University PVRT scores (m = 13.43, SD = 4.05): t(4.5697), df = 296, p = <.0001.

These results are relevant to the discussion of spatial abilities in computer graphics because they highlight a difference in PVRT scores that favours students with CG experience (IGAD students) over students with experience in other domains. However, Coventry University students also had CG experience, but their scores were not higher on average than scores from the six Purdue University groups. This might be due to the orientation of the IGAD programme, which is visual art for game development, in comparison to CAD for design applications at Coventry University.

A Spearman's rank-order correlation was run to assess the relationship between grades earned in the MD1 class and PVRT scores. Preliminary analysis showed the relationship to be monotonic, as assessed by visual inspection of a scatterplot. There was a statistically significant positive correlation between MD1MAX scores and PVRT scores, r_s (109) = .330, p <.0005. The test was also run with former MBO students excluded (n = 22), on the basis that they had prior experience with polygonal modelling and may have biased the result. Preliminary analysis of all remaining cases (n = 87) showed a statistically significant positive correlation between MD1MAX scores and PVRT scores r_s (87) = .217, p = .043. Although both tests showed a significant correlation, the significance was much lower when MBO students were removed from the sample. Like other tests reviewed so far, this demonstrates an experience effect, where experience correlates with performance. In this example, it indicates that experience as an MBO student enhances spatial visualisation ability.

After the PVRT was taken, students started work on the NURBS project in the MD2 class. At that time, all students had taken the MD1 class and had been taking technical drawing classes for two blocks. If they had continued practising their polygon modelling skills during Block B (an option but not a requirement), they would have had a minimum of two blocks (20 weeks) of experience as polygon modellers at the time the MD2 class started, in addition to any prior experience they may have had. Because retakes for Block A classes were turned in at the end of Block B, student progress prior to the start of the MD2 course in Block C was represented in the MD1MAX variable. This concludes the section on prior experience.

4.6 Novice Status and Spatial Ability

Findings in this section show that: (1) MBO students are over-represented in the study, but are the second-largest group of students for the period 2006–2013, (2) previous CG experience roughly correlates with an MBO education, (3) intake assessments favoured drawing skills over CG skills, which tended to be weak in comparison, (4)

MD1 polygon assignment scores made by MBO students were higher on average to a statistically significant degree than students from other education types, (5) IGAD student PVRT scores were higher on average, to a statistically significant degree, than average scores for students at Purdue and Coventry universities and (6) IGAD student PVRT scores correlated to a statistically significant degree with MD1 project performance

4.7 NURBS Project Grades

After student participants turned in their MD2 projects, they were graded by the co-lecturer for the class. For statistical comparisons, their grades were coded in the same way as MD1 grades: MD2original, MD2retake and MD2MAX.

At IGAD, a grade of 6 meets a minimum academic standard and an 8 or above is supposed to represent a professional standard. Six of the 20 student participants received grades of 8 or above on the original hand-in of the assignment, indicating that teachers thought that those students had developed a professional level of proficiency during the class. The distribution of grades for this group (Table 4.12) shows that the full range of academic performance is represented by the students who volunteered to be a part of the study.

Of the 20 student participants, eight received a failing grade on the original hand-in. On the retake, seven of these students earned a passing grade. Only one student failed both attempts. When compared to all IGAD students who have taken the MD2 class or all students from the same year, the participant pass rate is significantly higher than the mean for either of the other two groups (Table 4.13). This data is presented as a reminder that the group of students who volunteered as participants are not representative of failure rates at IGAD. This may be because there is a significantly higher number of more experienced former MBO students among them.

Table 4.12 Frequency of MD2 original grades

Valid		Frequency	Percent
	0	3	15.0
	1	1	5.0
	4	4	20.0
	6	2	10.0
	7	4	20.0
	8	2	10.0
	9	1	5.0
	10	3	15.0
	Total	20	100.0

Table 4.13 MD2 pass type frequencies compared

	Frequency, participants	Percent, participants	Frequency, 2012	Percent, 2012	Frequency 2006–2013	Percent, 2006–2013
Fail both attempts	1	5.0	40	43.0	281	45.0
Fail original pass retake	7	35.0	34	36.6	123	19.7
Pass original	12	60.0	19	20.4	221	35.4
Total	20	100.0	93	100.0	625	100.0

4.7.1   MD2MAX Compared to Previous Education

A Kruskal-Wallis test was conducted to determine if there were differences in MD2MAX scores between four previous education group types: MBO (n = 164), HAVO (n = 267), VWO/GYM/LYC (n = 101) and Foreign (n = 76). Distributions of MD2MAX scores were not similar for all groups, as assessed by visual inspection of a boxplot. MD2MAX scores were statistically significantly different among the different types of previous education, X2(3) = 17.291, p = .001. Subsequently, pairwise comparisons were performed using Dunn's (1964) procedure with a Bonferroni correction for multiple comparisons. Adjusted p-values are presented. This post hoc analysis revealed statistically significant differences in MD2MAX scores between the HAVO (mean rank = 272.67) and MBO (mean rank = 325.42, p = .008) and the HAVO (mean rank = 272.67) and Foreign groups (mean rank = 347.93, p = .008), but not between any other group combination. The MD2MAX grade mean between HAVO and MBO students favoured MBO students by 0.99 grade points. The MD2MAX grade mean between HAVO and Foreign students favoured Foreign students by 1.33 grade points.

To determine what effect missing files had on results, a Kruskal-Wallis test was conducted to determine if there were differences in MD2MAX scores among six previous education group types if scores of 0 and 1 were excluded. The groups compared were: 'MBO' (n = 123), 'HAVO' (n = 167), 'VWO/GYM/LYC' (n = 74), 'Foreign' (n = 58), 'over 21' (n = 11) and 'HBO' (n = 1). Distributions of MD2MAX scores were not similar for all groups, as assessed by visual inspection of a boxplot. MD2MAX scores were not statistically significantly different between the different types of previous education, X2(5) = 7.925, p = .160. This result is different from when the same test was run on MD1MAX scores with grades of 0 and 1 excluded. In that test, MBO students (mean = 6.48, n = 162) had a 0.95 grade point advantage over HAVO students (mean = 5.53, n = 264) and foreign students (mean = 6.13, n = 76) had a 0.60 grade point advantage over HAVO students. This finding is relevant to the influence of prior experience and the relative difficulty of the two projects. This is discussed in more detail in the next chapter (p. 157).

A Kruskal-Wallis test was conducted to determine if there were differences in MD2MAX scores among the four intake groups. Distributions of MD2MAX scores were similar for all groups, as assessed by visual inspection of a boxplot. MD2MAX scores were statistically significantly different between the different intake groups, $X2(3) = 9.977, p = .019$. Subsequently, pairwise comparisons were performed using Dunn's (1964) procedure with a Bonferroni correction for multiple comparisons. Adjusted p-values are presented. This post hoc analysis revealed statistically significant differences in MD2MAX scores between the C (mean rank = 101.24) and A (mean rank = 141.25) intake groups ($p = .017$) but not between any other group combination. This test was also run with grades of 0 and 1 excluded. In that test, the results were not meaningfully different, but several outliers were created so it is not used here. This result is similar to the comparison between intake ranking and MD1MAX grades. Taken together, these results are inconclusive, indicating that intake group membership is not a reliable indicator of performance on the NURBS modelling task.

4.7.2 MD2MAX Compared to PVRT

A Spearman's rank-order correlation was run to assess the relationship between grades earned in the MD2 class and PVRT scores. Preliminary analysis showed the relationship to be monotonic, as assessed by visual inspection of a scatterplot. There was no statistically significant correlation between MD2MAX scores and PVRT scores, $r_s (109) = .185, p < .052$. This is quite different from the result from the MD1MAX comparison with the PVRT results, which strongly correlated ($r_s (109) = .330, p < .0005$).

Together, the comparison of MD2MAX scores with previous education groups and PVRT scores show no statistically significant correlation. This finding is different from when the same comparison was made with MD1MAX scores. Thus, performance on mental rotation tests and prior attendance at an MBO programme appeared to correlate with performance on the polygon project, but not on the NURBS project.

4.8 Summary of Phase One Findings

IGAD students' previous experience was estimated based on previous school type (polygon modelling), intake assessment (drawing), first block grades (polygon modelling) and spatial ability tests. Results of these comparisons are able to predict, to a statistically significant degree, performance in polygon modelling tasks. The same results are not predictive of performance on NURBS modelling tasks. This finding is important because it distinguishes between two types of modelling tasks that are in many ways similar. For instance, they use the same software, are used to build the same types of objects and are used in related industries. In the following chapter, qualitative results shed some light on the difference between polygon and NURBS modelling.

References

Bodner GM, Guay RB (1997) The Purdue visualization of rotations test. Chem Educ 2(4):1–14

Brown A, Moerkamp T, Voncken E (1999) Facilitating progression to higher education from vocational paths. Eur J Educ 34(2):219–235

Ericsson KA (2014) Why expert performance is special and cannot be extrapolated from studies of performance in the general population: a response to criticisms. Intelligence 45(1):81–103. https://doi.org/10.1016/j.intell.2013.12.001

Osmond J, Turner A (2007) Measuring the creative baseline in transport design education. Paper presented at the proceedings of the 15th improving student learning symposium, Dublin, Ireland

Osmond J, Bull K, Tovey M (2009) Threshold concepts and the transport and product design curriculum: reports of research in progress. Art Des Commun High Educ 8(2):169–175

Resnick LB, Nolan KJ, Resnick DP (1995) Benchmarking education standards. Educ Eval Policy Anal 17(4):438–461

Chapter 5
Qualitative Findings

5.1 Overview Qualitative Findings

Data collected during the nine-week observation period of this study are presented in this chapter. This data is most relevant to the primary research question, 'What are the principal contributing factors to crossing the proficiency skill threshold among digital art students?' and the third question, 'What is the relationship between spatial ability or spatial visualisation and development of proficiency among digital art students?' Seven students out of 10 (70%) who noticed a transition in their work implicated a type of visualisation as the principal obstacle and ultimately the means by which proficiency was obtained. The types of visualisation they described are different from the forms of mental visualisation tested for in the spatial visualisation tests given to IGAD students and those discussed in Chap. 2 (p. 29) (Bodner and Guay 1997; Eliot and Smith 1983; Vandenberg and Kuse 1978). The types of spatial visualisation identified by students can be distinguished from the technology used to express them because they can be expressed in multiple mediums such as drawings on paper, paintings, fabric patterns, or NURBS modelling. In addition, the data also suggest that proficiency in this skill was developed rapidly.

This chapter is organised to follow the development process among the students during phase two and three of the study. It starts by describing the MD2 class structure, then continues with week-by-week student progress. Student case study briefs and employed graduate interview results conclude the chapter.

5.2 MD2 Class Structure

At the beginning of Block C, first-year IGAD visual arts students must take the NURBS modelling class, MD2. To better understand student reflections on the class, its structure is described here. The MD2 class is composed of two mandatory

© Springer Nature Switzerland AG 2018
A. Paquette, *Spatial Visualization and Professional Competence*,
https://doi.org/10.1007/978-3-319-91289-9_5

components: lectures and workshops. The lectures take place once a week and are one-hour long. They are based on material from the textbook *Computer Graphics for Artists, an Introduction* (Paquette 2008). The NURBS lectures discuss NURBS modelling at a conceptual level, without reference to specific software applications or tools used in NURBS modelling. For example, the components of a NURBS curve are described, but the application-specific tools needed to make them are not mentioned (Fig. 5.1).

To provide a better teacher-to-student ratio, students are split into three or four groups of approximately equal size (between 17 and 22 students per group, depending on the year) to be taught in separate workshops. Workshops were given between one and four days after each weekly lecture and were three hours long. For the first four of seven workshops, students were introduced to NURBS modelling tools in the software Autodesk Maya 2012. This was done by providing students with example files at the start of every class. Students were then asked to solve NURBS modelling problems contained in the files by using the available NURBS tools, which were first demonstrated at the beginning of each workshop. A senior lecturer and a junior lecturer were available in each of the four classes to assist students.

Class work was designed to familiarise students with NURBS modelling tools to prepare them for the main project of the class: to build a model of a vehicle. This project was given at the beginning of the first workshop for students to work on at home. At the same time, students were given weekly milestones they were expected to meet. Progress was checked weekly in workshops. After the fourth workshop, there were no more exercises in class and students worked exclusively on their vehicle progress.

In addition to the lectures and workshops, there were optional after-hours gatherings known as 'NURBS parties' each week that were supervised by the junior lecturer. These were usually well-attended and lasted approximately as long as a normal workshop. Students brought their vehicle models to these gatherings and worked with other students and the junior lecturer for the purpose of deepening their understanding of NURBS modelling techniques.

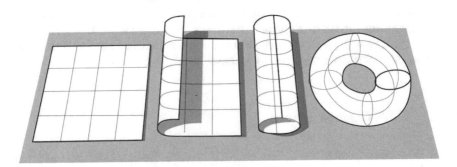

Fig. 5.1 An application-independent example from the NURBS text, illustrating the polymorphic nature of NURBS surfaces

The findings in this section are primarily qualitative and derive from a combination of student learning logs, student questionnaires, interviews with students and copies of student milestone deliveries. Grades on the MD2 project are the only quantitative data collected during this phase, and they were added to the phase one quantitative data for analysis. Whenever quotes are presented, pseudonyms are used to identify the speaker. These form the basis for thematic analysis presented in the discussion chapter.

5.3 First Three Weeks: Reactions and Problems

To examine whether students' prior experience and/or attitude towards the class affected their performance, questionnaires and interviews were used to gather their early reactions to the NURBS project over the first three weeks.

Overall, only one student (n = 19) reported being 'somewhat comfortable' with the NURBS project at the beginning. The rest were either 'neutral' (n = 5), 'somewhat uncomfortable' (n = 6), or 'uncomfortable (n = 7) (Table 5.1). All considered the NURBS project to be the most difficult assignment of any kind they had encountered at any school.

A key finding to emerge from the first three weeks was that students noticed that while working on the NURBS project, their way of thinking about form was different from when they built the illusion project out of polygons in block A, ten weeks earlier. The difference was significant to them.

5.3.1 Attitude Towards MD2 Class

Many students were not eager to work with NURBS at the beginning of the class. One student, Ward, claimed that his initial progress was slow because he was not scheduling his time well, admitting that 'at the start, I really hated the whole idea of working with NURBS.' Maikel felt the same way, saying, 'I don't feel like NURBS is really going to be useful in my future in the gaming industry'. Other students

Table 5.1 Questionnaire answers to 'How did you feel about working with NURBS at the beginning of MD2?'

	N	Percent (%)
Uncomfortable	7	36.80
Somewhat uncomfortable	6	31.60
Neutral	5	26.30
Somewhat comfortable	1	5.30
Comfortable	0	0.00

resisted using NURBS because, as Bjorn explained, '[polygons] are easier to edit, for me at least, than NURBS.'

The difficulty of working with NURBS was a frequent source of frustration. Sebastian expressed his feelings this way: 'It felt like you had asked me, milk this pineapple.' Another student wrote in an anonymous questionnaire from the previous year, 'It was the most challenging thing I ever had to do after being able [to] understand girls.' Others used terms like 'evil', 'nightmare', 'screwed' and 'worst time of my life' to describe the difficulty of the project, at least in the first few weeks. During the interviews, students consistently rated the NURBS project as the most difficult they had ever encountered in any school.

Despite the difficulty, some students reacted positively to the class from the beginning. According to Lisette, she 'like[d] looking for a sort of puzzle in something…I like challenges like that.' Paula admitted that the project was intimidating, at least partly due to warnings given to first-year students from upperclassmen, but after a couple of weeks Paula wondered, 'Why are they saying that? This is cool.' To her, it was a challenge and a 'fun exercise'. She felt that a negative attitude toward the project led to failure, so she made a conscious decision that she would not fall into that trap and would enjoy the project instead.

5.3.2 The Problem of Reference

The first problem students faced was to find reference for their vehicles. This imitates standard industry practice, where artists are normally responsible for finding their own reference. The purpose of reference is to assist students in achieving a likeness of their target vehicle.

Students mentioned reference for two reasons. Firstly, some students complained of the difficulty of acquiring reference, particularly for the undercarriage of their vehicles. Secondly, students wanted to explain why reference was important or problematic. Some students, like Lisette, did not initially think that reference would be an issue. In her learning log, she described having found 'a lot' of reference in her first week as if this aspect of the project had been dealt with. However, in her third week she mentioned finding new reference for the axle and transmission in her vehicle and then in the following week that she had found better reference for these things.

Maike wrote in her learning log that her 'orthographic reference images' (line drawings) were from the wrong version of her car. She later wrote that she found some images, but 'the quality is not as good as I hoped.' Still later, she wrote of sending a request to a local auto dealer for reference, but a week later there was 'still no answer from the car seller. I doubt that there will be any.' In most cases, students were able to find only incomplete reference from any one source. Maike never found more reference than she had started with in the first week.

Another student concern was when reference images did not match. Sebastian noticed this when he saw that the 'back wheels in my kit are the same size as the front wheels. While in the blueprints, the back wheels are slightly bigger.' He followed that comment with his solution, which was to measure the wheels of his model kit with a toothpick he had divided into millimetres. He expressed the difficulty of working with reference by describing a project he had worked on at an internship during his previous MBO education. On that assignment, he had been asked to build a model of a submarine. He did not expect it to be difficult because he had earlier made models of a cup and a bottle at the same company without any problems, but 'the bottle and the cup were in my hands so I could really look at it. The submarine is a bit difficult to hold in your hand.'

When students went looking for reference, particularly when they had chosen unusual or rare vehicles, they found that, as Wietse says, 'I just couldn't get my hands on a decent reference. Dimensions were also a pain to get. I only managed to get the length and the width and the wheels.' According to Maikel, even when he had reference, there was a problem with using it: 'You have front and side view and such and you have a tape model but the gap between those…I think that was [the] harder problem.'

Timothy described his solution to working with mismatched reference as a matter of estimation: 'I would look at other reference images and I would check which ones actually matched each other, which ones were most comparable and if they weren't I would go with something in between.' According to Roel, seeing the shapes in a vehicle was problematic regardless of reference because 'when you look at the image you might think at first that it's a reflection, but if you look at different angles of the car and it's still there, you know that it's built into the surface and if you look at the diagram you think it's all flat. The bonnet, for example, the hood of the car, it has a curve in there that you can't see by the diagrams themselves.'

The problem was that no one reference contained all of the information needed to recreate the depicted vehicle in 3D graphics and students had to mentally fill in the gaps. Reference images might be low quality, inconsistent, or lacking information about certain parts of the vehicle. Students solved these problems by seeking more detailed reference, cross-checking different references, or taking their own measurements and observations, but it was still a challenge to accurately visualize the vehicle based on the information they had gathered.

After students had finished acquiring reference for their vehicles, they had to build them. It was at this point, in the second and third weeks, that they started confronting differences between polygons and NURBS.

5.3.3 Thinking in Polygons

Some students stated that prior experience with modelling in polygons did not facilitate the NURBS modelling task. One student, Pim, had received an MBO education prior to IGAD and was one of the six student participants who passed the Carton project. He also earned a 9 on the Illusion project. When asked whether that experience helped on the NURBS project, Pim said that 'NURBS is a different way of thinking and [polygon modelling] didn't help me in that way of thinking.' Martin had attended an MBO, passed the Carton project and earned a 10 on the Illusion project; but when asked whether NURBS was any easier due to his prior experience, he said, 'No, because it's different than polygons—it's totally different.' Bart did not have previous experience at another institution, but he had completed the Illusion project at IGAD. When asked whether his work modelling in polygons at IGAD benefitted him on the NURBS project he said that it only informed him of the Maya interface rather than modelling techniques useful to NURBS modelling. Only one student, Roel, felt that polygons and NURBS modelling were not that different. In his words, 'they are both modelling classes.'

Yet the two types of CG modelling were largely characterized as being so different that experience in one could actually impair ability to work with the other, as Maike suggested in the following comment: 'In NURBS, the polygon experience didn't really help us…it even prevented us from having good results sometimes because polygons and NURBS are different.' Other students described why they thought NURBS were different from polygons. According to Janet, the two are 'fundamentally different' because 'I think my thinking process, my analysis of the form, is different.' She then described how she can 'just see' the shape she is working with when polygon modelling, but in NURBS she must mentally extend the shape and think of how it must be cut to get the shape she wants. Paula described it as being like making a rough drawing and then gradually adding detail: 'I saw NURBS as the same, like you start with, yes, surfaces, like, very large, and I cut away things.'

Both of these students described a type of spatial visualization as a requirement for working with NURBS; instead of building an object from scratch by adding shapes until it began to resemble the desired form, NURBS demanded that they 'mentally extend' the form and then visualize how to 'cut' it so that it took the shape desired, like the difference between a carpenter assembling an object from assorted parts and a sculptor carving it out of a block. The majority of students found the latter type of visualization more challenging and that any attempt to use the easier type of visualization was a hindrance to the task.

Wietse said that when he worked with NURBS, he was still using polygon modelling techniques: 'trying to connect surfaces, and not cutting at all.' Pim said that with NURBS, 'it's like thinking three steps ahead instead of just doing whatever at the moment and a polygon is more like doing what you do at the moment.' Thus, working with NURBS required an advanced type of spatial visualization in which students had to think ahead to how their object would look at multiple stages in its development, rather than only the most immediate one.

5.4 Weeks 4 Through 6: Difficulties Encountered on the Project

When asked to describe difficulties found in the next three-week span of the NURBS project, students focussed on two things: tools and visualisation. Some reported that their problems were solely tool-related, while others found that the tools highlighted a different problem: the tools wouldn't work unless the student was first able to visualise the form of the object they were trying to make. This second problem proved quite difficult for most students, who frequently described it as a problem of 'seeing' the shapes they needed to make. If they could see them in their mind, they could make them. If they couldn't, they experienced many problems.

The visualisation problems described by students fell into two principal categories: order of construction and topology. In the first category, students explained the importance of having a good idea of how they intended to approach a shape-related problem before trying to build it. Because of the inter-related character of the way NURBS objects are defined, they could not, as they could with polygons, simply iteratively modify a shape until it matched their target shape. The second category, topology, is a visualisation-related problem that defines how different surfaces are connected to each other. Students found that if their topology wasn't well-designed, the likeness would be poor. Both of these challenges required some form of visualisation to solve.

The difficulties students described were learning to command the NURBS toolbox itself and/or with forming a mental image of how they would create the desired shape of their object, without which they found the tools were useless.

5.4.1 Tool Problems

Students had to understand what the NURBS software tools did before they could determine how to use them to create the desired shapes. Alexander said that working with NURBS was a simple matter of learning the tools introduced in the class. In answer to a question about visualising solutions to the shape problems he faced, he said, 'if you know what tools there are and how to use them, you can imagine how to create those patches and surfaces.' Alexander's learning log had a tendency to describe tools as not working 'properly', which caused Maya to 'crash more frequently'. Such crashes were typical of tools being used without understanding of their function.

A more detailed view of tool problems faced by students was provided by excerpts from Maike's learning log, which included many examples such as: 'These [patches] are separated by hard edges, and I cannot find a way to soften/align them. Aligning destroys the functional fillet shape, while fusing all projected curves into one results in a slightly distorted fillet.' Throughout the logs, she described building and rebuilding her shapes multiple times as she experimented with the tools. Other students were observed experiencing the same or similar problems in class.

Lucas described the majority of problems he encountered as 'tools that didn't do what I was expecting.' Until he got to the end of the project, his primary occupation was simply 'figuring out how NURBS exactly work'. In doing so, he realised that 'it's a completely different way of thinking than if you're working with polygons, because with NURBS you have to take into account a lot more.' Maikel separated the problems he experienced into two categories: 'When you solve the tools problem, when you understand them, well, you have that problem solved and every time you start something new, well, you know how the tools work but you still have that problem of creating the shape, the second problem.' For some, then, mastering the tools was a step that revealed the second problem, which required visualisation to solve.

Pim described the problems he faced as magnified by the types of shapes he had to make rather than as problems with the tools used to make them. To him, in comparison to simpler vehicles chosen by other students, his was 'a thousand acre[s] of problems' due to his vehicle's complexity. Because of this, he said that he had to 're-evaluate the problem every time and that really helps your problem-solving skills because you're busy solving problems the entire time of the project.'

Maike said the difficulty of working with NURBS tools was that

> The knowledge didn't really sink in immediately. I had to try it myself. So, it's basically trial and error…When something isn't working, instead of asking how can I do that, I like to edit it with a hammer until it works.

To understand the toolset, students found it necessary to experiment with the tools and see the results for themselves. Timothy mentioned solving problems by similar trial-and-error, claiming that the difficulties he faced were

> a mixture of how I was using the tools and looking at the shapes. [I] had to re-do parts of the car quite often which forced me and probably most of the students to try out different ways of creating the car.

For Bjorn, understanding how NURBS tools functioned was separate from the primary problem he faced on the NURBS project. As he put it, 'I knew how the tools worked pretty all right but yes, the shape was just…how am I going to make a certain shape?' Although workshop tutorials had covered how to build non-specific or generic shapes which did not need to match specific dimensions or proportions, learning how specific shapes were made was a much greater challenge mentioned by several students. In Bjorn's case, he echoed Roel and Janet when he said in his interview that 'it was still very hard to see the shape you wanted.' This was frustrating for him because it interfered with his ability to 'plan how the shape should be'. At a cognitive level, he felt that he had to take the lessons from his classes and then 'work out' how they applied to his specific car. This required visualisation of how the tools could be used to create the desired shape.

5.4.2 Visualisation

5.4.2.1 2D Understanding of Curvature

Students had a tendency to describe problems as either tool errors or a problem with 'seeing shapes'. During the interviews, I pursued both types of answers to try and determine exactly what was meant. The frequent comments about the difficulty of 'seeing shapes' sounded to me like they were describing likeness errors: the difficulty of matching the 3D model to the appearance of the target vehicle. However, when questioned more carefully, students in some cases were describing an aspect of seeing that they found difficult to put into words.

The first indication of the problem was visible in some of the early vehicle models, called 'tape models', when they were still made of curves, prior to making surfaces. In some of these models, the curves were not 3D. Although the curves had been generated in 3D space, they were planar (Fig. 5.2) and then rotated to create a three-dimensional form in the same way that a flat sheet of paper can be rolled into a cylinder. Students found these 2D curves easier to work with than fully 3D shapes. Bart acknowledged this of his own model in the following exchange:

Bart: Well, the wheels part went pretty well, I think, and the carriage was all right too. Those were really obvious shapes.

AP: Why were those easier than the body?

Bart: Well the wheel is just a cylinder actually and [the] under-carriage is really flat. And the body I had to really think in 3D.

Students had little trouble building 2D curves based on their two-dimensional reference; however, problems arose when they had to create 3D shapes based on flat images. Like Bart, Maike found it more difficult to work with curves that were fully 3D. Her reference required the use of non-planar curves, which caused a likeness mistake that she described as the product of a curve that 'didn't line up with [her] top reference, […] caused by the side plane not being bent enough at the back.' This type of error was frequently observed during workshops, where students would build a curve so that it looked like the reference in one view, such as the side view, but they would not adjust the curve to match the other two views, front and top.

A comparison between Maike's and Roel's vehicles (Fig. 5.3) shows that Maike's is built of simple 2D curves and is less defined than Roel's vehicle built of 3D

Fig. 5.2 Bart's model in week 4 contains nothing but 2D curves

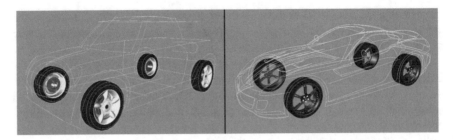

Fig. 5.3 Two tape models from week 3, by Maike (L) and Roel (R), show layout curves and wheels

curves. In Maike's case, the likeness error meant that she would either have to make significant changes to other parts she had already made, or 'patch that up'. When asked to explain why it would be a problem on the vehicle, Maike said that 'if you don't really define what something looks like […] then nobody would understand it.'

Maike's answers helped explain at least part of what was meant when students used the words 'see' and 'seeing' when talking about the vehicle project. It was difficult for them to 'see' 3D details when using 2D reference, which caused problems when they tried to define the shape in 3D for viewers to understand. However, this did not completely explain student mentions of the word 'seeing'.

Alexander made the following effort to define it:

> I know what it was, it was spatial visualisation. You had to put a plane somewhere, a line on the side of the tape model or something like that and then it looked correct on the side and the front and I put another one over there and then there was a curve inward somewhere and then I thought, how is that, do I now put another plane there or curve it in? And I thought, curving it in isn't really possible.

The scenario Alexander described sounds like an attempt to describe his thought process as he visualised alternate means of achieving a desired shape. He added to this by saying the issue was twofold: not only was he trying to visualise the shapes, but also 'the way they should be laid out'. Thus, visualising the way the shapes connected to each other was just as important as how to build the shapes themselves.

The problems students had with visualising or 'seeing' shapes were threefold: the difficulty of understanding a 3D object based on 2D reference, of creating the desired shapes using the tools provided, and of connecting the shapes to each other so that the resulting object accurately represented the intended vehicle.

5.4.2.2   Visualisation of Shapes

To connect surfaces to each other, 'blends' are used to join separate 3D surfaces. It is a challenge to decide how to place a blend so that the surfaces are smoothly connected. Paula said that the problem was 'seeing where are the blends…where are they supposed to be. That's kind of difficult for people to see.' To help visualise a solution to 'seeing the blends', Paula bought a plastic model kit of the car she was building, covered it with tape and then drew lines on the tape to create a visual representation of potential solutions. According to Paula, this exercise 'made [her] see the overall shape of objects, instead of focussing on a certain part of the object.'

To 'see' how his vehicle was built, Wietse described the mental visualisation technique he used: 'Just imagine just a plain surface here and imagine something else, a bread knife cutting it through like this, and how would it look if you did it like that'. After visualising the resulting shape, Wietse had to determine how groups of shapes could be blended together smoothly. The problem was that 'when you finish one surface and you work on another surface that is right next to it and patched together, the one you finished before might go wrong.' It is because of this quality of NURBS modelling, that surfaces have an effect on the shape of previously made surfaces, that Lucas and other students emphasised the importance of 'thinking ahead' when working with NURBS.

In NURBS modelling, two shapes that look nothing like the desired shape can be manipulated to create the intended result, such as two planar squares being used to form a circular depression. Figure 5.4 illustrates how the two squares are laid over each other and the centre of one square is drawn out while the other is pushed in, so that they intersect in the middle. The smaller square pushes the larger one inward and vice versa, so that when the smaller square is removed, a circular depression is left in the now curved surface of the larger square. This is the type of sequence that students must visualize in order to solve how to use shapes like these to create an accurate 3D representation of a vehicle.

Thinking ahead was described by Daniel as 'playing a video' in his head where he plans out the steps of a solution: 'Sometimes it doesn't work but then I'm already making another video in my mind with what I have to do then.' The way Janet explained it, 'If it's just a likeness error then it's easy to fix, just rebuild it. But if the topology is not right you probably have to review a lot of other things because the connection is not that right.' To solve for the connections, Janet created two versions of her model: one for 'research' and one to work on the likeness after she

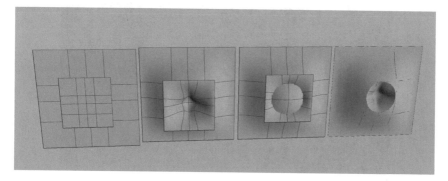

Fig. 5.4 Two square surfaces are intersected to create a circular hole

had determined with the research model how patches should be connected. Multiple solutions to this type of problem are possible, as shown in Fig. 5.5 which depicts three different ways to represent the same shape using varying patch layouts.

5.4.2.3 Student References to 'Seeing'

Students consistently chose to use the word 'seeing' when discussing problems, they experienced on the NURBS project. As they described it, the principal challenge of the project to them was 'seeing' shapes in their vehicle. This term was not intended to be taken literally, because all students were able to see the reference they used. The issue was that they had a hard time extrapolating from their reference a coherent 3D mental visualisation. It was this kind of internal 'seeing' that they meant. Here, it is called 'projection visualisation' because it is the projection of 2D information into 3D space.

When the methodology for this project was designed, it was unknown what students would have to say about their learning experience after the project concluded. It was expected that they would in some way reference the topological problems encountered during the modelling process, but the results proved to emphasise the problem of 'seeing' more than any other factor. Students' word choice and more detailed answers indicated that they associated visualisation with the NURBS problem more strongly than problem-solving. It may be that solving the topology problem required an adequate visualisation first, but even in that case, students who referenced topology did so in the context of 'seeing'. So even then, they understood the problem to be first an issue of visualisation and second, a puzzle-like problem-solving exercise.

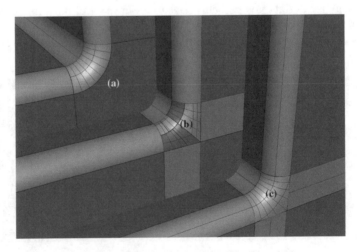

Fig. 5.5 Different topological treatments for three corners, (**a**), (**b**) and (**c**)

5.4.2.4   Order of Construction

Because NURBS surfaces interact with and affect the shape of previously made surfaces, the order in which they are constructed is important. Alexander's learning log from Week 6 contains the following entry: 'I have a few isues [*sic*] with the order of witch [*sic*] I create surfaces. The main problem is that after I have builded [*sic*] a part of the car, I find that other parts would have been easier to make first.' This statement highlights an issue hinted at in the interviews with Daniel, Lucas, Wietse and others when they talked about the importance of 'seeing ahead' when working with NURBS. Martin gave an example of the consequences of not planning ahead when working in NURBS: 'If your art director or someone on your team says now you have to change some part and you have already made all the details, you are going to have to delete them.' This is because the details depended on larger structures that, if altered, also affect all connected sub-structures.

Lisette knew that she should not focus on details before working out the larger shapes of her vehicle, but did so anyway because 'I got impatient so I wanted to see the progress in it right away. And by working with the big shapes, it felt to me like it took too long so I tried focussing on smaller parts.' She was not the only student to do this, nor the only student who ignored lecturers' warnings against approaching the NURBS problem this way.

Martin acknowledged he was aware that teachers had advised him to work with large simple shapes to start with, but said, 'I was not listening, you know, I have to make the headlight like this [first].' After he discovered his error, he tried to inform other students that the order of construction was important, but they also ignored his advice. 'I didn't listen to you and they don't listen to me, so, they have got to get this, have this moment of, oh, he's right.' Many students disregarded this advice until they came to understand it from seeing the results of their own experimentation.

Like Martin, several students reported that after spending long hours on the NURBS project for weeks, they threw away what they had made until that point and started over. After Timothy did this in Week 5, he reported in his learning log that he was then 'able to make the basic shapes of the car in 30–60 min. [It] used to be 5–7 h.' This was a typical result. Many students who rebuilt their projects from scratch reported that they could rebuild their vehicle to a higher-quality standard in a fraction of the time it took to make the original shapes.

Jacqueline compared the process of modelling in NURBS and polygons this way:

> With polygonal modelling, when you make a square, it's a square and you can add another thing to it and another thing…but NURBS, you know that this result of yours will not be the last. You may throw this away when you have a better thing, and it's like it isn't final; it's one step by another and…it's like, you have this huge paper and you have to write a [step-by-step] plan, and one by one, that's NURBS.

In Week 6 of the project, Paula submitted a model file that contained at least three different treatments of the front corner of her vehicle (Fig. 5.6). Paula's explanation was that 'as a whole object it doesn't flow nicely, like it is supposed to be very simple, the lines have to be all […] flowing nicely.' With this in mind, the variety of

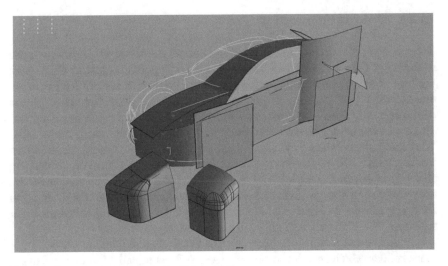

Fig. 5.6 Corner treatment tests by Paula in week 6

solutions she tried were attempts to improve the 'flow' of surfaces. This is the 'fluid surfacing' mentioned by Meyer and Land (2012) in their description of threshold concepts related to design education (see §5.1). Fluid surfacing refers to groups of NURBS surfaces that flow seamlessly into each other at common boundaries. When done well, it is not possible to detect that multiple surfaces are present. Instead, an object built this way appears to be a single unbroken surface.

5.4.2.5   Topology and Connections

Topology, or the way that parts of an object connect to form the overall structure, was a significant challenge for students to understand. Like Lisette, Daniel's description of the modelling process was reminiscent of solving a puzzle:

'In the beginning it was just basic long planes, and okay, that's a plane, that's the side view, that's the top part and that's it. But in the end, I had to break up every single part. I first had to think of it, if I trim it, like, these sections will have enough sides to connect it again, or will I have too many sides and not be able to connect it anymore?'

The connections between parts make up the topology of the model. Ensuring that connections are smooth, or flow, is called 'blending'. A 'blend' is a special type of surface that bridges a gap between unconnected surfaces. For Janet, blending surfaces was the most difficult part of the project. She said that she had been building 'random shapes' to test various blending techniques until she discovered which combinations worked. This happened in Week 5, after which she said that blending shapes 'went really fast'. This was supported by the files she turned in at that time, which showed rapid progress (Fig. 5.7).

Fig. 5.7   Janet's vehicle, Week 5 (L) and Week 6 (R)

Lisette claimed that, for her, the primary problem was that she did not know how NURBS modelling tools worked. However, when asked if she meant that she did not understand tool options or the way patches related to each other, she answered, 'The way the patches have to relate to each other. I mean the options were a problem at first but then I started slowly understanding them.' Lisette said that she also had to pay attention to the way she built things in polygons, but that in polygon modelling, 'you have a direct confirmation of whether you did it right, and with NURBS you might have to go through a lot more steps to really get that.'

Again, students found that they had to visualize several steps ahead in order to find effective methods of connecting the parts of their object. Until such methods were found, there was much trial-and-error, but as seen in Janet's example, students could afterwards make rapid progress.

5.5   Final Weeks: Visualisation and Performance Transition

In the last weeks of the NURBS project, students learned that better quality visualisations led to simpler, better solutions that were more easily executed than the complicated solutions they started with. They also reported a spontaneous change to the way they saw structure in objects found in their immediate environment. Dubbed 'NURBS vision' or 'seeing in NURBS', some students described how they found themselves reflexively conducting shape analyses of objects in their surroundings, particularly vehicles and examples of industrial design.

5.5.1   *Visualisation*

Towards the end of the project, more students were beginning to understand NURBS. This understanding came paired with an enhanced awareness of mistakes. As Martin said, 'For me it was kind of frustrating because I had to delete almost half of the car just to change the width of the…I think the back lights' (Fig. 5.8). But rebuilding the model was less of a problem for students than it might seem, as Roel explained: 'When I started, I made surfaces and I connected them in such a way that they looked like crap, and every time I look at [it] now, as in I've made my diffuser in less than a day, where I used to be working on it for like two or three weeks, because I know the right approaches now.'

Timothy described the moment things changed for him on the NURBS project as related to understanding the patch layout of his model: 'Since the car has very complex curves I tended to think a lot more difficult [sic]. And that part was exactly a part that I didn't have to think difficult [sic] and just use simpler tools and simpler connections.' Once he realised this, his approach to the project changed suddenly and he progressed more rapidly because he had learned how to 'put the base together that you don't run into problems later on with the final.'

Thus, students claimed that their way of thinking about shapes and their connections changed between the start and end of the NURBS project. After the change their progress was more rapid. Once they understood how to approach the problem, they found solutions much more quickly and could more easily recognize and solve their own mistakes.

5.5.2   Reflexive Shape Analysis

Students talked about changes to the way they 'see' as a result of the NURBS project. They claimed to have developed enhanced sensitivity to detail, structure and surface tension. Another modification to the way they saw things during the NURBS class was typified by this statement from Sebastian: 'Well this morning I walked over the street and looked at all the cars and I literally saw fillets in between some of the things.' Timothy agreed in his interview that the same thing had happened to him. He put it this way: 'I see everything in NURBS now.' According to him, it was automatic.

(a)   **(b)**   **(c)**

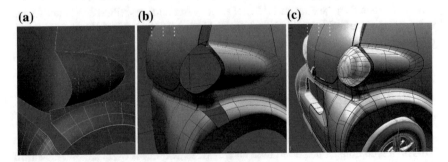

Fig. 5.8 Tail light by Martin, Week 4 (**a**), Week 5 (**b**) and Week 6 (**c**)

Maike had this to say on the subject:

> A friend of mine, always when I walk to the, to the train station, we just constantly see NURBS in everything, just look at, we look at cars and he just, you know, he only says, just from there is a hard edge, that's a NURBS.

She added that this was involuntary. She or her friend would look at designed objects in the environment around them and immediately visualise the topology or order of construction of the object. In Ward's case, 'I can't turn it off. It's really hard and especially when I see a car that kind of looks like mine I really start to think from a…how would I build that if I had to do that particular car.'

In previous years, students have described how they experienced this same involuntary or automatic shape analysis effect during and after the NURBS class. Students were observed during the study talking about this during workshops starting in about Week 5, but it became more prevalent in later weeks. Janet said,

'I just couldn't stop thinking of it. And actually, I see everything around me is kind of made of NURBS, all the shampoo bottles, everything. I just can't get it out of my mind. All the cars I see in the street, I just automatically analyse it; how can I cut it, how can I blend it?'

In her case, she said it stopped after the project was concluded, but for Martin, once he started seeing things this way, he could not stop and it persisted after the class was over. He said this about two months after he had finished the NURBS project.

At IGAD, this kind of reflexive shape analysis is called 'NURBS vision'. Not all students develop it, but many do. On this subject, Roel said that 'I would never have believed you if I didn't have this class, but it's actually true, you see patches.' For more examples of student statements relevant to this subject, see Appendix 4 (p. 212).

5.6 Student Reflections on the Project

Regardless of whether students completed the NURBS project, they tended to report that the project changed the way they saw things, the way they analysed form in objects and the way they made drawings. Some of these changes were described as 'eureka moments' by the students, who stated that their working methods suddenly changed after they understood how to visualise the shapes they needed to make. This was supported by weekly records of their progress in class. Students also credited the NURBS project with a positive influence on their approach to complex or difficult problems and their ability to focus their mental attention on a problem.

5.6.1 Identification of Transition Moments

Students were asked if they had experienced any 'transition moments' during the NURBS project. These were described to students as occasions where they felt that the way they worked, the quality of their work, or their understanding of the project had noticeably changed. Eleven of the 20 student participants said they had noticed something like this while working on the NURBS project, but it happened in different weeks and for different reasons.

Roel said that he had made a couple of breakthroughs at the after-hours NURBS parties where students gathered to do extra work, one of which was focussed on making large patches and cutting them down to the right shape and size. This technique is called 'intersection' because it involves positioning two or more surfaces so that they intersect and then using the intersection boundary to cut the patches. Figure 5.9 shows layers of patches intersecting each other in such a way that when the outer patches are removed, the shape of the side of a car will be left, according to the same principle that allowed a circular depression to be carved using two squares in Fig. 5.4.

When the patches are trimmed away, the remaining surfaces will have sharp edges where they were cut. Hence, Roel also mentioned the importance of learning how to use blends to bridge gaps between surfaces. This allows surfaces to transition seamlessly into each other and give the appearance of a smooth curve. It can be very difficult to smoothly reconcile the edges of all surfaces at corners where they intersect, and to do so is dependent on a good patch layout.

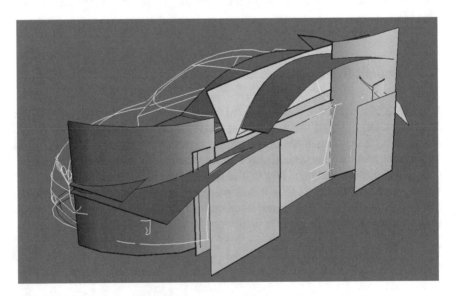

Fig. 5.9 Surface-to-surface intersections

Paula described the moment when she suddenly understood how intersecting surfaces can result in 3D curvature and a better likeness as a 'eureka moment'. Until then, she said that she had 'no idea what [she was] doing.' She said that her method of using intersected planes to create 3D curves was 'the change [to] my thought pattern [that] made a lot of things fall in place.'

According to Ward,

> Well, in the first weeks…I really hated the whole idea of working with NURBS and I thought it was damn foolish to do it with NURBS when you just could do it with polygons, but yes, that's because I really didn't know how to use the tools.

This changed after a workshop where students were shown how to use intersections to create the shapes they wanted. After this, he realised that he had been working 'the other way around' and changed his methods. Of this change, he said that when modelling in NURBS, 'you're really forced to think about what you want to get and then how you're going to build it.'

For Maikel, the most significant improvement he made on the project came in Week 6 or 7. 'What caused that improvement was finally totally understanding the work flow of NURBS. I'm used to work[ing] with Sub-D modelling, so I needed to find that switch.' He understood the importance of making large shapes first and then cutting into them for details, but he was not used to the intersection workflow. According to him, he did not come to understand this through gradual development, but as a 'switch' or 'eureka moment', where his method and ability changed suddenly for the better.

Koen described a sudden change in his thinking that occurred in Week 7. Like others', it was related to using surface intersections, which is related to using the correct order of construction. He said that when he saw how shapes could be intersected with other shapes to create the shapes he wanted, it made it easier to visualise how he would build his vehicle. However, as he put it, by Week 6, 'I knew the tools, and yes, that was just it, just the tools. So, the transition was really fast, but in order to go to the transition it took me seven weeks.' As a result of this change in the way he visualised his project, he was able to substantially rebuild his vehicle from scratch in one day (Fig. 5.10).

Maike said that her work style changed in Week 4, but the change was due to the natural development of tool knowledge. This happened because in Week 4, students switched 'from the preparatory exercises of wheels and chassis to dealing with the main object with all of its challenges.' Unlike most students, she did not experience problems with surface intersections or order of construction.

Wietse and Daniel both claimed that in Week 5 they had simply learned how to use the tools available to them and that this counted as a significant transition. As Daniel explained, 'we had a solid base on how to implement all the tools together to create the shape we are trying to create.'

Janet's transition took place in Week 4. Like Maike, she said that she understood surface intersections from the first week of classes. In her case, the transition was related to understanding how to visualise blend points, locations where different patches meet at their corners (Fig. 5.11). This is related to designing the patch layout or topology of the model.

Fig. 5.10 Koen's vehicle model, built in one day, week 7

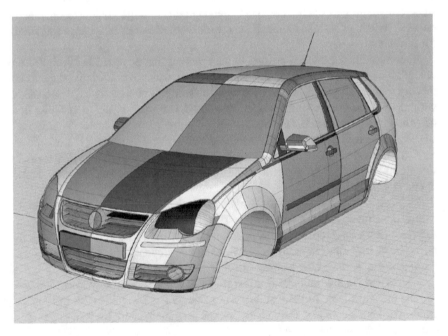

Fig. 5.11 Patch layout of Janet's vehicle

Although there were differences among these students, the significant thresholds they identified can be grouped as belonging to the following categories:

- Intersections/order of construction (n = 6)
- Tool knowledge (n = 3)
- Blends/topology (n = 1).

For some students, classroom interaction or specific lessons led to their transition, but others discovered them on their own as they worked on their project. Although these techniques had been covered in class, students found them counter-intuitive and resisted applying them until they saw for themselves why they were important.

5.6.2 Outcomes

5.6.2.1 Motivation and NURBS Project Completion

Three students did not turn in an assignment and the projects of five others were severely incomplete. In Week 7, Sebastian wrote in his learning log, 'I'm not going to finish this in block C.' He was not the only student who lacked confidence in his work. When asked why he did not turn in his assignment, Maikel said, 'I was ashamed of the one I had at the end.' Pim's reaction to the same question was that his project was too incomplete to be worth turning in. He then added, 'I didn't turn it in because I can't bring it over from my heart to turn in something I believe really looks bad.' Despite this, he stated that he enjoyed the project and now found himself interested in cars, though he had not been previously.

Jacqueline, who described herself as 'lazy', said, 'I didn't think I would make it until you said I wouldn't make it. I have this thing with people telling me I'll fail; I'll prove them wrong.' This defiance motivated her to work on the project for a time, but she gave up in the end because she thought it was more likely she would pass other classes if she diverted her effort from MD2.

The effort it took to complete the project was a factor some students singled out as a significant contributor to their reasons for enjoying the class. Jacqueline said, 'Oh, yes, I think the mind-set at the end that you actually did this and passed with this beautiful car, no matter the errors, it's just beautiful. You have this, like, huge feeling of accomplishment and NURBS is like the Mount Everest of the first year. So, if you pass that, you can really feel good about yourself.' Paula had a similar reaction, saying that although she was not proud of the Illusion project made for the MD1 class, she was proud of the MD2 project because the challenge made it more satisfying.

Koen, who did pass the class, said, 'In the last week of the project I had the feeling that I was going to fail this course, and that made me think, that made me care less about the result because I was afraid to fail, and that also made me try different things.' It was this fear of failure that he directly credited for his sudden understanding of

NURBS and the satisfying outcome of his project. The reason, he said, is that he had been 'afraid to touch that which already looks good', but he knew there were mistakes. He had built the model 'over and over again' and become very frustrated. Eventually he realised that he had to try something new. Because he thought he would fail if he did not, he looked at the problem in a new way and learned surface intersection. To get to that point took what he characterised as 'pure frustration' and that frustration helped him overcome what he called an emotional barrier that prevented further progress. The frustration, he said, was important because 'it gave me more willpower.'

In Koen's case, the 'feeling that [he] was going to fail' motivated him to try different solutions and succeed. Other students' predictions of failure seemed to have the opposite effect, discouraging them from trying any harder. Students who passed the class described the challenge as satisfying, implying that the difficulty and frustration of the project motivated them to keep looking for new solutions. Those who failed appeared to have been discouraged by this same difficulty and did not complete their work.

5.6.2.2   Observation Skills Enhanced

Seeing an object and understanding it are not always the same thing. As Pim said during his interview,

> every time I made a part of my car it was like I suddenly see another detail that I hadn't seen before, and now it just keeps forcing me to when I see cars everywhere to just really keep looking like, whoa, there's another thing that I didn't see there and I can really keep looking at them for a long time now.

The enhanced sensitivity to detail that Pim describes carried over to other observations because 'I basically got a lot of respect for shapes around me because even if I look at a chair I'm now looking at how was that really built.' For him, this was the most important lesson he derived from the MD2 class.

Alexander also said that his observation skills were enhanced by the class. When asked how this happened, he said that 'trying to identify from the car where to cut the boundaries for the patches, how to cut up the car into separate patches' was the principal method that contributed to improved observation skills. This is similar to Janet's statements about 'blend points' being critical to a major transition in her understanding of NURBS.

Roel described how he could 'see' things better after the MD2 class. He quantified this by remarking that

> I see shapes in like a day now, or even in a matter of time, like hours or something, instead of having to look at it for three days and then trying it and still see like it's the wrong way, the wrong approach.

Bart explained that, for him, the quality of his observations improved after a class critique. He was told that the metal of the exhaust pipe he had built was too thick, 'and that was the moment I thought, whoa, is this the criteria he is looking for? And at that moment, I really wanted to create the car as real as the real one and more.'

The project's exacting criteria encouraged students to develop much more accurate observational skills and greater understanding of the construction of objects.

5.6.2.3 Attitude Changes

Some students credited the NURBS project for development of confidence, problem-solving skills and attention to quality. Wietse claimed that the MD2 class had an effect on his attitude towards craftsmanship. He said that 'just making it look good isn't everything. It has to be good, it has to function good, and… Yes. It has not only changed my work, the stuff I do, but it has also changed my attitude.'

Bart said that 'a few days before the interview' he was thinking about how the NURBS class had had a significant effect on the way he worked. On this subject, he said that 'I usually am very frustrated when I encounter a problem and I get very mad at, mad if I don't get to solve it in the next 10 min.' Later, he surprised himself when he realised that he had 'worked at the NURBS car for almost an entire day', at the same problems that had caused him to quit almost immediately the previous week. Now, he was more willing to spend time searching for solutions. According to Bart, 'this attitude I received from and gained in this project, I think it can be very useful in other courses.'

Maike said, 'I think my confidence also has changed because everybody kept saying that the NURBS project was a very difficult one and that it was like the worst thing I have to do…but I think after having done this project and not failed on it, I think I can do everything, sort of. I just need to learn the process.'

Lisette agreed that her increased confidence was more important than any skill she developed as a NURBS modeller. This was because, 'sure, you can say this is a new skill now, but it doesn't really make a difference if you still have your previous faults. If you don't improve on anything that is wrong with the way you work in general, I don't think it really helps much to know how to do something more.' Koen agreed, saying that 'confidence is pretty much everything. If you believe that you can do something, then you can.'

The difficulty of the project was a formidable hurdle for students, but once they had overcome it, they claimed to have much greater confidence in their ability to handle future challenges.

5.6.2.4 Drawing Skill

Students were asked if they noticed whether the NURBS class had affected their performance in other subjects. Apart from statements in the previous section regarding attitude, confidence and general observation skills, at least six students thought it helped their drawing skill. According to Janet, 'when I draw from observation I started to notice the important points. Yes, and it actually simplified my lines. It's simplified, but actually looks more solid because the structure is right.' She started noticing this effect in Week 4 and was 'quite surprised because I didn't really practice. How come my drawing skills improved?'

Pim said that he started to notice

> lines on cars that I never noticed before and when you start drawing and you suddenly notice that you noticed all those lines back on the street and now you have to draw them, it's way easier to draw a line because you understand it.

When it came to drawing, Pim said that MD2 was more useful than the perspective drawing classes he also took. Thus, he felt that understanding how to model objects in 3D had a greater influence on his drawing skill than what he learned in traditional drawing classes.

Bart discovered that he had started using NURBS visualisation techniques in his drawings after finishing a drawing one day: 'I [had] walked away and when I came back, I saw the drawing laying [*sic*] on my desk, and I just saw that part where I used that technique and said, hang on.' The drawing showed that he had drawn large shapes and then erased parts of them to derive other shapes, as he had done when intersecting patches with NURBS. Daniel had a similar experience when he realised that he was now drawing by starting with simple shapes that were then made progressively more detailed. The strategies used for understanding and representing an object's structure were similar both in NURBS modelling and traditional art.

Lisette said that she had not given much thought to it, but when asked, realised that she had started drawing 'through' objects after the MD2 class. 'Drawing through' is a technique that is particularly common among professional designers and animators, where both visible and hidden sides of an object are drawn together to improve the alignment of dependent shapes. Lisette gave the example of complete ovals she found herself drawing to represent details in the back of the car, only some of which were visible in the front. Daniel said that he had started drawing through objects also, but added that he had noticed

> I was more comfortable with drawing a line than I used to be. There's supposed to be a time when you draw it, and it's not right, and you draw it again and draw it again, you get this really big fat ugly line, and now I could just actually make it in one straight [attempt].

Maike said that drawing and NURBS were complementary subjects:

> Now that I built the car, what I discovered [was] that the modelling cars helped my drawings of the car and the other way around. So, whatever I did first helped me in the second step of doing the other subject.

According to these students, working with NURBS improved students' observation skills, attention to important details and understanding of structure in ways that aided their traditional drawing ability. Maike's report suggests that drawing skill also helped in her understanding of NURBS, implying that knowledge in one subject informs and reinforces skill in the other.

5.6.2.5 Overall Progress as Digital Art Students

During the nine weeks of classroom observations, in combination with learning logs, weekly progress files and interviews, a portrait of student progress emerged. It was not homogenous in the sense that not all students progressed at the same rate or described their problems in the same way, but some general comments can be made. Firstly, acquiring reference was a significant problem for students, not just because it was extra labour, but because students tended to describe it in ways that made it look like it was related to visualisation problems. Secondly, students mentioned 'seeing' and 'tools' as significant issues, but it is possible to interpret some of their complaints about tools as visualisation problems that were not evident until their visualisation skill had improved. During the project, several students started reflexively performing shape analyses on objects in their immediate environment. Lastly, some of these students identified their transition to proficiency as contingent on one of two visualisation skills: visualising surface to surface intersection, or understanding blend shapes.

Taken together, the data from this chapter strongly supports a link between spatial visualisation and performance in NURBS modelling tasks. It also provides some insight into the kind of spatial visualisation that was most needed or exercised on the project.

5.7 Introduction to Post Study Period

Data collected from study participants during questionnaires and interviews are presented in this section. This material is focussed on the second research question 'What criteria are used to determine student performance levels?' as a way to validate whether students have become proficient and if IGAD assessment methods are consistent with industry standards. Secondly, statistical comparisons of past performance and performance in the MD2 class address the fourth research question 'How does the NURBS problem differ from the polygon problem?'

All industry participants agreed that the work they were shown was proficient. This allowed the identification of students who had developed proficiency and an investigation of how they developed it. Projects that received grades below an eight were not shown to industry participants on the basis that they were either too incomplete or had too many serious errors to be rated on a professional scale. The number of proficient students was smaller than the number of those who did not become proficient. Three of the eight students (37.5%) who became proficient had prior experience that aided their development, but this was not true for the remaining five students (62.5%).

This chapter concludes with brief representative case histories of the students who became proficient and those who did not.

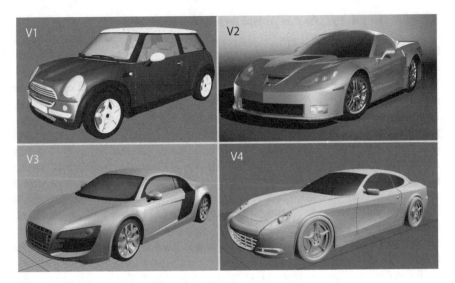

Fig. 5.12 Images of the four vehicles submitted for industry grading

5.8 Validating Proficient Performance

In total, there were four vehicles submitted to each of the five industry participants to be graded (Fig. 5.12). Three of the vehicles were made by student participants Maike, Koen and Ward. A fourth model made by a student from the previous year, Johannes, was added to control for the possibility that the different teachers who graded the projects applied different standards. Industry participants were observed and recorded as they evaluated each vehicle during interviews. The material that follows is derived from interview transcripts of those sessions. Pseudonyms are used for all industry participants.

5.8.1 Industry Grades

The industry grades were transformed so that the minimum 'professionally competent' grade of 6 on the industry scale was equal to the minimum 'professionally competent' grade of eight on the academic scale. After scaling, the academic and industry means were very close, a 9 for the academic grades and 8.84 from industry participants (Table 5.2). Each of the five industry participants was asked to confirm that they intended their grades to be interpreted as professionally competent. All participants confirmed that none of the vehicles was below a professional standard. These results establish that the four files presented to industry assessors were 'professionally competent' and therefore 'technically proficient' using the definition provided in the literature review.

Table 5.2 Industry grades scaled to match academic grading scale and means compared

	Vehicle 1	Vehicle 2	Vehicle 3	Vehicle 4	Mean
Industry 1	8.00	8.50	9.00	9.00	8.62
Industry 2	9.00	8.75	9.00	9.25	9.00
Industry 3	8.00	9.00	8.50	10.00	8.88
Industry 4	8.50	9.00	8.75	9.00	8.81
Industry 5	9.00	8.75	8.25	9.50	8.875
Mean	8.50	8.80	8.70	9.35	8.84
Academic grade	10.00	9.00	8.00	9.00	9.00
Difference	1.50	0.20	−0.70	−0.35	0.16

No claim was made that student files demonstrated expertise, but industry assessors stated that they would not be able to distinguish these files from work by other professionals in the workplace on the basis of quality. According to the definitions provided in the literature review, the difference between proficiency and expertise is that the proficient performer can solve a problem correctly by engaging in a problem-solving process, as these students did. The expert performer would know the solution from experience and would not need to engage in problem-solving. The student performers did not know the solution in advance and had to engage in problem-solving, so they cannot be defined as 'expert', according to that definition, regardless of the quality of their solutions. The results were, however, impressive to industry participants, who stated they had not often seen results of this standard from graduates of similar programmes, let alone first year students.

5.8.2   The Importance of Likeness

Every industry assessor asked to see the reference the vehicles were based on. The reason, as explained by Wouter, was that

> the shape is the most important thing that you have to set up, it's not the technique. There are a lot of people dive into the techniques very deeply, but in the end, you want to have a really cool shape, because that's what people see.

Wouter said that if a vehicle model were not a good likeness, it would be excluded from consideration for use in a professional context.

Comprehensive reference was not available for all of the vehicles because it was not anticipated that assessors would ask to see it. Because the assessors wanted to see reference for specific parts of the vehicles, attempts were made during the interviews to find reference on the Internet or among the students' hand-in materials. These were usually successful, but at times the reference found did not contain a view of the vehicle part that the assessor was curious about. In those cases, the reviewers focussed on the craftsmanship, whether the vehicle was plausible, or checked other parts of the model they did have reference for.

The first observations Bas made were related to the 'shape, size and silhouette' of the vehicle he was examining. He explained that he did this because 'that's the first shape that they need to get right.' If successful, then he concentrated on details. Stefano was primarily interested in what he called 'the contrast of the details'. He defined this as the tendency found in modern automobiles to have 'a very nice contrast of things that are very smooth and then things that are actually very detailed, and that's one thing that is always a little bit tricky to capture with NURBS.' Of the IGAD models, Stefano said that 'the things that I like about some of the first models that I saw is that they had [this] type of contrast.' Josh explained that when building cars, clients are 'particularly picky about any little divot, any tiny little thing'. To illustrate what he meant, he mentioned an example at his workplace where another artist had to spend 'an hour trying to get one little divot out' to satisfy a client.

On the subject of likeness, all reviewers seemed to decide within a minute or less if the likeness was adequate. Stefano agreed this was the case: 'A lot of times the first impression that you get when you look at something is that very quick, like, is it right or is it wrong. 'The models from IGAD, he said, were done well enough that 'I couldn't find too much whether there, where these models could actually go.' The bottom line for Josh was that 'whether it's a drawing, or a sculpture, or a 3D model, I want to see if it looks right to begin with, you know. If I put that... if I put this car in a scene, is it going to look right?'

An accurate likeness is a crucial aspect of commercially used models, because customers seeing the model must be able to recognize and believe in what it represents. Industry assessors therefore checked this trait in the submitted models before any others, and in every case identified it as professional quality.

5.8.3 *Patch Layout Checked*

All of the industry assessors asked to look at the models in 'wireframe mode'. This allowed them to examine the patch layout of each vehicle (Fig. 5.13). A good patch layout tends towards having patches of similar size and accentuating the structure of the object. After looking at the models in wireframe, Josh commented,

> The thing I really like about these last three as opposed to the first one was if we just had a wire-frame to go with, you can tell [what] these cars are with the wire-frame. I'm afraid with the first one, if I had just a wire-frame to go by, there are so many tiny, little patches all over the place that it makes it difficult.

It was important for cars to be easily recognizable even in the wireframe mode. This was true of three of the four vehicles.

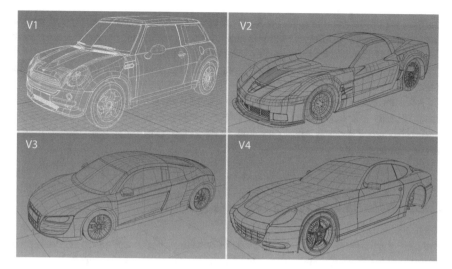

Fig. 5.13 Wireframe view of industry-assessed vehicles

5.8.4 Industry Expects High-Quality Models

In his interview, Stefano mentioned the importance of maintaining high quality standards. Graduates are now expected to meet the same level of quality met by professionals because

> our industry is constantly evolving. What a seventeen-year-old could do ten years ago is very different than what a seventeen-year-old could do now...when we actually get our little portfolios and everything, you see a lot of people who are capable to do amazing models now.

Due to ever-advancing technology, models that would have been considered impressive ten years ago are commonplace now. To differentiate between these applicants, Stefano looked for 'that extra one thing that makes them just that special.' These increasing quality standards make it important for graduates to be able to meet professional standards, because the standards become continually higher as technology progresses.

5.8.5 Technical Errors a Lesser Problem

While evaluating models during his interview, Wouter had a tendency to first comment on the likeness and then more carefully examine the model from various angles for technical errors. However, when asked about this, he said he was less concerned about technical problems than with the aesthetic quality of the model. Bas and other assessors did the same thing. According to Bas, technical errors are less difficult to fix than aesthetic problems, so he was less concerned about them. However, he did say that it is important for artists to be able to 'spot your own fault and clean up your own mess'. Josh noticed technical errors but said, 'I think those are fixable, I don't think that's going to be a difficult…I mean all the geometry was there in the right place.'

Accurate likeness and overall aesthetic appeal were thus considered more important to quality assessment than technical details. The ability to make self-assessments and self-corrections was highlighted as an important trait for a proficient or expert performer to have.

5.8.6 NURBS and Visualisation in Industry

Industry participants acknowledged the importance of 3D visualisation. Josh provided background information on a modelling training programme provided on-site at his company for a number of years, saying that they had the most trouble with artists who 'just couldn't see in 3D. You know, we had a girl and she was fantastic at drawing, but all the stuff she drew was flat, she couldn't translate it to 3D.'

Bas said that NURBS are a

> good way to at least start thinking in 3D because that's one of the things that I liked about NURBS when I was working with it. They give you a real good notion of how stuff works in a three-dimensional space. So, working with NURBS, even though it wouldn't necessarily be required of you here or we never ask people about it, they come out and tell it during [the] interview. It's always a plus.

Stefano looked at NURBS modelling as an 'extra' as well. He said, 'I think it's a very important skill to teach. It's not just because of modelling NURBS, it's because of understanding how to actually work within, you know, these parameters.' This was important to Stefano because artists who have been introduced to alternate methods of making CG products 'seem to be more welcoming when some of these other [technologies] come into play.' As far as tool knowledge is concerned, Bas did not care how an object was made or what tool it was made with as long as the artist was comfortable with it and the results looked good.

Bas's statement reinforces that working with NURBS can improve understanding and awareness of how objects function in three-dimensional space, while Stefano values artists with NURBS knowledge because they tend to be more adaptable. Both considered NURBS training to be a positive factor for an industry applicant.

5.8.7 The Balance of Likeness and Technique

Based on their interviews, industry participants stated that likeness was more important than anything else when evaluating proficiency. They pointed out the importance of good reference to accomplish this, implying a dependency on strong observation skills. They were unanimous in describing technical problems as a lower priority than problems with likeness and that errors of craftsmanship are more easily fixed than likeness errors. All four of the models presented for evaluation were deemed to be professional quality.

5.9 Case Histories

The case histories that follow are representative examples of student development, with an emphasis on students whose work was seen by industry assessors and assessed as proficient. The first examples are students who did not pass the class, then a student who passed but was not proficient, followed by students who were deemed proficient by industry assessors. The last example is from a student whose work was not seen by industry assessors but would likely have been rated as proficient based on criteria described in assessment interviews. This section also provides more detailed comments from industry assessors on the vehicles they assessed.

5.9.1 Wietse: Former MBO Student, Did not Pass MD2

5.9.1.1 Starting Position

Wietse had four years of previous drawing experience at an MBO but no experience working in 3D. The drawing experience was not evident in the drawings provided for the intake. His submission score was 2.0 and his intake rank 65. He failed the Carton project and received a minimum grade of 1 on the Illusion project, indicating that it was turned in but that it was grossly incomplete. His score on the PVRT was 16 (out of 20), indicating comfort with mental rotation tasks, which is common among IGAD students.

5.9.1.2 Development

The progress of Wietse's project involved what appeared to be a sincere effort, if assessed on the basis of the number of NURBS parties he attended (all of them), his perfect attendance in lectures and workshops, and his serious demeanour in class. However, he ran into the first possible stumbling block: insufficient reference images. He acknowledged it as a problem, and then without fixing it, proceeded with his project. The lack of reference was reflected in his tape model, in which there were numerous likeness errors. He also chose inappropriate curves to build in the tape model (Fig. 5.14). This indicated an observation problem because he did not seem to be aware of the structure underlying the curves he built.

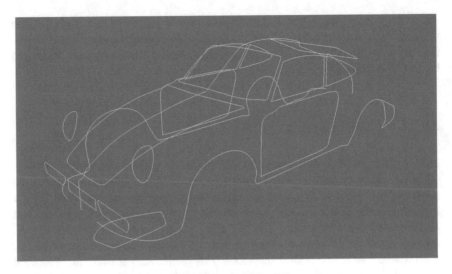

Fig. 5.14 Wietse's tape model contains cut boundaries but little structure

For the duration of the project, Wietse's focus was on achieving tangency. This objective was marred by his weak patch layout, which introduced many inconsistencies in the likeness. He insisted on maintaining tangency even when the likeness was compromised or the patch layout became inefficient or messy as a consequence. The weak likeness evident in the tape model was carried forward into the patches. This could have been the product of poor or inadequate reference, or it may have been partly the result of weak observation skills. He may also have decided to temporarily ignore the likeness while he worked on the patch layout, with the intention of correcting the likeness later.

5.9.1.3 Final Result

This file was incomplete, had many likeness errors and a large quantity of technical errors (Fig. 5.15). The final grade was a 4. Wietse earned only 6 ECTS out of 60 in the first year and was given a negative binding recommendation (NBR) due to inadequate credits. Because of this, he had to leave the IGAD programme after the first year.

5.9.1.4 Comments

In his interview, Wietse stated that

> NURBS…opened my eyes, and yes, how should I say this? It was just, like I said before, it was like a barrier I had to go through and I feel like I've overcome that barrier. And, it made me think that I was capable of doing much more. I had the capacity to learn much more, and I'd be able to do better.

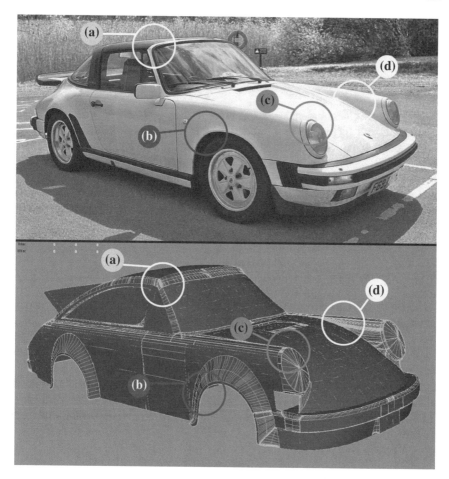

Fig. 5.15 Wietse's final model, with likeness errors highlighted

What he learned, according to him, was the importance of quality craftsmanship, something he did not achieve on this or any other project I am familiar with. He said that class critiques were the most valuable learning opportunities available within the MD2 class. Wietse claimed that his greatest difficulty was trying to divide the shape of the vehicle's body into separate patches that together could represent the vehicle without tangency or likeness errors. This is a spatial visualisation problem that requires blend visualisation to solve.

Although Wietse stated that he had learned a great deal, his difficulty with this type of spatial visualisation appeared to prevent his work from achieving proficiency. It is possible that the MD2 class prepared him for the project and that he would have performed better if given a second opportunity, but later performance in other classes suggests otherwise.

5.9.2 Sebastian: Former MBO Student, Initially Failed MD2, Passed on Second Retake

5.9.2.1 Starting Position

Sebastian is an older student with four years' previous 3D experience at an MBO. Despite this, the 3D project he submitted for the assessment was much simpler than the first polygon project assigned to students at IGAD. More telling were his drawing samples, both of which were made after more than four years' prior experience. The drawings were naïve, and did not reflect strong observation or tool handling. His intake score was the same as Wietse's: 2.0, but his ranking was lower, 77. His PVRT score was 14. Sebastian failed the Carton project but passed the Illusion project on the first opportunity with a grade of 7.

5.9.2.2 Development

Sebastian clearly stated that he found it difficult, 'impossible', to visualise 3D curves based on orthographic planar curves in 2D reference. Despite this, the rough structural outline of his vehicle was reasonably well-represented in his tape model (Fig. 5.16). Sebastian said that he found it difficult to visualise correctly shaped precursor surfaces that would result in the desired shapes when intersected. To finish the project, he attempted to ignore tangency issues, but his incorrect patch layout would have made any attempt to blend between patches nearly impossible without severe distortion. He did not discuss tangency much as an issue, mentioning visualisation problems instead.

5.9.2.3 Final Result

The vehicle turned in earned a failing grade of 4 (Fig. 5.17). The retake turned in the following year earned a 6 (Fig. 5.18). The retake grade did not indicate proficiency but that the model met the academic standard. The academic standard consists of the following: (1) the file is complete, (2) the file was built according to the instructions given and (3) there are no severe technical or likeness errors. In this case, the problem was the likeness.

5.9.2.4 Comments

According to Sebastian, 'previous classes at this school also had [problem solving], but those you could solve eventually. And this project, some I could solve and some I was really staring at dumbfounded.' This statement sums up many of the comments he made during his interview, one of which urged that his reply be interpreted 'in

Fig. 5.16 Sebastian's tape model

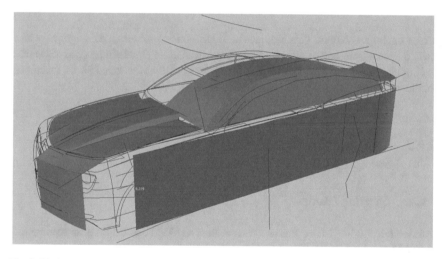

Fig. 5.17 Sebastian's original final delivery

the most sarcastic way possible'. His frustration with the problems he faced on the project was clearly enhanced by the diligent efforts he made to complete it. In the end he wasn't satisfied with the end result, but appreciated the value of the exercise.

Sebastian's original file was not completed because he was unable to create blend surfaces. This was caused by inattention to the patch layout, which was not constructed to accommodate blending. Sebastian learned how to create blends and had an improved patch layout for his final retake, but neither was perfect. Of greater concern was that the likeness could have been considerably improved. Based on the weekly progress files, Sebastian never mastered how to use intersected surfaces to

Fig. 5.18 Sebastian's successful retake vehicle

create the target shapes. This indicated a visualisation problem that hindered performance. He complained of this more than once in class and made humorous references to it during his interview. In the end, he recognized that the problem he faced was that he had a hard time seeing, or visualising, a solution.

5.9.3 Timothy: Previous Interests Did not Prepare This Student for an Art Education

5.9.3.1 Starting Position

This student studied to become an accountant at a HAVO institution prior to enrolling at IGAD at 17 years old. The drawings and CG model submitted for the intake were the first drawings from life or CG art he had ever made. Despite this, the drawings he submitted for the intake show that he had made an effort to carefully observe the subjects of the drawings. This was unlike many students; whose naïve or primitive drawings were not the product of observation but of imperfect memory mixed with superficial observation. Timothy's drawings showed that he was not comfortable with drawing tools but had fairly good attention to observed structure and detail.

Timothy had a low intake rank of 86, indicating low expectations. In the first block he failed the Carton project but passed the Illusion project with a 7. This is an average performance for the class. Based on the foregoing, this student could have been described as a beginner with potential.

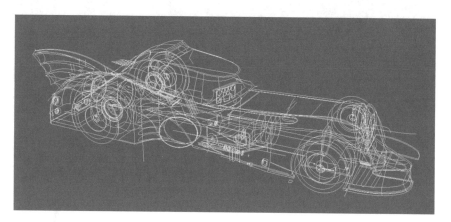

Fig. 5.19 Timothy's tape model

5.9.3.2 Development

Progress on this student's vehicle was regular and good. He claimed that the reference for his vehicle was inconsistent. This was probably true because he chose a fictitious vehicle that had been modified several times in a series of films. To get around this, Timothy created a version of the vehicle that blended elements from the reference he had.

The tape model was more important than he expected. He discovered during the construction process that mistakes in the tape model could have strong effects on the final project (Fig. 5.19). For this reason, he had to rebuild surfaces on multiple occasions. He claimed that the primary problems he experienced were tool-related, but in the interview, he frequently made reference to the problems in such a way that it was also possible to interpret them as visualisation problems. This was because he solved them by making a simpler patch layout (a visualisation-related strategy) as opposed to mentioning a tool or tool combination that led to the solution.

He claimed that his visualisation skills were improved because the project forced him to pay attention to shape in a new way that allowed him to better understand structure.

5.9.3.3 Final Result

The project earned a 7, a good grade for this class, but not high enough to be described as 'proficient'. His model did not have any serious tangency errors, but the likeness suffered from his interpretation of the reference he had, making it look more like a toy than a full-size vehicle (Fig. 5.20). The effect was of a vehicle that has a bias toward planar or single axis curves in the patches. This meant that the blends he made were

Fig. 5.20 Timothy's final vehicle

less complicated than they would have been in a car possessing more complex curvature and the vehicle lacked the 'contrast of detail' mentioned by industry participant Stefano.

5.9.3.4   Comments

Early on, Timothy ran into the problem of translating his reference into 3D. As he put it,

> a lot of the reference…is different from each other, so you never know which is the real example of the official car. So, it helped me do a lot more research and visualise a lot more, like, what is the correct… what are the correct proportions of this part, for example.

Throughout his interview, Timothy made references to visualisation and how it was an integral part of 'seeing' multiple alternate solutions to various problems. Timothy made excellent progress, particularly when considering that he had no prior 2D or 3D experience before attending IGAD and no particular interest in visual art. Although not proficient, the final result showed solid potential and a good attitude toward meeting deadlines and approaching one's responsibilities seriously. Like other students, he said that he 'sees everything in NURBS now', meaning that he was automatically analysing the structure of shapes in the context of NURBS limitations. This, combined with evidence in his work, indicated that Timothy had learned to analyse shape in a new way that improved his spatial visualisation skills.

5.9.4 Maike: Strong Drawing, No 3D Experience, Proficient on First Attempt

5.9.4.1 Starting Position

Maike's 2D intake assignments demonstrated very well-developed observation skills. There was no 3D assignment presented, in keeping with the student's questionnaire answer that she had no previous 3D experience. Her PVRT test score was 17, one point below the highest in the class. Her grades from her previous education, a VWO equivalent, were uniformly high. She was ranked first in her intake group, passed the Carton assignment and received a 10 on her Illusion project for the MD1 class.

5.9.4.2 Development

Each weekly hand-in showed progress and was generally ahead of expectations, but her tape model had very little detail (Fig. 5.21). This, she said, was partly due to lack of good reference. Maike's learning log and her interview recorded numerous specific problems related to tool use in the context of 'solving' certain shape-related problems. She stated that lack of knowledge regarding the tools was the reason for difficulties experienced building her vehicle. However, part of using the tools properly is learning how to craft a patch layout. The patch layout cannot be made without knowledge of tools, but the tools will not work if the patch layout is faulty. Seemingly without realising it, she worked on solving both problems at the same time.

5.9.4.3 Final Result and Industry Analysis

Maike's project earned a grade of 10. It was one of four vehicles shown to industry participants (Fig. 5.22).

One of the first comments made by industry assessor Wouter about Maike's vehicle had to do with reference. He was puzzled that she did not have more:

> Why? There's like millions and millions of photographs and really good reference. That's not an excuse. I'm sure I can find this. It's not really correctly, it's a close call, but there's some parts, and I think it's due to the reference she used. Like the wheels, they're really way too thin.

Wouter continued criticising the likeness of this vehicle during most of the time devoted to grading it. His conclusion was that, on the basis of likeness alone, this model would be sent back for corrections but 'it's fixable'. Bas agreed with Wouter, saying that he found the likeness of the headlights unconvincing: 'it could be cleaned up and it should be cleaned up.'

Josh started his review of Maike's model by saying, 'I'd love to see the wire-frame on this. I mean so far it looks pretty good.' After the wireframe view was enabled,

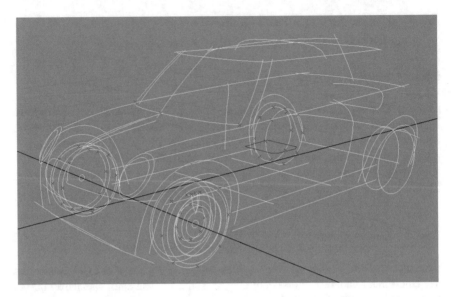

Fig. 5.21 Maike's tape model

Fig. 5.22 Maike's final vehicle model

Josh was able to see the patch layout. At that point he commented, 'Wow, that's a lot of blended surfaces!' Overall, he said that it was 'a good job', but that he would have used fewer blend surfaces because 'sometimes when you animate it and you've got so many surfaces, if you tried to deform that thing it can get really ugly and hairy quickly.' Josh also commented on the likeness: 'The ring around the headlight, it

Table 5.3 Industry grades for Maike's vehicle

Vehicle 1	Assessor 1	Assessor 2	Assessor 3	Assessor 4	Assessor 5	Average
Raw	6	8	6	7	8	7.0
Adjusted	8	9	8	8.5	9	8.5

seems a little uneven. It's not as even as I would like, you know, as a Hero car that would be pristine.' When he commented on other IGAD vehicles, Josh said, 'These two guys seem like they're more artistic. They have a better grasp of artistic shape and I think that's what was bothering me with [Maike's] Mini, it just didn't feel as artistic.'

When Caleb first opened Maike's vehicle, he said that 'on first look, the proportions look good; let's see, most of the shapes look pretty clean…The first problems I saw were on the left front fender, it looks like there are some dimples which, in the geometry where it looks like it should be a smooth shape and it looks like it's getting some dimpling; right by the headlight there.' Like the assessment made before his, Caleb's first impression was of good proportions but a likeness error near the headlight. He characterised the errors as 'mistakes that I see in junior- and mid-level modellers, usually.' He added that it was useable but that it would need adjustments before it was finished.

Stefano, like the other industry participants, noticed a likeness problem near the headlight. Despite this, he said that 'it actually feels pretty good, you know, it actually seems, you know, to have a level, a very nice level of sophistication to it.' He said of the wireframe that the patches were 'pretty nicely distributed' apart from the region near the headlight. Overall, he said it was a 'very complete model'.

All of the industry participants commented on either a likeness or patch layout problem near the headlights in Maike's car. Wouter thought there was a likeness error in the tyres, but was the only industry participant to mention this. All industry participants said that, despite the errors they noted, the file was professional. However, they all felt that the headlight region had to be rebuilt to fix the likeness and patch layout. The positive reaction was primarily due to good overall proportions and flow between surfaces. The grades for this project varied more than for any other model (Table 5.3).

5.9.4.4 Comments

Maike was asked how she felt about her observation skills after the MD2 class. She answered that 'when I would be asked to make another car in NURBS or something, I would immediately know what to do. I wouldn't sit there and try to figure it out. I would immediately see there's a patch.' In this statement, she implicates visualisation rather than problem-solving as the important factor in NURBS modelling. Maike's excellent observation skills were compromised by inadequate reference. Despite this, she managed to use surface intersection correctly and had very few tangency errors and only one serious likeness error. She did not explicitly acknowledge the role visualisation plays in using NURBS tools when asked, but implied it in other statements.

It is clear that Maike was a strong student in the generic sense, because she earned high grades regularly in all of her classes. This could be seen as an 'academic' skill separate from spatial visualisation. It was an advantage in that it helped Maike organise her time and effort to ensure that she completed her projects to a good standard, but it could also have been a weakness that interfered with the development of visualisation skills learned by other study participants. In Maike's case, the only major weakness in her file, a weakness immediately spotted by every industry assessor, had to do with the inefficient patch layout around the headlight of her car. This layout was functional, but not ideal. Presumably, if she had 'seen' the structure of the vehicle more clearly, a more efficient layout would have been the result.

5.9.5   Koen: Former MBO Student, no Drawing Experience, Proficient on First Attempt

5.9.5.1   Starting Position

Koen attended an MBO institution for several years prior to attending IGAD. He did not receive drawing instruction there and his questionnaire answers showed that he had no prior drawing experience. The quality of the drawings submitted in the intake were mixed. The landscape was fairly well-observed and well-composed. The self-portrait was less well-observed and contained traces of naïve interpretation of observed details, such as in the eyes. The vehicle drawing was too heavily biased toward distorted perspective guidelines he had drawn. In all three examples, it was evident that Koen tried to make observations of his subject but was hampered by lack of knowledge and practice. The 3D toy train model submitted for the intake was simpler than assignments given to IGAD students in their first block of the first year. As such, this demonstrated less knowledge of modelling than expected of IGAD students in their first 10 weeks. Koen did not pass the Carton project but did pass the Illusion project on the first attempt with a grade of 7.

5.9.5.2   Development

Koen thought that his previous experience helped him at IGAD because he 'knew the terms' and was able to quickly transition from using one application (Max) to another (Maya). This was accomplished in only one week, but most IGAD students also learned Maya in the first week. Many of these had no previous knowledge of any 3D software or the terminology involved.

Koen's progress on the NURBS assignment was serious and regular, though with mistakes. This continued until the seventh week, when a dramatic improvement in the project was evident. Koen stated in his interview that this was because he suddenly understood how to use NURBS the night before and had rebuilt his vehicle from scratch using the new method.

The solution involved visualising the vehicle differently in order to improve the patch layout. With this done, the tools worked as expected and he was able to get the result he wanted. This is a crucial point because the tools do not work as expected if the patch layout cannot accommodate the goal. In that case, it may look to the student as if it were a tool problem (because they do not behave as expected), but it is actually a visualisation or patch layout problem because the tools require a patch layout that follows the rules of NURBS construction.

5.9.5.3   Final Result and Industry Analysis

Koen's file earned a grade of 9 and was submitted to industry participants for review (Fig. 5.23).

Industry participant Wouter asked for reference before commenting on the likeness of Koen's vehicle. After it was found, he compared the two. His initial impression was that 'it feels far more correct as a shape [than Maike's model]; it doesn't feel off…with the right shading, this would fit into something like a Gran Turismo [a popular video game].' Wouter was then asked whether the model was fit for use. He said that 'this wouldn't be sent back, I think. It's a complex model. It looks easy, but

Fig. 5.23 Koen's final vehicle project

there's enough happening in the shape…there's some nice blends in here, over big lengths. That's not so easy to do.'

The first comment from Bas on this model was, 'I'm going to be nit-picking because overall it seems like a well-modelled car', and then he asked for reference so that he could make a more in-depth assessment. While the reference was being located, he said that the model was good enough that he would not send it back 'without looking at the reference'. After the reference was found, Bas started noticing errors in the likeness, such as the absence of some filleted edges [he used the word 'bevelled']. After comparing the model to the reference photographs for a few minutes, he said, 'I guess it would boil down to a bit of the same, fixing, giving it back to the same artist, fixing proportions, but it being game-ready, yes.'

When Josh opened the file, his first impression was, 'This looks pretty good. Looks like whoever did this had good knowledge or [a] good picture of this car. I think they did a pretty good job overall.' Josh then enabled wireframe mode to analyse the patch layout (Fig. 5.24).

Josh said Koen's wireframe was not

super heavy in the scene and for me that's really important for a couple of reasons. Just because I think the less patches you use, you don't have to worry about where those patches meet, that there's going to be any little, crazy, funky things going on. And so, you know, I really like what he's done with this.

Caleb's first impression of Koen's vehicle was that

this car looks nice and clean; from just the shaded view I'm not seeing any artefacts that look like some strange shapes; it looks really clean. Nice, evenly spaced mesh. Okay, this is looking pretty good. This looks really nice and clean. This model looks great.

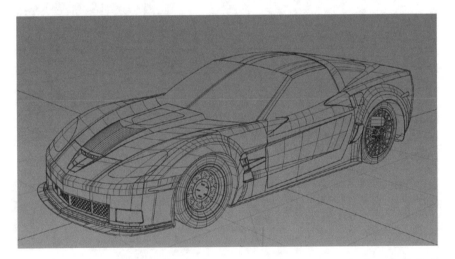

Fig. 5.24 Wireframe view of Koen's vehicle

Table 5.4 Industry grades for Koen's model

Vehicle 2	Assessor 1	Assessor 2	Assessor 3	Assessor 4	Assessor 5	Average
Raw	7	7.5	9	8	9	8.1
Adjusted	8.5	8.75	9.5	9	9.5	9.05

Stefano compared Koen's model to models used in a popular racing game by saying, 'If I actually was to put this in Need for Speed or something, I think it will hold up very well.' When asked for more detail, Stefano said

> I can see kind of things where you have attention to detail. It's attention to detail. You know, I particularly know this type of car obviously. I know it doesn't have that many bells and whistles on the actual body, you know…But the thing that actually is captured very well on this particular one is the contrasting between the actual soft curves and the actual sharp angles.

Stefano then changed to a wireframe display of the vehicle. Of this, he said, 'I actually really like the distribution of this one.' Stefano noticed missing details, such as windshield wipers and door handles. Because of this, he said, 'As beautiful as the craftsmanship is, you know, I cannot use something if it's missing details.' He lowered the grade due to the missing details but asserted that it was professional but unfinished rather than being not professional.

Koen's scores from industry assessors reflected a more positive impression of this vehicle than the previous one (Table 5.4).

5.9.5.4 Comments

Koen stated that the NURBS modelling assignment was 'the most challenging assignment so far' in comparison to every school experience he'd ever had. This could be attributed to the fact that he was a beginner NURBS modeller and a naïve drawing student when he started at IGAD, but he also had three years previous experience working with polygon modelling tools at his previous education, an MBO school. However, he did not credit this experience for helping him on the NURBS project. Koen agreed that he learned much more in the first weeks at IGAD than in his years at an MBO.

Koen progressed from having no knowledge of NURBS modelling to being a proficient practitioner within the nine-week period given to the class. According to him, the change from non-proficient to proficient performance depended on a single realisation regarding surface intersections that resulted in a change to the way he visualised structure; this in turn led to improvement in the way he interacted with the NURBS tools.

The quality of observation in Koen's final model was strong and was the major factor responsible for the unanimous assessment by industry participants that the work was proficient. Beneath the praise his model received, was implicit recognition of Koen's visualisation ability. This allowed him to correctly project 2D curves into

3D space for his tape model, then to visualise patch intersections to create the primary surfaces needed for the vehicle and last, to come up with a patch layout that served the form and likeness of the finished vehicle.

5.9.6 Ward: Former HAVO Student, Proficient on First Attempt

5.9.6.1 Starting Position

Ward enjoyed drawing prior to starting at IGAD but had only occasionally dabbled in unsupervised 3D modelling. He supplied a textured 3D character model of a fantasy creature as part of his assessment. It was not an excellent example of this type of modelling, but it did demonstrate familiarity with basic polygonal modelling and texturing tools, more than other submissions from former MBO students. Ward came to IGAD directly after finishing his HAVO secondary school. These facts indicate a beginner's level of experience prior to joining IGAD. On this basis, he was classified as a beginner. He did not pass the Carton project and earned the minimum passing grade of 6 on the Illusion project. Ward's intake submission drawings indicated attempts at observing his subjects, but they were all compromised by a naïve approach.

5.9.6.2 Development

The tape model for this vehicle was incomplete. It did not adequately describe the form of the car (Fig. 5.25). The student did not turn in his project for evaluation in Weeks 5 and 7, but showed definite progress throughout the group of files.

The most notable improvement occurred between Weeks 4 and 6. Ward said that the reason for this change was that in approximately Week 4 I told him to throw away his file and start over because he was building it incorrectly. He said this forced him to 'look at it differently', causing him to appreciate the need for determining a good patch layout for the vehicle. In Week 6 the model appeared to be well-observed and tangency errors were minimal.

5.9.6.3 Final Result and Industry Analysis

The file earned a grade of 8 and was submitted to industry participants for review (Fig. 5.26).

Wouter's first impression of Ward's file upon opening it was that 'the shape is right'. He continued by remarking that 'everything is really cool and slick', but then complained that the level of detail in the grille seemed lower than in other parts of the vehicle. He summed up his evaluation of the car by saying

Fig. 5.25 Ward's incomplete tape model

Fig. 5.26 Ward's final NURBS vehicle model

this is game-worthy, this model. In the PlayStation 2 era, this would be like thrown in any racing game in a heartbeat, so… especially with the detail on the back. He has a good feel of shape, the artist. The model again doesn't feel off. It feels pretty consistent, really.

Bas started his review of Ward's vehicle by first loading reference images and then he loaded Ward's file. After comparing the two, his first statement was, 'There's nothing really, really to fault with this one.' To explain, he said, 'In terms of curvature, it follows the curves of the car nicely, and I know that these kinds of curves are really, really hard to get right, especially in 3D.' In comparison to the previous models, Bas said 'First impression on all the cars is good and then you dive in and find faults as you would. But this is a good model, probably the better one of the three up until now.'

Fig. 5.27 Wireframe view of Ward's final vehicle

Josh said he liked the car when he opened it, and then modified the lighting to make it harsher, in an attempt to reveal mistakes that would have been less easily spotted in softer light. After performing this test, he reaffirmed his original impression: 'I think this is a pretty good car. I think it's usable.' After making these comments, Josh rotated the virtual scene camera to evaluate the rear of Ward's vehicle, where he found a tangency error.

> There is some discontinuity in the back of the car on the fender, near… it's hard to see on your screen, but there is some. I see a distinct line where with two patches meet and that's not good. That's pretty ugly so…

Josh said that the tangency error would have to be fixed but that it was not a serious concern compared to the excellent likeness.

Caleb examined the reference for Ward's car in an attempt to determine whether a fillet was the right size. He found it difficult to assess with the photo he had, but regardless, said, 'I think I'm being really nit-picky. It looks really clean…like it, just a few fixes and it's perfect.'

On opening the file, Stefano commented on details missing from the model that were present on the other models, such as the windshield wipers. Because of this, he said that 'it needs more work, you know, that it needs to actually keep moving forward, you know, to actually start bringing it to the same level of detail that the other ones had.' He described it as a 'first pass' rather than a finished model. This impression was confirmed when he looked at the wireframe (Fig. 5.27) and saw the windows.

Table 5.5 Industry assessor grades for Ward's vehicle

Vehicle 3	Assessor 1	Assessor 2	Assessor 3	Assessor 4	Assessor 5	Average
Raw	8	8	7	7.5	6.5	7.4
Adjusted	9	9	8.5	8.75	8.25	8.7

> I mean, they're basically just a single patch. You know, maybe I would actually have given a little bit more detail there to allow for better shading. The problem is that…the problem is that even a bad distribution will actually cause bad shading in many different situations.

Despite this, he said it would 'fit right in' at his company, but would have to be finished.

Grades from industry assessors positioned this vehicle between Maike and Koen's vehicles (Table 5.5).

5.9.6.4 Comments

> I really hated the whole idea of working with NURBS and I… the only thing I could think of was, like, oh man, just wait, like, one hour more and then I'll start or… I just was postponing, and I think if you had more time that it wouldn't have mattered that much.

The successful conclusion of this student's project could not reasonably be attributed to pre-existing knowledge of NURBS, other CG techniques, or drawing skill. All evidence available for this study indicates weak-to-poor drawing skill, weak polygon modelling skill and a total lack of knowledge regarding NURBS tools and techniques prior to the start of the MD2 class. Ward credits feedback received in class as materially altering the way he 'saw' the NURBS project and that this led to a dramatic improvement in the quality of his work. The principal change made to his workflow was that he switched to intersecting surfaces rather than filling in curves (similar to polygon modelling). During the class, Ward discovered that he had developed NURBS vision and that he could not 'turn it off'.

The final project supports the view that Koen's ability to project 2D curves into 3D space was good, but that he struggled with visualising the shape of surfaces needed to perform successful intersections. Koen's patch layout shows a fair but imperfect ability to visualise blend patches. Based on feedback from industry assessors, a good ability to project and intersect surfaces to produce a good likeness are requirements for proficiency in NURBS modelling. Visualisation of blends, as indicated in the assessment of Maike and Koen's files, appears to be a desirable skill, but one that is not required for proficiency at a junior or mid-level.

5.9.7   Roel: Started as a Complete Novice, Proficient After Retake

5.9.7.1   Starting Position

Roel had a low intake rating (82), low PVRT score (10) and naïve or primitive drawings as part of his intake assessment. However, in his favour, the self-portrait appeared to be the product of genuine observation. This tends to be a good sign, particularly among students who have no prior drawing experience, as was the case here. Another good sign was that the 3D object presented for the intake was complex, if imperfect. It was more complex than any other model made by former MBO student participants admitted to IGAD in his year. Roel's intake model, however, was the first 3D model he had ever made. In his interview, he said that the drawings submitted were not the first he had ever made, but that the first he had made were inspired by a lecture I had given a few months earlier at an open day for the school. Therefore, the amount of experience he had upon entering the IGAD programme was minimal and none of it had the benefit of instruction or supervision. He attended a HAVO school prior to IGAD. On his first day at IGAD, he was 17.

In his first block, Roel failed the Carton project and the Illusion project, but then passed a retake of the Illusion project with a grade of 7.

5.9.7.2   Development

Roel presented progress every week but clearly struggled throughout the block to obtain perfect results. In the first hand-in, his tape model was very well-made and observed (Fig. 5.28). From that point on, quality of observation typified this project, though he continually deleted and then rebuilt elements of the file.

From the earliest stages of Roel's project, it attracted attention from other students due to the quality of its likeness. Despite problems with tangency, the likeness never suffered a great deal. The vehicle itself was among the most complex he could have attempted to make, because it had many complex blends.

Roel said that he suddenly understood how to work with NURBS in about the fourth week after attending a workshop with the co-teacher, who demonstrated how to intersect surfaces. He tested the method immediately, as is evident in his hand-in file for that week. After roughing in the vehicle's shape using this technique, Roel then worked on solving the blends. This showed in the gaps stripped out between surfaces as he worked out how to blend between them (Fig. 5.29).

5.9.7.3   Final Result

Roel did not turn in a file by the deadline because he was 'ashamed' that it was not complete. Instead, he utilised the next block to finish his vehicle. This file was very

Fig. 5.28   Roel's tape model

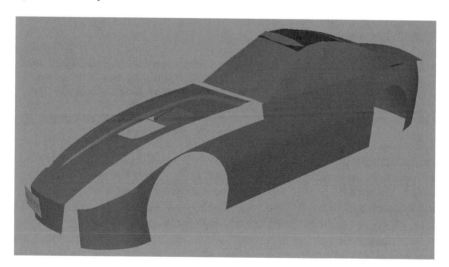

Fig. 5.29   Gaps between patches, waiting for blends

well-observed and did demonstrate proficiency. Although his grade was reduced due
to simple technical errors, it was perhaps the best-observed project made in his class
(Fig. 5.30).

Fig. 5.30 Roel's final vehicle

5.9.7.4   Comments

> I dislike the car in the fact that it challenges me so much and it's like my nemesis right now, and we keep fighting each other and in the end, I feel like I will win from it, but the way it went when I started, well, it was a difficult car really, there are a lot of shapes that you need to see before you actually go out and make the patches and lay them out. And when you have the diagram of the car, like the four image planes, a lot of stuff is hidden in there…

Roel said that he was too obsessed with details to finish the project on time and that focussing on details interfered with his ability to work out a patch layout. If Roel was correct to assert that his polygon modelling experience was of no benefit to his work on the NURBS project, then he progressed from a beginner to being proficient within a period of 18 weeks. This represents the time elapsed between the first day of the MD2 class and the date he handed in the retake.

Roel's case is particularly interesting because he started with less experience, less apparent ability and lower scores than any other student participant. In the end, he proved to have developed very strong observation, visualisation and technical skills that were at least on par with the best of the other projects. To do this, he clearly was not reliant on any type of prior experience checked in this study.

5.9.8   *Case History Themes*

Students described their progress in many different ways, and in some cases disagreed, most notably concerning the importance of tool knowledge vs. spatial visualisation-related tasks. However, their accounts make it possible to identify spatial visualisation as an important factor in their development. They also indicated that not being able to 'see' a solution interfered with or prevented them from completing the project. Students did not think that prior experience (when they had some) was of any use, nor their prior education. To them, NURBS modelling was a new experience, and they felt they had to learn it from scratch.

5.10 Employed Graduates

Each interview with employed graduates started with a series of questions designed to elicit whether they were treated as experts by their employers. The key elements used to determine whether employed graduates were treated as experts were the following:

- Assigned pipeline creation tasks
- Titles reflecting senior status
- Work product used as template for other employees
- Supervision responsibilities
- Problem-solving for groups rather than oneself only
- Responsibility for prominent assets.

Based on answers to questions on these subjects, four of the five employed graduates, Maarten, Fidde, Robbert and Frank, could be described as domain-level experts at the time of their interviews. All of these participants had responsibility for pipeline-related tasks, their work served as an example to more junior employees, and they were engaged in problem-solving on behalf of teams of other employees at their place of work. Two of these participants were given senior-level titles within two months of their interview, but none had a senior title at the time of the interview. The fifth employed graduate, Roy, did not have the kinds of responsibilities that lead to supervision or evaluation of colleague's work, but he was highly regarded by his employer on the basis of his skill. For this, he was given a heavy workload consisting of many important assets for various projects.

Each of the employed graduates was able to distinguish between their first example of proficient work made at IGAD and when they transitioned to being domain-level experts, on the basis of knowledge of industry standards learned at their workplace, duties assigned to them and their general knowledge of solutions to various problems. Although all of the employed graduates reported a period of as many as three years between their first proficient work at IGAD and their later transition to being experts, a closer look revealed that the transition to becoming experts was not wholly dependent on the full span of intervening time for the purpose of accumulating experience. Instead, the transition began only after they made the decision to explore a subject more thoroughly and then it was followed through on with full immersion in the problem, or 'deliberate practice'. If the decision was made close to when their first proficient project was made, then they transitioned to domain-level experts sooner than if the decision was made after a lengthy period of time had passed.

Maarten described his NURBS vehicle project as 'professional quality' (this agrees with his grade, a 9), but said that he did not become an expert (in a different specialty) until several years later. In his third year at IGAD, he took a nine-week class on procedural modelling that he performed well on. In the following year, he decided to spend a month intensively studying procedural modelling for the purpose of securing employment at a popular game development studio. He was successful in this endeavour and was hired at the end of his month of intensive study. At the time he was hired, he estimated that he had spent a total of 14 weeks studying procedural modelling to develop proficiency. Maarten said he realised he had become an expert about two and a half years later (six and a half years after initiating his study of digital art techniques at IGAD). This happened during a meeting at his office when

> we started with the big R&D phase after the project and that's when actually I started, like, diving into all different areas of the effects. I can just read the task or just hear from the producer and I'm already starting to think about all the ways I can achieve this and I can already sort it out.

Maarten contrasted this with junior employees who could follow directions but could not create the directions, as Maarten now discovered he could do. In this example, Maarten's progress followed closely the stage development model of Dreyfus and Dreyfus (2005) as well as the model of deliberate practice proposed by Ericsson (1993). This was because Maarten first developed proficiency, then expertise (stage model) and did so over a span of six and a half years of deliberate practice.

Maarten took longer to reach domain-level expert status than other employed graduates. In contrast, Robbert was hired directly after graduation in a critical role at one of the world's largest game studios. His position required him to build procedural art solutions for other artists that were then distributed to multiple teams within his company. This particular type of knowledge is rare in game studios and highly sought-after because procedural methods, like automation in manufacturing, allow one solution to perform more work on a per-employee basis than would be the case for non-procedural methods. In his case, he had a domain expert's level of responsibility as soon as he started working, which was only six months after he started studying procedural modelling. The difference, according to Maarten, was that at school he was responsible for every aspect of a project, but in industry, he had to focus on a smaller portion of the process. However, that portion had to be based on the work of other teams and his results would be delivered to yet other teams. The team aspect of professional work is what provided the opportunity to more fully explore the constraints he had in the context of using material that had to be shared with others on staff. The 'sharing' aspect of the work required him to understand what he was doing and why he was doing it because he would be called upon to explain his reasons for doing something and how a specific solution would work. Prior to this, as someone who was proficient at a task level, he did not have to explain his work to anyone. As long as the end result was fit for use by professional standards, that was enough.

According to Fidde,

> if you want to take a leadership position you need to be involved in things like pipeline and multiple disciplines within the company. You need to be able to know the steps that are in front of you, and come after you…if you live in this glass bubble where you just make great 3D models, but you don't really care or see what's going on before…you can only be asked to make great looking content, that's like the maximum people can expect from you.

Roy stated that his first professional-quality work was done at the end of his first year at IGAD (this agrees with his grade for the project, a 10), but that the discipline he eventually specialised in was learned during a three-month-long internship in his third year. Like Maarten and Robbert, he developed task-level proficiency rapidly, and then used that as the basis for gaining entry into industry when he graduated. A year after starting his job in industry, he was given full responsibility for a number of feature film- and television-related projects.

Although not reflected in his title, his employer seemed to be treating him as an expert by giving him responsibility for prominent projects at his workplace. In my interview with his supervisor, Roy was described in terms that were consistent with but stop short of identifying him as an expert.

Roy described himself as technically competent but not as an expert because he felt that he had not worked on sufficiently complex projects to earn that distinction. His studio specialised in small- to medium-sized projects, but 'if you work at a bigger studio the work is much more specialised.' At his company, he simply had not seen projects that required a higher order of skill or knowledge beyond what he had. He said that the bigger projects provided necessary opportunities to significantly raise one's skill and become an expert at a higher level by focussing on narrower aspects of the project. In other words, he felt that the standard of the project limited how far it could be taken and how much one could learn from it.

Wouter, an industry participant, expressed his idea on the difference between proficiency and being an expert in the following way:

> if you train a monkey really hard you will be able to model, but understanding where the modelling part is fed into the entire process of creating a game or creating an animation, special effects…is something no student can learn if you haven't lived through the process.

This statement agrees with statements from employed graduates who all said that they did not become domain-level experts until after they had begun working in industry, but that they were technically competent (proficient) prior to graduation.

5.11 Conclusion

In Chap. 4 and this chapter, I have presented data relevant to determining (1) how students develop proficiency as NURBS modellers, (2) what quality inherent to learning or using NURBS modelling tools is of generic practical use in industry, (3) how proficiency in NURBS modelling is assessed by industry professionals and (4) how proficient former IGAD students transitioned to being experts.

To study the development of proficiency, I first had to determine whether any students developed proficiency. This was done with the aid of industry professionals, who agreed to assess the same group of four student files. The outcome of their assessments was that all of the files they reviewed were proficient to varying degrees. With this established, records of progress, interviews, questionnaires and other data collected during the study allowed for the creation of case histories of each student's development, including those identified by industry participants as proficient.

The data presented here begin by attempting to establish what level of skill or knowledge each student had upon entering IGAD. This information was then checked against a variety of performance indicators to see what, if any, influence prior experience had on performance at IGAD. According to these data, students who entered IGAD after attending an MBO or foreign education had higher polygon modelling grades than students in all other categories. PVRT mental rotation tests also correlated to a statistically significant degree with polygon modelling performance. Both of these findings demonstrate that prior experience and spatial ability as measured on a mental rotation test correlate with performance levels in polygon modelling tasks. However, neither factor correlates to a statistically significant degree with NURBS modelling tasks.

Students stated in their interviews and questionnaires that knowledge of polygon modelling did not help them with NURBS modelling and even retarded their progress, although both NURBS and polygon modelling was done in the same software, Maya. When asked about differences between polygon and NURBS modelling, they gave a narrow range of answers, the majority of which centred on visualisation-related subjects. Ten students said that they had experienced 'eureka moments', after which their ability to work in NURBS was significantly enhanced. In seven examples, those moments were associated with visualisation tasks that cannot easily be matched to the type of visualisation tested for in many existing tests.

In the next chapter, the meaning of these data is explored more fully in an attempt to better understand (1) why NURBS modelling seems to rely on different skills than polygon modelling, (2) how to define the difference, (3) why visualisation is meaningful to digital art careers and (4) implications for theory on the development of proficiency and expertise.

References

Bodner GM, Guay RB (1997) The Purdue visualization of rotations test. The Chem Educ 2(4):1–14
Dreyfus HL, Dreyfus SE (2005) Peripheral vision: expertise in real world contexts. Organ Stud 26(5):779–792. https://doi.org/10.1177/0170840605053102
Eliot J, Smith IM (1983) An international directory of spatial tests. The NFER-Nelson Publishing Company Ltd, Windsor, Berks UK

Ericsson KA (1993) The role of deliberate practice in the acquisition of expert performance. Psychol Rev 100(3):363–406

Meyer JHF, Land R (eds) (2012) Overcoming barriers to student understanding, First paperback ed. Routledge, Abingdon, Oxon and New York

Paquette A (2008) Computer graphics for artists: an introduction, 1st edn, vol 1. Springer UK, London

Vandenberg SG, Kuse AR (1978) Mental rotations, a group test of three-dimensional spatial visualization. Percept Mot Skills 47(2):599–604

Chapter 6
Discussion

6.1 Overview

In this chapter, development of proficiency and mental visualisation are discussed. These two subjects are closely linked, as shown by the findings in this study and the data they are based on. Some IGAD students became proficient NURBS modellers during the nine-week MD2 NURBS modelling class. Of those students, none had prior experience of NURBS modelling and some had no prior experience of CG tools or of drawing before enrolling at IGAD. Because these students started with little or no prior relevant experience, it was possible to observe very close to the full process of development from a beginner's lack of knowledge and skill to proficiency. One of the key findings of this research is that the development of certain kinds of spatial visualisation ability was essential to becoming proficient. These spatial visualisation abilities performed the same function as threshold concepts.

6.2 Development

6.2.1 Students Became Proficient

To verify that students had become proficient according to industry standards, industry professionals were asked to look at student work and provide their own assessment of their quality, using standards that they would apply to work produced in their own studios (p. 122). The industry participants in this study came from five companies headquartered in four countries and did not know each other. The consistency of grades and grading criteria among the five industry participants was strong evidence that their assessments were reliable indicators of industry norms. There were no disagreements in their methods, and only slight differences in the grades they gave. In all cases, the slight grade differences between industry participants did not change

© Springer Nature Switzerland AG 2018
A. Paquette, *Spatial Visualization and Professional Competence*,
https://doi.org/10.1007/978-3-319-91289-9_6

the status of any of the files produced by students, all of which were rated as 'professionally competent' (technically proficient) by all industry participants. Although the students who produced these files were first-year students, they satisfied the criterion that 'graduate skills meet predictable, industry-accepted standards of performance' insisted upon by King et al. (2008).

Each of the industry participants first made a brief review of the overall appearance of the vehicle models (p. 124). This was done by rotating a virtual camera in 3D software around the model for the purpose of ascertaining whether the model was 'convincing' as a rough measure of likeness. After completing their review of the likeness of each model, they checked the patch layout of each model for 'flow' across patches, then checked for technical errors and last, missing details. The total process took between 5 and 10 min for each model, but the grades they gave did not change much after they had developed a first opinion of the model in the first minute of evaluating it. They explained that technical flaws were 'easy to fix' in contrast with likeness errors that were easy to find but difficult to fix.

The implication of comments regarding likeness was that 'fixing' a likeness amounts to first learning how to create a likeness. In Maike's case, the general opinion was that her likeness suffered from weak reference rather than an inability to create a likeness (p. 136). Technical problems were viewed differently, as overlooked remnants of the modelling process, like typographical errors, that were easily cleaned up.

Although likeness was known to be important to any assessment of modelling skill, it was not expected that industry participants would be so casual in their evaluation of technical defects. Instead, they scrutinised the likeness carefully, even to the extent of requesting reference to make a comparison. This behaviour mirrored student concerns about 'seeing' the structure of their models (p. 112). This revealed a bias on my part, because I had not prepared reference material for industry assessors to view when grading student projects. Fortunately, most students had submitted good reference with their final assignments and for those who had not, reference could be found quickly (in most cases) online based on the make and model of their chosen vehicle. This caused a slight delay in the first two interviews, after which reference material was more readily accessible for assessors to use if they wished.

6.2.2 The Path to Proficiency

According to the literature, rapid development of proficiency may be caused by previous development of skill in a related domain (Ericsson 2014). Students were thus examined for prior experience with 3D modelling, drawing and mental rotation ability, in order to determine whether these factors were predictive of class performance (pp. 82–93).

The IGAD students in this study entered the programme from a variety of other schools, were of different ages and had differing levels of experience and spatial ability. Prior experience and PVRT scores did correlate to a statistically significant degree with polygon modelling tasks (p. 90), but there were no common characteristics found that reliably predicted success in NURBS modelling. Students on the whole found NURBS modelling to be difficult. Many confirmed it was the most difficult single project of any kind they had ever attempted (p. 99). Despite this, several completed the project successfully, including some of the most pessimistic students. Those who succeeded appeared to develop the requisite skill over the course of the single project, suggesting that their transition to proficiency hinged on a factor present in the class itself rather than prior experience (p. 146).

6.2.2.1 Understanding of Tools (Broad Knowledge)

The 'broad knowledge' definition of expertise expects that one must have considerable experience in a domain or related domains to be considered an expert (Ericsson 1993). Because the work product of proficient and expert performance can be identical (p. 13), and this study only rated performance, the broad knowledge standard is considered here in brief. For IGAD students, there are two types of relevant broad knowledge they could have: (1) NURBS modelling, or (2) a domain related to NURBS modelling. While none had prior experience with NURBS modelling, some did have prior experience with the seemingly related tasks of polygon modelling and drawing (pp. 81–84). However, the data shows that neither of these previously acquired skills had any consistent impact on their NURBS modelling performance (pp. 85, 93). Their development of proficiency in NURBS appeared to be unrelated to transfer of knowledge or ability from previously developed skills.

6.2.2.2 Prior CG Experience

Students who had received previous MBO education were found to perform better on the polygon projects (Carton and Illusion) by nearly a full grade point (p. 84), but prior training did not appear to affect performance on the NURBS project (p. 94). In this study, some students had up to four years' prior experience with polygon modelling, either because they had attended a technical high school (MBO) or through self-study. However, former MBO students said that NURBS modelling was not taught at their previous schools and all student participants denied having any exposure to NURBS modelling prior to the MD2 class. This provided an opportunity to test whether prior modelling experience with polygons had an impact on the development of general modelling performance and NURBS modelling skills.

For the Carton project, a project described in the methodology chapter (p. 45), students were asked to perform a deceptively simple task: to build and then fold a folding carton. Most students failed this project (67%, n = 625), but students with a secondary vocational education (MBO) diploma passed more often than students with general secondary education (HAVO) diplomas by a 7.2% margin (p. 87). On the MD1 polygon modelling project (the Illusion project) described in Chap. 3 (p. 45), a comparison revealed statistically significant differences in grades earned by the

MBO and HAVO student groups ($n = 426, p = .001$). The difference favoured MBO students by .95 of a grade point over HAVO students, but for the MD2 NURBS project, there was no statistically significant difference between any student groups. This finding suggests that prior experience in polygon modelling, the type of modelling taught at MBO institutions, does benefit students on polygon modelling assignments but not on NURBS assignments. Data from qualitative interviews with students about how their previous educational experiences affected subsequent development at IGAD supported this finding. In fact, some students even talked about their previous learning being detrimental to their efforts on the NURBS project (p. 102).

In summary, prior polygon modelling experience has a statistically significant positive relationship to eventual success in producing a polygon-based modelling project, as represented by the two MD1 projects (Carton and Illusion). The same experience, however, does not benefit a NURBS-based project, as represented by the MD2 project grades. This indicates that there is something about the MD2 class or NURBS modelling that is meaningfully different from polygon modelling.

In this light, it could be argued that polygon modelling is a specific skill rather than a general modelling ability. Therefore, one would not expect it to transfer, and it does not appear to. Of interest, though, is that the skill in question, polygon modelling, is superficially similar to NURBS modelling. Both are methods of creating a 3D facsimile of a real-world object in a computer, and both use the same software: Maya 2012, to do it. With this in mind, one might expect to find that the two are related enough to allow accelerated learning in NURBS modelling due to polygon modelling or software experience. Based on the student interview data and the statistical evidence gathered for this project, however, the answer appears to be no. In this group, polygon modelling experience did not enhance the acquisition of NURBS modelling skills.

If Ericsson's (2014) answer to Ackerman (p. 21) on the subject of rapid development of expertise is considered in this light, that previous experience as an athlete contributed to performance in the specialty of rowing, we have an example where experience in one CG specialisation, polygon modelling, does not transfer to a related specialty, NURBS modelling, of the same domain: digital art. However, when the students' backgrounds are taken into consideration, there remains the possibility that another previously developed art-related skill may have contributed to the development of ability in NURBS modelling: prior drawing experience.

6.2.2.3   Prior Drawing Experience

To be considered for admission into the IGAD programme, students were required to provide intake assignments consisting of three drawings and an optional 3D model (p. 85). The drawing component of the intake project was worth a total of six points but the 3D component was worth only two points. This resulted in intake assessments that were weighted in favour of previous drawing experience over CG experience. For this reason, intake assessment scores were used as an indicator of prior drawing experience. Intake scores were then used to assign students to four groups; A, B, C and D, where the 'A' group was the most desirable group and the 'D' group the most likely to be rejected.

To determine if previous drawing skills affected performance at IGAD, intake group membership was compared to MD1 and MD2 grades using a Kruskal-Wallis test (p. 85). It was expected that MD1 and MD2 grades earned by students assigned to adjacent intake groups (AB, BC, CD) would not be significantly different, but that students whose intake groups were more distant (AC, AD, BD) would receive significantly different MD1 and MD2 scores. If true, this would indicate that prior experience in drawing contributed to performance in 3D modelling tasks.

The results showed a statistically significant difference between the A and C intake groups for MD1MAX ($n = 93$, $p = .01$) and MD2MAX ($n = 93$, $p = .017$), as expected. The difference between the A and D groups came close to significance for MD1MAX ($n = 102$, $p = .054$) and MD2MAX ($n = 102$, $p = .058$). Last, the difference between the B and C groups was significant ($n = 125$, $p = .041$) for MD1MAX only. This result, unlike the previous two, was the opposite of what was expected. A possible explanation is that the intake groups are not simple rankings, but categories (Table 6.1).

Table 6.1 Intake assessment groups and corresponding categories

A	B	C	D
Accept	Accept if space available and interview satisfactory	Reject unless interview material changes grade and/or space available	Reject regardless of space

Based on these categories, it was expected that all A- and B-group students would be accepted but that all D-group and most C-group students would be rejected. This placed pressure on assessors to be particularly careful distinguishing between B and C, because it was the boundary between almost certain acceptance and rejection. This may have led them to be more cautious when discriminating between these groups, with the effect that the composition of the groups was more similar than other group pairs.

Because the test results did not rank the intake groups as expected, they do not support the hypothesis that previous drawing skills as measured by intake group membership have an effect on performance in MD1 or MD2. This could also be explained by the generally low level of drawing ability found in submissions. It is difficult for assessors to effectively distinguish quality levels among drawings by students who have little to no experience. The effect of this is that although assessors must sort using four groups for administrative purposes, the work presented fits more logically into only two groups: skilled and unskilled. A method available to check this hypothesis was to examine the drawings provided by student participants.

Eight of the 20 student participants had previous drawing experience but no CG experience. Of this group, four students each earned grades between 8 and 10 in MD1 and MD2. If the actual drawings submitted by these students as part of their intake submission are examined, it is found that only two students, Maike and Janet, had developed their drawing skills to a high level. This is reflected in their assessment scores, 9 and 10 respectively, the two highest scores possible. In both cases, the students earned a 10 on the MD2 project. It is easy to infer from this that a relationship exists between the well-developed drawing skills of Maike and Janet and their MD2 results. However, both students also performed well in other classes at IGAD and their previous schools. There may be a connection, but this could be due to general academic aptitude rather than drawing skill.

6.2.2.4   No Prior CG or Drawing Experience

In contrast to Maike and Janet, Roel had no prior experience with drawing or CG, yet he also became proficient at NURBS modelling (p. 146). A check of his intake drawings reveals that they are quite weak, almost on the opposite end of the spectrum from Maike or Janet's work. His success cannot be explained on the basis of prior drawing skill or CG knowledge, nor is Roel unique in this. An examination of students who received grades in the range of 8–10 on the MD2 project reveals that their backgrounds include every possible combination of experience or lack of experience in CG and drawing. In summary, there was a relationship between drawing ability and admission into the programme, but there was not a clear relationship between drawing ability and eventual success in NURBS modelling.

6.2.3   Drawing and Visual Thinking

Janet was one possible exception to the lack of correlation between drawing ability and NURBS modelling performance (p. 146). Of the student participants, she was the only one who had any industrial sketching experience prior to attending IGAD. Industrial sketching is a type of technical drawing in which products are designed from scratch and shown in detail from many different angles, with an emphasis on clarity of form. Janet's interview data showed that she thought NURBS modelling was similar to industrial sketching. She claimed that her experience with the latter was the reason she had avoided certain mistakes other students made in the early weeks of the project. As Janet said, 'In the beginning, I tried to [solve NURBS problems] only in my brain, but I can't remember everything so I started drawing it and I found that was clearer.'

Janet's explanation that prior industrial sketching experience helped her learn NURBS modelling was credible on the basis of (1) her final NURBS project, (2) her working method, which showed an early appreciation of form and (3) the sketches she made in class to solve shape-related problems. However, with this exception noted, there is evidence that proficiency was developed by other students without any prior experience of NURBS, CG, or drawing. Further, experience with polygonal modelling was not a factor in developing proficiency in NURBS modelling (p. 94).

It is possible that drawing experience did contribute to the proficiency Maike and Janet eventually developed in NURBS modelling, but based on the available evidence, this is only true because in both cases their drawings showed considerable achievement, well above anything produced by all other students. However, this does not explain how six other students developed proficiency without developing equivalent drawing skill.

The literature of engineering design provides a possible explanation for Janet's observation about the connection between her drawings and NURBS modelling. Ferguson (1992) describes how '…engineering designers convert the visions in their minds to drawings and specifications' (pp. 2–3). This is not the same process that artists undertake when they make drawings for the intake submission. Submission drawings are 'drawn from life', meaning that no design is taking place, but they are attempting to record what they see before them. In contrast, design problems and their solutions rely on mental visualisation to create a mental image of the design prior to making a drawing. To convert a 'vision' from their mind, or to engage in 'visual thinking' as Ferguson describes it, students must first be able to create that vision. The type of drawing Ferguson describes is the same kind that Janet called 'industrial sketching'. 'Visual thinking', as described by Ferguson (1992) and Henderson (1999), is necessary for engineers and designers. This study shows it is true of digital artists as well, though the type of visual thinking may be different.

Maike's drawings were strong and she earned a 10 for her NURBS model. However, her model did not show the same fluid patch layout found in Janet's model. This was pointed out by several industry participants (p. 135). In her case, an argument could be made that her drawing experience was relevant to her observation skills but not to her understanding of the shape problems presented in the NURBS project. This is supported by her learning log entries, which emphasised tool problems over visualisation. The fact that Roel and Koen managed to succeed without strong drawing skills demonstrates that drawing experience, while helpful to Janet, was not required to successfully complete the NURBS project. Among students who failed the MD2 class, the same variety of previous experience was found as in the group of students who passed.

Like the difference between polygon and NURBS modelling, where topology is meaningful to one and not to the other, the tools available in the software, such as component translation, interface, file organisation, etc., may be the same, but the process is different. This is because polygons do not require a carefully organised patch layout to establish smooth blends between shapes, nor do they require all shapes to be constructed out of four sides defined by curves, as is the case with NURBS. The same difference can exist between different types of drawings, thus opening the possibility that the crucial skill that led to proficiency among IGAD students was not specific to NURBS modelling or drawing, but was a more general skill: visualisation. In the case of Maike and Janet, one could say that their general visualisation skill was expressed in their drawing ability but that the visualisation skill developed by Roel and others was not dependent on prior drawing experience. Instead, visualisation was a separate skill that could be developed through drawing, NURBS modelling, or perhaps other methods as well.

6.2.4 Motivation

6.2.4.1 Students Claim Importance of Motivation

Of the factors mentioned by students or observed in class as important to their progress, motivation was the most prominent (p. 117). This was visible in slow progress on the project and comments from students such as Ward, who thought that NURBS was 'damn foolish'. Motivation is a powerful factor in the development of proficiency (Alexander 2003), because without it, students may not persist to the point where they overcome threshold concepts that stand in their way. This becomes even more important in the context of individual work conducted outside a classroom, where students often find they do good work because 'you need to sit down and think about what you're doing', and 'sit down and work it out on paper and really understand what happens' (Boustedt et al. 2007 p. 507). This is reflected in data collected for this study, where Koen, Martin and Janet overcame threshold concepts on their own. Other students overcame threshold concepts in 'patch parties' after class while working with others, which was done as a way to motivate the students in these groups, and according to them was effective (pp. 127, 162). Overall, successful students felt that one of the more valuable takeaways from the NURBS project was improved confidence and motivation because, in the words of Koen 'if you believe you can do something, you can.'

6.2.4.2 Failure and Frustration as Motivation

One incentive students had available to them was that prints of student work from previous years had been framed and mounted on walls throughout the IGAD building. These served as a reminder that it was possible for students to accomplish the feat of building a NURBS vehicle, but it also resulted in considerable frustration, as reflected in interviews with students, like Sebastian, who likened the project to milking a pineapple (p. 99).

Students who performed well, like Ward, refused to give up, no matter how difficult the project seemed to be (p. 142). For these students, frustration and tenacity became their motivation to complete the assignment at a high standard. According to Roel 'I found myself frustrated, but in that frustration, I found motivation.' This statement and others like it provides counterpoint to Sternberg's (1998) theory that ability differences lead to motivation differences, because 'meeting with success, those with more ability may practice more; meeting with lesser success, those with lesser ability may give up' (p. 14).

In the case presented by IGAD students, some, like Roel and Koen, accustomed to failure, became motivated by the failure itself until they became successful. Other students, like Johannes, were accustomed to academic success, but lost all interest in the project very early in the process and did not make a serious effort in class after encountering the intersection and blend problems presented in weeks three and five, respectively. These results, despite student claims to the contrary, do not strongly support an argument for motivation playing a causative role in proficiency development.

6.2.5 Learning and Transition

The transition from novice to proficient performance was repeatedly described as a sudden, not a gradual, change (p. 114). Student participants Paula and Roel both claimed to have experienced their 'eureka moments' in class during class critiques. Other students, like Koen, described their eureka moments (or 'transitions') happening outside of class or at home while working on the project. This is consistent with Sternberg et al. (2000), who describes tacit skill as typically acquired with little environmental support, on one's own. He writes that this is usually the case because learners must test solutions themselves to truly understand them.

According to Roel, 'the light went off' [meaning fired, as in a flash] when he saw files made by other students; Paula had 'no idea what I was doing' until she started using intersection and then she experienced 'the change [to] my thought pattern that made a lot of things fall in place'; and Janet suddenly found herself analysing the structure of every manufactured object in her environment: 'I just can't get it out of my mind...I just automatically analyse it'. Each of these students experienced a significant change in the way they approached the NURBS project, but they and others, experienced this change in different circumstances: in class, patch parties, at home, with friends and alone. What they all share are descriptions of a shift in the way they see or visualise the problem. They are not talking about learning new information that was unknown until that moment, but about understanding the problem in a new and irreversible way that meaningfully altered their perception. In each case, it was a matter of 'seeing', but with the mind, not the eyes, because the seeing they described was a mental image that became the plan for subsequent work.

Roel pointed out that although he attended the after-hours patch parties and had experienced more than one transition in his understanding of NURBS there or during class critiques, it would not have been possible to explore the problems without the work he did at home. Without that, he said, 'I would forget [the answer] because I hadn't solved it.' This comment and others like it emphasise the importance of understanding and of providing students an environment that allows them to fully explore and understand a problem on their own. Too much support, as Roel said, would have prevented understanding. To illustrate his point, he described how, when I would 'take [his] mouse' and show him something, he would have to do it over again by himself because if he didn't perform the actions himself, he wouldn't remember them. A demonstration of the solution, thus, did not teach him how to arrive at it himself. Roel had to learn through his own experimentation why certain solutions were effective and others weren't in order to develop the understanding that allowed him to find solutions rapidly once he knew how to approach the problem.

Gamble (2001) describes 'modelling behaviour' as learning situations where students closely follow, or 'model', the behaviour of their instructors as they demonstrate techniques to their class or individual students. At IGAD, students are given demonstrations in tool functionality, but as they report, this is not enough to solve the problems they face. Rather, 'individuals often must engage in these processes on their own in order to make sense of and respond to situations' (Sternberg et al. 2000, p. 107).

The IGAD teaching method is designed to avoid the 'software-only' style of CG education that industry complains of as inadequate (King et al. 2008; Livingstone and Hope 2011) by encouraging students to explore solutions on their own. While this supports the potential development of a tacit skill (Sternberg et al. 2000), it means that students have little access to instructors who could model exact methods for problems, and therefore students have few opportunities to model their performance based on those examples. IGAD instructors do provide general principles and tool-use demonstrations, but the difference between understanding principles, seeing how the tools work in a generic context and actually using them to create a specific shape was one of the core problems reported by students (p. 106).

The problem described by Koen was that he was afraid to take the risks required to advance his visualisation ability. At first, Koen was unsure what the result would be if he took the 'risks' he knew he should be taking. He was, in Osmond et al.'s (2009) language, not tolerant of design uncertainty. When Koen finally overcame the hurdle regarding intersection visualisation, the quality of his work immediately became proficient (p. 138). Other students described the trial-and-error process as fraught with anxiety, in many cases coupled with reluctance to attempt unfamiliar strategies to solve the NURBS problem. The counterpart to this anxiety was the confidence that other participants reported after successfully completing the project, all of whom had to try new methods to get the results they wanted.

Simonton's (2014) discussion of risk-taking as an essential element of successful design was reflected in comments made by Koen in this study. He noted that he felt as if a lack of risk-taking behaviour stymied his efforts to progress to a solution. In Koen's case, as with other students, 'risk-taking' entailed iterations of the problem-solving process. Observations of participants as they learned new ways to see things via trial and error are similar to observations made by Atman et al. (2007) and Schön (1992), who discuss iteration and the design process as key to changing the way students see things.

During their interviews, students were asked to name factors that they felt contributed the most to their learning experience. They were expected to reference classroom materials or learning opportunities created for students by lecturers or the university. However, many students mentioned the importance of working together in groups of friends off-campus. Roel went so far as to write two emails after his interview to remind me of how important this was to his learning experience and to insist that I include the item in my research. He was not the only student who thought that this was important and among study participants there were two prominent groups of friends who worked together throughout the project. According to various members of these study groups, working with peers had the following advantages: (1) they helped them stay focussed on the work, (2) they made the process more fun, thus improving motivation and (3) they were able to learn from each other.

Despite the statements from students regarding the importance of working in peer groups as described above, in each of the two known groups involved in this study, results were uneven for group members. Not all members of each group passed the class. One member of one group of about five students became proficient (with a retake). In the other, two members of a similarly sized group became proficient, and again, one of those became proficient only after a retake. Two students worked at home and avoided group work sessions but both became proficient. It is possible that working in groups was helpful up to the limits of each student's ability, but the evidence does not support a conclusion that working in groups such as these produces uniformly good results.

These data presented here provide an example of a domain where broad knowledge is less important than a tacitly acquired skill, spatial visualisation, to the development of proficiency and expertise. Some assertions in the expertise literature come across as sceptical of claims that expertise can be developed without broad knowledge, but this study indicates that it might be accomplished by acquiring certain threshold concepts that are critical to a particular domain of practice, just as the artificial intelligence in Epstein (1995) became 'expert' after encountering a key node when playing tic-tac-toe and other (more complex) games.

6.2.6 Experience Mediates PVRT Performance

The literature provides an example of why PVRT scores may not correlate with performance in certain conditions. According to Keehner et al. (2004), the more experience a surgeon has, the weaker the correlation between performance in laparoscopic surgery and PVRT scores. This is similar to Bodner and Guay's (1987) claim that the PVRT is expected to correlate with examples of novel problem-solving, 'questions that differed significantly from those students had seen previously in the textbook, in lecture, or on homework assignments' (p. 6), but not with rote answers to questions they had previously studied.

If applied to the IGAD results the theory that experience mediates performance presents two possibilities: (1) PVRT scores do not correlate with performance of NURBS modelling tasks because NURBS modelling is familiar or 'rote' due to prior NURBS modelling experience or ability, or (2) PVRT scores do not correlate with performance on NURBS modelling tasks for an unknown reason.

It is known that NURBS modelling was unfamiliar to all students at the start of the MD2 class. This argues in favour of eliminating the first possibility, that lack of correlation is due to experience or familiarity. One could argue that polygon modelling experience from the MD1 class allowed performance in MD2 to become rote and thus explain the PVRT results, or that spatial visualisation is not relevant to NURBS modelling. However, these explanations directly contradict how students described their experience of the MD2 class, observations made during class, statistical comparisons between MD1 and MD2 performance and the evidence of students' weekly progress hand-ins, all of which emphasise the novel nature of the NURBS project to students and the importance of visualisation (p. 99).

The PVRT mental rotations test, described in detail in Chap. 2 (p. 29), was given to visual art students at IGAD. The IGAD students' mean score of 16.68 was compared to the means of six separate test groups at Purdue University and a seventh group from Coventry University using an unpaired t-test. The assumption driving this comparison was that if IGAD and Coventry student scores were statistically significantly higher than median scores found in the Purdue studies, the higher scores would support the arguments of Hegarty et al. (2009) and Bodner and Guay (1997), who claim that experience mediates the effect of spatial ability and performance. This is because IGAD and Coventry students would likely have had more exposure to mental rotation-related problems than students not accustomed to working with 3D imaging software.

The difference between IGAD scores and all of the Purdue groups was statistically significant at $p = < .0001$ for all but one group, which was also statistically significant at $p = < .0005$. When Purdue scores were separated by gender and the higher, male-only means were used instead, the same results were obtained. In all cases, the IGAD mean was higher than the Purdue and Coventry University means to a statistically significant degree. This indicates the possibility that there is something different about the IGAD visual arts students' mental rotation ability and that of students enrolled in different domains of study. It also suggests that the relationship between mental rotation and spatial task performance among digital art students is different from tasks performed in the domains studied at Purdue and Coventry.

6.2.7 Mental Rotation Ability Can Mask Visualisation Deficits

Two possible explanations for the high scores at IGAD come from the literature of spatial visualisation. The first explanation is that, because playing video games has the effect of improving mental rotation scores (Terlicki and Newcombe 2005), IGAD students, who are enrolled in a video game development programme, have developed this skill due to their interest in and practice with video games. The second explanation is based on research findings that the use of CAD software has the effect of improving mental rotation test scores (Kurtulus and Uygan 2010). Most vocational secondary school (MBO) students entering IGAD, 25.8% of all students, receive some computer graphics training before enrolling at IGAD. This training, where they are constantly engaged in processes that train their mental rotation ability, could improve their mental rotation test scores. This does not, however, explain the PVRT mean reported by Osmond at Coventry University, where students use similar software to that used by IGAD students but had significantly lower scores than IGAD students.

The literature on spatial problem-solving indicates that high ability in mental rotation tasks can predict high ability in solving novel problems with a spatial component (Bodner and Guay 1997; Pribyl and Bodner 1987). IGAD students' relatively strong measured ability in spatial visualisation (compared to other university students') should have predicted their performance in modelling tasks if those tasks were novel to the students. Instead, mental rotation test scores (PVRT) predicted performance in familiar modelling tasks (polygon modelling) but not in novel modelling tasks (NURBS modelling).

Prior to the pilot study, it was expected that the PVRT and other spatial visualisation tests would predict performance in modelling classes. These were initially compared to the MD2 class, where no correlation was found. This was unexpected, but even more unexpected was that in this study, PVRT scores correlated with MD1 but not MD2. This clearly distinguished between the two classes on the basis of mental rotation as a presumed valid indicator of spatial visualisation ability. The inconsistency between these two results modified the analysis of study findings to include the possibility that spatial visualisation either does not contribute to NURBS modelling skills, or that it is a type of spatial visualisation that is not captured by mental rotation or other spatial visualisation tests given to IGAD students.

6.2.8 PVRT Explained by Non-rotation Dependent Visualisation

One explanation for the lack of correlation found between PVRT results and NURBS grades is that mental rotation ability is more closely related to the problem-solving process of working with polygons than NURBS. This is supported by the present research which shows that the nature of the visualisation problem in NURBS modelling is unrelated to mental rotation (p. 104). With this in mind, the lack of correlation between PVRT scores and performance at IGAD and Coventry can be explained because NURBS modelling tasks are not dependent on mental rotation ability, nor is mental rotation-related problem-solving a concern when most students score high on mental rotation tests.

The importance of projection and intersection highlight that the commonly used PVRT mental rotation test is not effective when used to predict performance in domains where the relevant type of visualisation is not dependent on mental rotation. NURBS modelling is such a domain. Proficiency and expertise in NURBS modelling is less dependent on knowledge of the domain than on strong mental visualisation ability. Mental rotation is pertinent to navigating the 3D environment of a CAD program or a video game, but not to NURBS modelling. It is, however, the basis for many commonly used tests of spatial ability and consequently affect how this ability is measured.

6.2.9 Development Claims

Industry assessors agreed that the work they were shown met professional CG industry standards (p. 122). Statistical tests were sufficient to verify that there was a significant difference between polygon modelling and NURBS modelling. Interviews with students in combination with spatial visualisation tests made it possible to conclude that NURBS modelling has three important visualisation components. Each of the types of visualisation identified: projection, intersection and blend, are requirements for progressing on the NURBS project. What this shows is that knowledge of NURBS tools alone is not sufficient to succeed on the project.

Industry participants did not emphasise the importance of the software or the tools. If anything, that topic was ignored. This is consistent with King et al. (2008) who writes that 'software certification is a useful metric regarding knowledge and familiarity with common industry applications but does not address the creative nature of authentic industry problem-solving abilities' (p. 1). What these statements imply is that the NURBS project provided a means to evaluate skills of interest to industry that were different from technical knowledge of software.

The difference between PVRT results and performance in MD1 or MD2 highlight a difference between the two classes that is relevant to mental rotation. In addition, students made references to problems related to 'seeing' or 'seeing shapes' during their interviews, in learning logs and in the questionnaire. As described in Chap. 5 (pp. 104–112), thematic analysis of qualitative data from students showed three different stages of the modelling process, each of which could be described as visualisation. To better understand how they relate to each other, in the next section I will discuss aspects of the NURBS visualisation problem in the context of mental rotation and what was discovered in this study.

6.3 Visualisation

The NURBS problem was shown to be different from the polygon modelling problem in three ways. Firstly, PVRT tests correlated with polygon modelling performance on the Carton and Illusion projects, but not with the NURBS vehicle modelling task (p. 95). Because the PVRT is a test of mental rotation ability, this indicated that mental rotation was less relevant to NURBS modelling than to polygon modelling. Secondly, previous experience with polygon modelling did correlate with performance on the polygonal Carton and Illusion projects, but not with performance on the NURBS vehicle modelling project (p. 87, 94). This indicated that the usage of a common software application Maya 2012 and knowledge of its common tools was not a meaningful factor in predicting performance. Thirdly, students' subjective impression of the modelling process was that NURBS modelling required more planning and visualisation than polygonal modelling (p. 106). Some students felt that knowledge of polygon modelling interfered with their ability to execute the vehicle project because the polygon projects did not require the level of planning or visualisation required by the NURBS project.

Data from student participants who were working through the process of learning NURBS modelling revealed three specific types of visualisation that are not currently reflected in the literature of spatial visualisation, largely due to a dependence on mental rotation tests (Maeda and Yoon 2013; Samsudin et al. 2011; Vandenberg and Kuse 1978). They are described here as (1) Projection, (2) Intersection and (3) Blend (p. 114).

6.3.1 Projection

The first of these visualisation types is described in data from student interviews regarding the difficulty of finding 'good' reference, of using the reference they had and of 'seeing' the shapes contained in their reference images. When prompted to describe their comments in another way, students articulated the difficulty of taking 2D views of their car and then mentally combining them into a coherent 3D representation of the vehicle as a whole. This is similar to what happens when an architect or engineer 'projects' multiple orthographic views of an object into 3D space to create a perspective drawing (Ferguson 1992). The difference is that IGAD students were taking the equivalent of multiple perspective views and trying to extract from them the original design plans. This is the opposite of the design process engaged in by architects, engineers and industrial designers. Because of its similarity to architectural projection, the term 'projection' is used here to refer to this type of mental visualisation. At this stage of the process, students were trying to 'see' (mentally) what their vehicle looked like so that they could build it. This task involved mental rotation as the student visualised each section of the vehicle from the reference, then had to mentally adjust the orientations or positions of the individual parts to fit them into a coherent whole.

Projection is not as simple as it might sound because, as some students noted in their interviews, reference photos and drawings contain artefacts that can spoil their mental image of the vehicle. For instance, highlights or reflections in a photograph can create the appearance of non-existent structure, lens distortions would affect the shapes portrayed in photographs, important details might be cropped from the reference, or over-simplified orthographic drawings could hide important detail.

In NURBS modelling, digital artists are called upon to extract salient information about their subjects using a variety of reference types. Appearance alone, as students discovered from working with photographs and drawings, is not enough. They need to understand their subject in a different way: not what it looks like to a camera, but the relationship between blended shapes and its structure that creates its outward appearance. This is akin to Anderson and Leinhardt's (2002) example of a cartographer drilling between two points on a globe, then transforming the 'line' created on the surface by peeling it off and flattening it out to reveal a curve (see Fig. 2.2, p. 28). A straight line drawn on a globe does not remain straight, but becomes a 3D curve because it is on a globe. In this study, data showed that students learned that 2D reference of 3D structure similarly disguises information necessary to make the transformation from 2D reference to 3D space.

The process of learning to interrogate reference to create a consistent vision of the object students wanted to make was described by students as learning to 'see shapes', but it was also mentioned in the context of observation skills. The students felt that learning to project, or create, a mental visualisation of their vehicle improved their observation skills because it helped them discriminate between relevant and irrelevant visual information contained in their reference (p. 108). This aspect of projection visualisation might utilise mental rotation, but more importantly involves the investigation of conflicting images to establish the validity of perceived structure, by comparing and cross-referencing the images with each other.

6.3.2 Intersection

The findings chapters describe how most students preferred to try and build shapes directly by outlining shape boundaries and then filling them in (p. 101). This is how models are made with polygons, but it does not work with NURBS because it prevents smooth alignment of structural features. Students referred to the problem as 'polygon thinking' and said it got in their way at first. This visualisation problem was encountered by students after the projection problem, usually in Weeks 4 and 5, when they started building the body of their vehicles. If they intersected surfaces instead, using the 'intersection' workflow, key boundaries to define surface structure could be found by intersecting larger precursor shapes (p. 109). For this method to be effective, students had to visualise the precursor shapes first. If the shapes were wrong, the intersection boundary would also be wrong.

An analysis of student interview data showed that learning to 'see' precursor shapes, plan which shapes need to be cut, identify which shapes should be used as cutting tools and understand the order in which the cuts must be made are all important elements of the visualisation process. Because the solutions to this type of visualisation problem are associated with the intersection tool set in Maya 2012, it is called 'intersection visualisation' here.

For some, like Koen, Roel and Paula, learning to 'see' intersections was a 'eureka moment', when they felt like they suddenly understood 'how NURBS work'. In Koen's case, he claimed that it led directly to developing proficiency as a NURBS modeller (p. 138). His assertion is supported by similar statements from other students, his weekly progress and grades given by industry participants, all of whom agreed that his vehicle met a good professional standard (p. 139).

Student learning logs and student interview data show that students started talking about NURBS vision, or reflexive shape analysis, around the time they started dealing with the intersection problem or just after they had solved it (p. 112). After students began reflexively analysing the shapes of manufactured objects in their environment and were consciously aware this was happening, it became reasonable to conclude that the NURBS modelling problem is novel (because the experience of NURBS vision was novel) and that visualisation skill is required, regardless of mental rotation test results that do not correlate with NURBS performance.

Of the three visualisation types, intersection visualisation received the most attention from students. The focus on intersection may have been not only because achieving a likeness is dependent on it, but also that it forced students to visualise shapes that did not exist in their reference. This was only possible if students had already worked out a good projection of the target as represented in the tape model, just as blend visualisation relies on shapes created by the intersection process. Each of these forms of visualisation is a stage that leads from one to the next.

6.3.3 Blend

The last stage of visualisation pertinent to NURBS modelling identified by this study is 'blending'. Blending is the process by which non-adjacent patches are blended together with the use of a 'bridge', or 'blend', patch. Blending was described by some students as a eureka moment that meaningfully changed their approach to the project (p. 110). In the interview conducted with Lisette, she explained that she dealt with blend shapes in the following way: She bought a toy model of her car, covered it with tape and then drew test patch layouts on the tape. This process involved no mental rotation at all, but interaction with a static externalised visualisation of the blend problem. Although not all students commented on 'blend visualisation', those who did consistently described it as the most difficult part of the NURBS project.

The NURBS blend visualisation problem requires digital artists to determine how best to represent a specific shape using nothing but deformable four-sided patches. At this stage of the visualisation process, the shape has already been determined through the projection and intersection visualisation processes. The blend problem is to take the shape in question and convert it into an efficient layout by blending surfaces together. Students must interrogate their object to determine how many patches are optimal and where their boundaries are located. There are many equally correct solutions to the problem, just as there are many incorrect or non-optimal solutions. Data collected in student interviews indicate that discrimination among these options is largely a mental process, though at least two students (Lisette and Janet) augmented their mental visualisations with drawings.

The process of blend visualisation can be compared to topological problems presented by McLeay and Piggins (1996). In their study, illustrations of knots and 'unknots', arrangements of cord that form loops that appear to be knots, are paired as knots, unknots, or the same knots, with one rotated. Test-takers were asked whether the paired knots were indeed knots and whether they were the same knot, though rotation of the drawings and alterations to their shape made them appear to be different. When mental rotation tasks were combined with a modification to the topology of the knot being rotated, test-takers experienced significantly more difficulty than when they were asked to compare rotated knot pairs that were not altered topologically. The study found that topological changes in knot designs increased the effort required to solve the problems.

McLeay and Piggins (1996) describe the knot solution process as the ability to 'mentally unravel knots' (p. 143). This ability is distinguished from mental rotation, which is described as a strategy used by subjects for solving some of the problems, but not all. What their study showed was that a visual problem (determining whether deformed knots are topologically identical or not) has at least two visualisation-related solution strategies, rotation and unravelling, only one of which has been extensively studied: rotation. The other, mental unravelling, is described as an important but separate mental visualisation ability used to check the topological structure of knots. This was the only study found as part of this investigation that discussed topology in the context of spatial visualisation.

6.3.4 Deformation and Problem Difficulty

In NURBS modelling, digital artists must be sensitive to topology, but unlike the participants in McLeay and Piggins' (1996) study, they are designing the structure from scratch rather than interpreting an existing design. This may not be obvious to the general reader because digital artists and the students in this study start with a pre-designed vehicle. However, the 'design' is not the shape of the vehicle. The design of the 3D NURBS model is the topology that shows how the pieces fit together to form the final shape of the vehicle, just as the 'design' of a jigsaw puzzle is the way the pieces fit together, the shape of the pieces and the number of pieces, not the image on the puzzle. The topology of the design is hidden in the original design documents used to manufacture the vehicle. Those documents are not available to students. Without this information, the vehicle becomes the equivalent of a vehicle-shaped whiteboard, upon which students must draw a sensible pattern of four-sided patches to arrive at an efficient topology. The fact that the topology can vary without changing the underlying shape is an example of how patch boundaries and the patch layout they are a part of are deformable.

This is like the problem presented by the Monster Change and Monster Move problems, where underlying structure is effectively hidden or distorted by its outward character as presented in the narrative. Similarly, students faced with the problem of building a vehicle using NURBS patches must be able to visualise a working structure beneath the outward appearance available in their reference.

Deformability is a quality that distinguishes NURBS from polygons. NURBS are deformable and polygons are not (p. 49). This means that moving any point on a NURBS surface will affect the entire object, causing the entire shape to change form, while moving a point on a polygonal object will affect only that point. This is similar to the difference between cloth and a sculpture of cloth made of marble. They may look the same, but one is flexible and the other isn't. Deformability in NURBS is controlled by manipulation of the topology, or patch layout. The ability to visualise deformable structure is described as separate from mental rotation by

McLeay and Piggins (1996). This is also relevant to problem difficulty, as reflected in the Tower of Hanoi isomorph problems discussed in the literature review (Kotovsky et al. 1985), where the 'Monster Change' problem is conceptually most similar to the blend visualisation problem in NURBS modelling.

The Monster Change problem asks test-takers to mentally solve a puzzle where spheres of different sizes must be scaled according to a set of rules, so that each monster is holding a sphere of the right size. The Monster Move problem asks test-takers to move several differently sized spheres according to rules, so that each monster is holding a sphere that matches their own size (Sect. 8.5, p. 216). The problems are isomorphic, they have the same number of steps, rules and variables, but the change problem is almost twice as difficult due to the mental representation of the problem (Kotovsky et al. 1985). The authors argue that this is a factor because moving the spheres is a familiar action, but scaling them mentally is unfamiliar (inconsistent with real-world knowledge) and requires greater effort to visualise. They conclude not only that the size of a problem space does not fully represent the complexity of a problem, but that modifications to the instructions affect the way the problem is visualised and that visualisation affects problem difficulty (p. 27).

In the McLeay and Piggins' (1996) knot problems, the deformability of the knots effectively disguises the similar knot topologies between some of the knots. The Monster Change problem requires test-takers to visualise changes to the shapes of 'globes' described in the problem and then to manipulate this property of the globes to solve the problem. In both of these examples, deformation is a common characteristic, and this is shared with NURBS modelling in two ways. Firstly, NURBS patches are highly deformable. The shape of a patch can be changed almost infinitely without changing its number of sides or their relationship to each other. Secondly, without changing the shape of the target object, the object may be divided into any number of topological layouts (Fig. 6.1). This is why Lisette drew potential layout solutions directly onto the surface of a model toy car, tested them and then changed the drawing on the car as necessary until she had a valid layout. This visualisation problem proved to be significant for students.

The combination of deformability and topological options makes the NURBS blend visualisation problem particularly complex. The trait shared by the knot problem (McLeay and Piggins 1996), chess movement visualisation (Chabris and Hearst 2003), the Monster Change problem (Kotovsky et al. 1985), and aspects of visualisation in NURBS modelling is that the subject of the visualisation does not have a constant shape or topological configuration. This differs from other types of spatial visualisation such as orientation and rotation, where the shape of the object visualised is constant and one's viewpoint relative to the subject is altered (McGee 1979) or the viewpoint is stable and the object is rotated to change the view (Vandenberg and Kuse 1978).

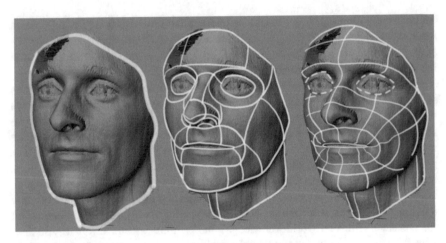

Fig. 6.1 Base shape and two alternate topologies for the same shape

6.3.5 NURBS Visualisation Types Compared

Three distinct types of visualisation were revealed and defined during this study: projection, intersection and blending. Only one of these requires mental rotation, projection, and it is the only one of these three visualisation types that is also found in polygon modelling. Any digital artist would have to go through exactly the same projection visualisation process to build a vehicle in polygons or NURBS. However, there is no equivalent need for intersection or blend visualisation in polygon modelling. In addition, although projection visualisation is utilised in polygon modelling tasks to extract information from reference to generate a likeness, the way it is done in NURBS modelling is meaningfully different. Students must work with curves when using NURBS, but curves do not behave the same as polygons, making the task more complex. With the linear shapes in the Illusion and Carton polygon projects, where all of the shapes are deliberately designed to be easily built, the shapes can be 'traced' by snapping to endpoints. This is not possible with curves, because the shape deforms considerably between endpoints and must be carefully controlled (Fig. 6.2). This raises the possibility that a polygon vehicle modelling project would entail exactly the same level of difficulty at the projection stage as in the NURBS vehicle project.

Just as the polygon project could be made more challenging, not all NURBS modelling tasks require projection, intersection and blend visualisation skills. There are simple types of objects that can be modelled without them. As Maikel said of his undercarriage and wheels (p. 100), they were easily made because the shapes were simple and his tools functioned as expected. This was because the shapes did not deform in multiple axes, but were constant. For example, a line can be made into a cylinder by rotating it in a circle around a pivot, but the hood of a car cannot be described by a constant transformation because the shape deforms in all three axes (Fig. 6.3). Therefore, the threshold concepts described by students are not general to

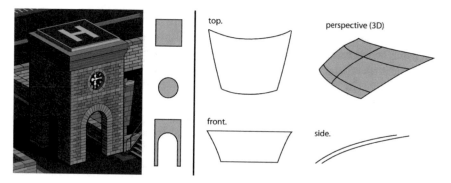

Fig. 6.2 Comparison complexity of polygon shapes (L) and NURBS shapes (R)

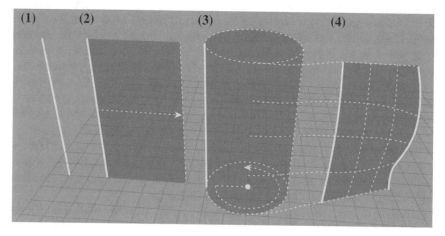

Fig. 6.3 Shape complexity (1) single axis line, (2) single axis plane, (3) single pivot cylinder, (4) multi-axis plane

all NURBS modelling, but specific to a type of problem faced by artists who must represent complex curvature in NURBS, the type found in the body of the vehicles made by students for the NURBS project. Until spatial visualisation abilities relevant to building complex curved surfaces were acquired, those skills represented barriers to further progress as NURBS modellers. Here, there is a real difference between polygon and NURBS modelling that transcends the type of target shape for the model, because NURBS requires intersection and blend visualisation for complex curvature but polygonal modelling does not.

When Lisette used a marker to draw experimental patch layouts on a toy model of her vehicle, she was creating an externalised visualisation of a problem she found too difficult to solve otherwise. Janet likewise made drawings and a separate version of her model to test patch layouts. Their test layouts were not dependent on the orientation of the vehicle to their eyes, or mind's eye, and could thus be made without rotating the object. What was useful was visualising alternate networks of boundaries between patches. However, this step was most useful after intersection visualisation was acquired. Students who tried to build the patch layout directly would fail because the patch layout was dependent on first having a true representation of the shape of the vehicle, and that required intersection visualisation. These types of visualisation are unlike what is found in mental rotation tests, but there are other types of spatial visualisation tests.

There are 392 spatial tests grouped into 13 categories reprinted in Eliot and Smith's (1983) comprehensive international directory of such tests. Although this directory is decades-old, the type of tests it contains remains in use today. Of the tests represented in the directory, six have some similarities to projection and blend visualisation, but all have pronounced differences as well.

The 'filling up gaps' test (number 061), form completion test (number 072), and intersections test (number 235) have some characteristics in common with intersection visualisation, but none involve rotation and all can be solved without reference to 3D space, unlike NURBS intersection. In addition, the intersection test provides what would be the answer to a NURBS problem within the question by showing precursor shapes. The shape analysis test (number 068) and figure construction test (number 082) are superficially similar to blend visualisation but are significantly different because blends only represent a problem for NURBS artists when three or more patches are involved, yet only two shapes are involved in the shape analysis test, and the figure construction test ignores the order of connection, tangency and the figure is planar, meaning there is no multi-axis curvature to deal with. 3D shape storage (number 225) is similar to mental rotation because it involves generating alternate arrangements of 3D objects in the same space, but it is much simpler than the PVRT because the shapes are all rectangular prisms.

Of all the tests included in the Eliot and Smith (1983) directory, none resemble the quality of working with CAD tools as well as the PVRT because the PVRT replicates the effect of rotating a virtual 'camera' to view multiple angles of an object. A review of these tests shows that none test for the kind of blend or intersection visualisation practised by IGAD students on the NURBS project.

The need to visualise intersection and blends forces artists to think ahead and plan for their results. This process is akin to design, where designers must first visualise the object they want to build, create an external visualisation of it, usually in the form of a drawing, and then plan out how the object will be made. This results in iterations of the design and then a final product. Although IGAD students were not tasked with designing a brand-new vehicle, they were tasked with interpreting an existing vehicle design from a flat 2D representation.

According to students' descriptions, this resulted in a workflow that resembled the design process. In this case, they were designing the topology of the vehicle.

According to Cross (1990), a designer's job is to create a description of the product to be made. The projection stage of the visualisation process in NURBS modelling could be described as finding the target shape, then intersection allows the definition of boundaries and tangents and blend visualisation is the final definition of the finished shape. Together, these three visualisation skills allow an artist to define an object using NURBS, a technology that allows an object to be manufactured based on the specifications in the NURBS file. In this way, the work of a NURBS modeller is like that of a designer. Developing the ability to perform that work requires a transition in skill, and that requires the acquisition of the spatial visualisation abilities described in this chapter. Are those skills a kind of threshold concept?

6.4 Threshold Concepts

6.4.1 Identification of Threshold Concepts

One way to identify threshold concepts may be inferred from Meyer and Land's (2003) statement regarding counter-intuitive knowledge, or 'troublesome knowledge'. They write that 'it increasingly appears that a threshold concept may on its own constitute, or in its application lead to, such troublesome knowledge' (p. 2). With this in mind, looking for troublesome knowledge can also lead to the discovery of threshold concepts. With IGAD students, troublesome knowledge was easily identified when students balked at their teacher's advice because it was counter-intuitive to them and as a result they failed to make progress (p. 109). Students who persevered were rewarded with success, but only after considerable frustration because the problem was not 'just the tools' as Koen put it (see Sect. 5.6.1), but a type of visualisation that was new to them.

A concern when identifying threshold concepts is that they could be mistaken for core concepts or significant states in the learning process. A core concept can allow progress in a domain, but a threshold concept leads to a qualitative change in the way a subject is viewed (Meyer and Land 2003). A significant state, such as a position in a game of chess, is a state where significant change can occur, such as a loss or victory. However, it does not necessarily follow that significant states are key nodes or threshold concepts. This is because it may be that a learning breakthrough is not required to understand its significance. In the same way, a position that is not significant can be a key node if it represents an opportunity to qualitatively change one's understanding of the game (Epstein 1995).

Student participants in this study helped identify three forms of spatial visualisation that they felt were important to their progress. However, only two of these, intersection and blend, caused a qualitative change in the way they approached the project. Projection visualisation could be described as a core concept because it was necessary to progress, but not a threshold concept because it did not lead to a qualitative change to the way the project was viewed by the student.

In addition to the projection, intersection and blend forms of visualisation, student and industry participants mentioned observation skills frequently as a subject of great importance to the quality of their work. This was not considered a threshold concept because it was more closely related to learning the level of finish needed for an object to be a good likeness than to changing the students' fundamental understanding of the project. If looked at as a scale where 98% accuracy was the threshold of proficiency, and the student had to work up from 30, 50% and so on, they understood from the beginning that they were learning to make measurements progressively more accurate. They may have found it difficult to meet the criteria of a high level of accuracy, but they understood the goal and were generally able to detect whether they had achieved it or not.

In contrast, when building the model itself, students could not complete the model without understanding intersection visualisation. This is mentioned to illustrate that a threshold concept like intersection visualisation can lie within a broad area, such as spatial visualisation (Boustedt et al. 2007). In this case, intersection and blend have emerged as the most likely threshold concepts on the NURBS project. One indicator that these are legitimate threshold concepts, unlike observation, which is development along a scale, is the suddenness of first overcoming the concept and then directly using it on their project. The suddenness of transformation, though not always present, is characteristic of threshold concepts (Meyer and Land 2003). Another indicator is the irreversible nature of the transformation (Meyer and Land 2003), as demonstrated by the 'NURBS vision' (p.112) developed by some students who found that once they'd learned intersection, they reflexively analysed the shapes around them. This also demonstrated that the effect was transformative, another trait of threshold concepts.

6.4.2   Visualisation as a Threshold Concept

All IGAD students initially found the NURBS project to be very difficult (p. 109). Some, like Lisette and Janet, became more comfortable working in NURBS after a few weeks, but other students, like Wietse and Sebastian, never became comfortable. All students, however, were at a loss for solutions when they started the project. This was because they had no knowledge of the workflow, and the knowledge they did have worked against their efforts to find solutions to shape problems presented by the project. Because of this, their initial efforts could be characterised as impasse-driven problem-solving.

Impasse-driven problem-solving occurs when an individual does not understand the rules or concepts necessary to solve a problem. To find a solution in the absence of understanding, a person engaged in this type of problem-solving will explore the problem space extensively, sometimes with a strategy, sometimes not, in the hope of finding something that works. This method is fraught with error, and suffers from the weakness of generally lacking direction (Anderson and Leinhardt 2002).

As observed among IGAD students in this study, efforts to solve the NURBS shape problems through trial and error only worked when combined with spatial visualisation-related threshold concepts (p. 99). Overcoming the threshold concepts was accomplished in a variety of circumstances, but could not be described as undi-rected, because students were repeatedly informed of the merits of the recommended workflow. As Martin said, many other students did not believe this advice because it was counter-intuitive to them. Because it was counter-intuitive, students failed to identify the problem type.

According to Anderson and Leinhardt (2002 p. 286) 'experts possess schemas built up over years of training in their discipline that allow them to quickly recognize the problem type and to employ sophisticated problem-solving strategies...'. In the case of NURBS modelling, visualisation ability is required to 'recognise the problem type', after which IGAD students found that 'years of training' were not required to develop practical solutions to the NURBS problem. Whether their solutions were 'sophisticated' is debatable, but some were proficient according to industry assessors, and that is the measure important to students seeking to graduate with marketable skills.

Students who did not overcome the threshold concept of intersection visualisation did not become proficient, and none, based on their interview responses and weekly hand-ins, recognised the nature of the problem they faced. Several of these students described it as a matter of their tools not functioning correctly or 'as expected' without noticing that the problem was the way they visualised a solution, not the tools (p. 130). This is just one example of how a threshold concept can prevent the development of proficiency or expertise, because overcoming the threshold concept in this case allows the practitioner to understand the problem. Without that understanding, a practical solution cannot reasonably be expected.

An example of the importance of visualisation to expertise (and thus to proficiency) is provided by Anderson and Leinhardt (2002) who make it clear that certain geography-related problems, such as the planning of airline routes, cannot be done without the ability to make an internal cognitive representation of a map. Without this ability, they would have no way of understanding the relationship of the map, a projection and the shape a path would follow on the object represented by the projection (see pp. 28–29). And yet, 'many college students failed to understand even the simplest cases of shadow projections' (Anderson and Leinhardt 2002, p. 285).

The ability to visualize how a map and the terrain it represents are related could be described as a 'threshold capability', meaning 'those capabilities that are in fact threshold to professional learning in a defined area of knowledge' (Baillie et al. 2013 p. 236), but as we will see in the next section, threshold capabilities can meet all of the requirements of threshold concepts. For the purposes of this study they fulfil the same function and will be treated as the same, on the basis that the difference between the two: knowledge vs. ability, is a domain-specific difference in the way expertise is assessed.

The discussion in this chapter has provided several explanations for the PVRT results when compared to polygon and NURBS project performance. Of the possibilities presented, the strongest is that NURBS modelling is meaningfully different from polygon modelling because it requires a kind of design-related visualisation skill, or skills, each of which is not well described in the literature of spatial visualisation. These visualisation skills: projection, intersection and blending, were crucial to the development of proficiency as NURBS modellers. Students were not dependent on precursor experience in polygon modelling or drawing to develop these visualisation skills, nor was knowledge of the NURBS toolset a significant factor.

In Chap. 7, the implication of these findings to pedagogical practice and curriculum design are discussed, followed by suggestions for future research, limitations of this study, and concluding remarks.

References

Alexander PA (2003) The development of expertise: the journey from acclimation to proficiency. Educ Res 32(8):10–14

Anderson KC, Leinhardt G (2002) Maps as representations: expert novice comparison of projection understanding. Cogn Instr 20(3):283–321

Atman CJ, Adams RS, Cardella ME, Turns J, Mosborg S, Saleem J (2007) Engineering design processes: A comparison of students and expert practitioners. J Eng Educ 96(4):359–379. https://doi.org/10.1002/j.2168-9830.2007.tb00945.x

Baillie C, Bowden JA, Meyer JHF (2013) Threshold capabilities: threshold concepts and knowledge capability linked through variation theory. High Educ 65(2):227–246. https://doi.org/10.1007/s10734-012-9540-5

Bodner GM, Guay RB (1997) The purdue visualization of rotations test. Chem Educ 2(4):1–14

Boustedt J, Eckerdal A, McCartney R, Mostrom JE, Ratcliffe M, Sanders K, Zander C (2007) Threshold concepts in computer science: do they exist and are they useful? Paper presented at the SIGCSE'07. Covington, Kentucky

Chabris CF, Hearst ES (2003) Visualization, pattern recognition, and forward search: effects of playing speed and sight of the position on grandmaster chess errors. Cognitive Science 27(4):637–648. https://doi.org/10.1016/S0364-0213(03)00032-6

Cross N (1990) The nature and nurture of design ability. Des Stud 11(3):127–140. https://doi.org/10.1016/0142-694X(90)90002-T

Eliot J, Smith IM (1983) An International directory of spatial Tests. The NFER-Nelson Publishing Company Ltd, Windsor, Berks UK

Epstein SL (1995) Learning in the right places. J Learn Sci 4(3):281–319

Ericsson KA (1993) The role of deliberate practice in the acquisition of expert performance. Psychol Rev 100(3):363–406

Ericsson KA (2014) Why expert performance is special and cannot be extrapolated from studies of performance in the general population: a response to criticisms. Intelligence 45(1):81–103. https://doi.org/10.1016/j.intell.2013.12.001

Ferguson ES (1992) Engineering and the mind's eye. MIT Press, Cambridge

Gamble J (2001) Modelling the invisible: the pedagogy of craft apprenticeship. Studies in continuing education 23(2):185–200

Hegarty M, Keehner M, Khooshabeh P, Montello DR (2009) How spatial abilities enhance, and are enhanced by, dental education. Learn Individ Differ 19(1):61–70

Henderson K (1999) On line and on paper. MIT Press, Cambridge

Keehner MM, Tendick F, Meng MV, Anwar HP, Hegarty M, Stoller ML, Quan-Yang D (2004) Spatial ability, experience, and skill in laparoscopic surgery. Am J Surg 188(1):71–75

King R, Weiss B, Buyyala P, Sehgal M (2008) Bridging the gap between education and professional production. Paper presented at the ACM SIGGRAPH ASIA 2008 educators programme, Singapore

Kotovsky K, Hayes JR, Simon HA (1985) Why are some problems hard? Evidence from Tower of Hanoi. Cogn Psychol 17(2):248–294

Kurtulus A, Uygan C (2010) The effects of Google Sketchup based geometry activities and projects on spatial visualization ability of student mathematics teachers. Procedia Soc Behav Sci 9:384–389. https://doi.org/10.1016/j.sbspro.2010.12.169

Livingstone I, Hope A. (2011) Next generation transforming the UK into the world's leading talent hub for the video games and visual effects industries. Retrieved from http://www.nesta.org.uk/sites/default/files/next_gen.pdf

Maeda Y, Yoon SY (2013) A meta-analysis on gender differences in mental rotation ability measured by the purdue spatial visualization tests: visualization of rotations (PSVT: R). Educ Psychol Rev 25(1):69–94

McGee M (1979) Human spatial abilities: psychometric studies and environmental, hormonal, and neurological influences. Psychol Bull 86(5):889–918

McLeay H, Piggins D (1996) The mental manipulation of 2-D representations of knots as deformable structures. Educ Studies Math 30(4):399–414

Meyer Jan H F, Land R (2003) Threshold concepts and troublesome knowledge: linkages to ways of thinking and practising within the disciplines. In: Rust C (ed) Improving student learning—ten years on. Oxford, Oxford

Osmond J, Bull K, Tovey M (2009) Threshold concepts and the transport and product design curriculum: reports of research in progress. Art Design Commun Higher Educ 8(2):169–175

Pribyl JR, Bodner GM (1987) Spatial ability and its role in organic chemistry: A study of four organic courses. J Res Sci Teach 24(3):229–240

Samsudin KR, Hanif Ahmad, Samad Abd (2011) Training in mental rotation and spatial visualization and its impact on orthographic drawing performance. Educ Technol Soc 14(1):8

Schön DA (1992) The theory of inquiry: Dewey's legacy to education. Curriculum Inquiry 22(2):119–139. https://doi.org/10.2307/1180029

Simonton DK (2014) Thomas Edison's creative career: the multilayered trajectory of trials, errors, failures, and triumphs. Psychol Aesthetics Creativity Arts 9(1):2–24

Sternberg RJ (1998) Abilities are forms of developing expertise. Educational researcher 27(3):11–20

Sternberg RJ, Forsythe GB, Hedlund J, Horvath JA, Wagner RK, Williams WM, Gigorenko EL (2000) Practical intelligence in everyday life. Cambridge University Press, Cambridge, UK

Terlicki MS, Newcombe NS (2005) How important is the digital divide? The relation of computer and videogame usage to gender differences in mental rotation ability. Sex Roles 53(5):433–441

Vandenberg SG, Kuse AR (1978) Mental rotations, a group test of three-dimensional spatial visualization. Percept Mot Skills 47(2):599–604

Chapter 7
Conclusion

7.1 Overview

Findings from this research point to the importance of spatial visualisation as a threshold concept for digital art students. The types of spatial visualisation found to be most important were different from mental rotation, the type most commonly tested for in paper-and-pencil spatial visualisation tests. These two findings are the basis for recommendations made in this chapter to (1) create new types of spatial visualisation tests and (2) add spatial visualisation training to curricula for digital artists. If successful, new tests will be able to measure spatial visualisation abilities that are relevant to NURBS modelling. Spatial visualisation classes that have been de-coupled from NURBS modelling can increase the likelihood that students will develop the threshold concepts required for proficiency as digital artists.

7.2 Digital Art Education and This Research

This research began as a way to better understand how students develop proficiency as digital artists. Proficiency is important to members of the CG industry, who are dissatisfied with the quality of graduates who apply for jobs (Livingstone and Hope 2011), to the schools that educate digital artists for industry and to the students themselves, who expect to be qualified to work in industry after graduation. The IGAD programme at the NHTV university of applied arts in Breda, the Netherlands, has a good track record of producing graduates who are qualified to work in industry, but at the cost of high numbers of students who do not advance beyond the first or second year. At IGAD, the problem is how to improve the graduation rate without compromising the established quality standards.

Industry-suggested remedies for the problems found in digital art education centre on curriculum design changes, such as separating animation from other courses as an

© Springer Nature Switzerland AG 2018
A. Paquette, *Spatial Visualization and Professional Competence*,
https://doi.org/10.1007/978-3-319-91289-9_7

independent subject (McCracken 2006), incorporating more visual art classes while dropping courses without a direct connection to visual art (Ip 2012), emphasizing science, technology, engineering and mathematics (STEM) courses (Livingstone and Hope 2011) and putting emphasis on visual design principles over the use of visual design software (IGDA 2008).

To better understand the problems faced by IGAD students, a single course with a reputation among students for its difficulty was observed as students developed proficiency. The class is called MD2, and it teaches students how to make 3D models using NURBS surfaces, a type of geometry that is notoriously difficult to control (Gao et al. 2006). This was chosen as a 'representative task' (Ericsson 2006) of a complex digital art specialty and of proficiency development in a class known to produce proficiency. In the NURBS modelling class, students were required to construct a NURBS-based model of an automobile, with a focus on the body of the vehicle. The NURBS modelling class fulfils three of the industry recommendations: it is (1) a visual arts class that (2) emphasises engineering and (3) visual design principles.

7.3 Research Questions and Answers

7.3.1 Methodology Summary

The principal research question developed for this study was:

1. What are the principal contributing factors to crossing the skill threshold from novice to proficient performance among digital art students?

To help answer the principal question, the following three sub-questions were developed:

2. What criteria are used to determine student performance levels?
3. What is the relationship between spatial ability or spatial visualisation and development of proficiency among digital art students?
4. How does the NURBS problem differ from the polygon problem (p. 45)?

These questions helped shape a methodology that investigated the development of proficiency among digital art students attending IGAD. To do this, I used a mixed methods exploratory design. Students were given spatial visualisation tests, observed as they progressed in class, copies of their work were saved every week to show progress, learning logs were kept by students, they took a questionnaire and were interviewed at the conclusion of the project. Student work was then evaluated by industry participants, who determined whether it met industry standards for proficiency. Employed graduates of the IGAD programme were interviewed regarding their transition from academic to industry-related work. Archival data provided information on prior experience and performance. In combination, this data allowed triangulation of archival quantitative performance data against qualitative data relevant to the learning experience of current IGAD students. Quantitative data was analysed with correlation and analysis of variance (ANOVA) tests. Qualitative data was analysed with case study methods.

There were 20 student participants, 5 industry participants and 5 employed graduate participants. The observation period lasted nine weeks. Archival data from previous years at IGAD were used for quantitative comparisons that involved records from as many as 625 students.

Data collected for this research provide some support for two of the suggestions provided by industry. The first is to emphasize visual art courses by dropping classes that are not directly linked to visual art, such as 'games and society' or 'audio design' (Ip 2012). The reason is that, as shown in this study, visual art students are faced with cognitively challenging visual arts-related concepts that must be overcome for proficiency to develop. Subjects that would take time away from that effort and are not directly relevant to their specialty are of little to no utility if graduates cannot enter the industry due to lack of visual art skills.

The second recommendation from industry that the present research supports is an emphasis on visual design principles over software training. IGAD students were able to use NURBS modelling tools without difficulty during classroom exercises but found it extremely difficult to transition from the examples worked through in class to applying those tools to their own shape problems at home. This showed that tool knowledge alone was not sufficient to deal with the problems students faced on the NURBS project.

The fact that graduates attempt to enter industry without the requisite skills, and that the schools they attended did not focus on visual art classes is clear from Ip's (2012) study of 242 game development programmes in the UK. The challenges faced by visual art students enrolled in IGAD's game development programme are an indication of the kind of challenges faced by students in this domain. This study showed that the challenges are unlikely to be solved through rote learning of software tools because the development of technical proficiency in digital art requires intensive creative problem-solving effort on the type of problems faced by working professionals.

7.3.2 Answers to Research Questions

In response to the research questions, this study has found that:

1. The principal contributing factors to crossing the skill threshold to proficiency in NURBS modelling are:

    a. Overcoming projection, intersection and blend visualisation
    b. A project that contains appropriate problems to solve
    c. Sensitivity to likeness errors.

2. Criteria used by industry assessors to evaluate student projects were: likeness and craft, with an emphasis on likeness, also described as observation skills.

3. The relationship between spatial visualisation and the development of proficiency is that the lack of certain spatial visualisation skills became a threshold obstacle for students that prevented further progress.
4. The NURBS problem differed from the polygon problem in that it was not dependent on mental rotation, but was dependent on two other forms of visualisation identified within this study: intersection and blend, that were not required for polygon modelling tasks. This made the NURBS problem considerably more complex than the polygon problem. This is why the NURBS problem was more difficult for students and a better project for the development of complex spatial visualisation skills.

In Chaps. 4 (p. 81) and 5 (p. 97), I reported findings that showed how data collected from students, industry professionals and employed graduates support these answers. The findings are the basis for five claims that have emerged from the data.

7.3.3   Five Claims Based on Data

Data from interviews with student participants, as well as data collected from their weekly learning logs, have given rise to the following claims:

(1) Learning to model a vehicle using NURBS geometry requires tool knowledge, but the primary difficulty of the project was unrelated to tools.
(2) Development of proficiency is dependent on acquiring between two and three forms of spatial visualisation ability: projection, intersection and blend.
(3) Development of these three spatial visualisation abilities, identified as tacit skills, requires that students have time and opportunity to practise iterated design strategies on their own rather than in a supervised environment, in addition to access to expertise in the form of feedback.
(4) Intersection and blend visualisation are threshold concepts or abilities.
(5) Mental rotation tests are not a reliable measure of the types of spatial visualisation identified in this study.

This next section discusses these claims, the research they are based on and how they contribute to the literature of expertise theory, proficiency, visualisation, transfer and threshold concepts.

7.4   Contributions to Knowledge

In this section, my original contributions to knowledge are described. What this section will show is that (1) proficiency among digital artists is partly dependent on threshold concepts, (2) that some of those concepts are related to spatial visualisation, (3) that spatial visualisation can be de-coupled from NURBS modelling, and

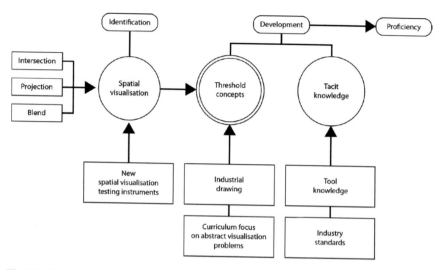

Fig. 7.1 Research implications for curriculum design

that (4) mental rotation tests are not adequate for measuring spatial visualisation as it relates to the NURBS problem. The outcome is a framework of learning that envisions spatial visualisation as a crucial element to the development of proficiency among digital artists (Fig. 7.1). To develop this critical skill as a threshold concept, new course material can be introduced that deals with it directly. In combination with instruction and tool knowledge developed in classes, proficiency should be the result. To measure the types of spatial visualisation identified in this study, new instruments will have to be designed.

7.4.1 Three Types of Visualisation

The three types of visualisation referred to earlier in this chapter are defined as:

(1) Projection visualisation, which allows two dimensional curves viewed from different angles to be combined into a coherent three-dimensional representation of a solid object (p. 147).
(2) Intersection visualisation, which requires the visualisation of deformed intersecting surfaces to plan how certain NURBS shapes are built (p. 114).
(3) Blend visualisation, which requires a mental visualisation of deformed NURBS patches to plan how different parts of a design are connected to form a seamless final shape (p. 116).

7.4.2   Generalisability of Visualisation

The visualisation types identified here: projection, intersection and blend, are non-software skills essential to success in NURBS modelling. This finding has a place in the literature of proficiency development as a potential means of enhancing the education of digital artists by encouraging educators to help students develop their visualisation skills. It also belongs in the general literature of proficiency and expertise development by identifying a domain where proficiency is dependent on a threshold concept.

7.4.3   Benefits of NURBS Modelling Project

There is some evidence from interviews that the way students made drawings in drawing classes was meaningfully changed due to the NURBS project. Lisette said that she was now drawing 'through' objects, where the hidden side of an object is drawn as if made from a transparent material, something she had not done before. Janet said that she had noticed just after the conclusion of the MD2 class that her drawings had changed for the better, though she had not been practising since before the NURBS project. Bart found that he had started drawing using the same techniques he had learned in the MD2 class. While these and other students found that the NURBS class had influenced their drawings, Maike pointed out that her drawings had also influenced her NURBS project. The impression left by these students' explanation of their learning journey is that the observation and visualisation skills developed on the NURBS project had a noticeable effect on drawing methods and on their skill level in drawing.

Interview data from both student and industry participants show that both believed that observation and visualisation skills are transferrable to domains other than NURBS modelling. This was reflected in numerous statements by student participants that their ability to 'see shapes', their projection, intersection and blend visualisation skills, improved due to the NURBS project.

The ability to see or understand a subject in a different way would inevitably influence and improve the results of any endeavour where an accurate visualisation of an object is required, or even when a fantasy object must be created that is grounded in reality. This was supported by employed graduates Fidde and Maarten, who described the importance of achieving a high-quality likeness and of finding or producing the reference needed to accomplish that goal. These findings are relevant to the literature of transfer in learning, by supporting theories that allow for transfer, such as Bransford and Schwartz (1999), who describes transfer as 'preparation for future learning', or Rosalie and Müller (2013), who found transfer between athletic disciplines.

Intersection and blend visualisation may be essential to NURBS modellers, but data collected for this study show that there are other benefits derived from the NURBS modelling project. These are: more efficient and accurate approach to drawing (p. 119), enhanced observation skills (p. 118) and awareness of the importance of securing good reference (p. 104). In addition, industry participants Bas and Stefano articulated how NURBS knowledge contributes to general 3D visualisation skills and conditions artists to work within constraints. Bas went on to say that artists who have NURBS skills adapt to new technology more easily (p. 126).

7.4.4 Prior Experience Less Important Than Spatial Visualisation

Some IGAD students had up to four years' prior experience in polygon modelling, yet this did not aid their efforts in NURBS modelling. Two students with strong drawing ability prior to IGAD performed at the top of the class in NURBS modelling, but so did students with no prior experience in drawing or modelling. Overall, strong performance could not be convincingly linked to prior experience or even experience within the nine weeks during which this study took place. Instead, proficiency hinged on overcoming a threshold concept: intersection or blend visualisation, after which tool knowledge became operational. After this, students were able to complete the project.

This result is reminiscent of descriptions of Galileo's work and reputation by Simonton (2012), who noted that his ability as an astronomer was a measure of the accuracy of his observations rather than the amount of time he had studied astronomy. In the case of IGAD students, their ability to see the problem mentally in the form of a visualisation was more crucial than any amount of tool knowledge, which they could not use correctly until they had this insight. This finding contributes to knowledge of the development of expertise and proficiency, both of which focus on experience and knowledge rather than tacit skills, such as spatial visualisation (Alexander 2003; Ericsson 2014).

The implication of these findings is that curriculum for undergraduate digital art students would better serve the students and industry if it emphasised observation and visualisation skills over tool knowledge, at least until students had developed sufficient observation and visualisation skills to make good use of tool knowledge.

7.4.5 Individual Differences

Experience, according to this research, may be useful to the development of expertise, but it does not appear to be all that is required. This is supported by Sternberg (1998), who agrees that practice may be necessary, but that it is not sufficient for expertise to develop. The cognitive ability to correctly structure experience derived from practice, according to Bradley et al. (2006) 'must also be present' (p. 77). This is why experience can be such a poor predictor of performance, as can be inferred from

Sternberg (1998): 'It seems less plausible that someone who practices composing will become a Mozart... other factors seem far more important in the development of creative expertise, in whatever field' (p. 15).

The 'other factors' referred to by Sternberg are individual differences found among learners and experts alike that undermine the deliberate practice framework developed by Ericsson et al. (Ackerman 2014b; Sternberg 1998; Wai 2014). Individual differences are not well understood, but they do exist, as Ackerman (2014a) makes clear when he points out that the subjects of expertise research tend to be highly selected for ability, rather than taken from the general population where one will find a mix of high, medium and low ability in addition to rare savants for whom practice is (apparently) unnecessary due to poorly understood cognitive differences between savants and the general population. Among expert subjects, it may be that the only clear differences among them amount to practice or experience, but in a broader sample, such as the students in this study of IGAD students, where none were proficient or expert to begin with, individual differences become more prominent. This contributes to the literature of expertise by showing how studying the development of proficiency among non-proficient participants highlights individual differences that would be hidden by methodologies that rely on pre-selected experts.

7.5 Pedagogical Implications

7.5.1 Threshold Concepts Can Streamline Education

For students enrolled in digital art programmes, it is important to develop the ability to translate their goals as artists into the medium of CG. The capability 'to draw on their learned experience to deal with new, real, previously unseen and, necessarily, more complex situations' (Baillie et al. 2013, p. 230) is important to learners, because without this ability, they are unprepared to deal with real world problems they will face after graduation. The value of threshold concepts to educators is that it presents the possibility of streamlining education for students by allowing for more efficient, concentrated learning experiences (Barradell 2013).

Earlier, when discussing impasse-driven problem-solving (p. 178) I wrote how lack of knowledge or understanding can lead a student to explore the problem space, either with or without a strategy, and that it is generally unsuccessful. The difference between a blind attempt to find the solution to a problem and a motivated, tenacious attempt to engage the problem, can be likened to the difference between the way computers and human grandmasters play chess.

Computers can beat amateur human players, but are much less successful against human grandmasters. Because humans cannot search the problem space as extensively as a computer designed to play chess, their success cannot be attributed to superior memory or search speed. Instead, the grandmaster is able to find a successful route to victory with a much smaller, more efficient search space. This indicates 'that the chess game tree, like the tic-tac-toe game tree, does not uniformly distribute the knowledge necessary for people to learn to play well across all its states' (Epstein 1995, p. 289). In the same way, proficiency for digital artists may require the acquisition of some threshold concepts that can be taught directly, rather than forcing students to search the entire problem space first, or a large portion of it, as an artificial intelligence chess program would.

7.5.1.1 Threshold Concepts as Key Nodes

According to Epstein (1995) it is possible for human players to perform better than computers by careful study of positions occurring in normal game play. These positions, or some of them, offer insight into the game and function as key nodes to understanding, much as threshold concepts do. Navigation of the full problem space is unnecessary if the pathways to victory, or the strategies that make victory possible, are known and understood by the player. A computer can only search out every path, and this can waste considerable resources. If this same idea is applied to higher education, the value of threshold concepts as key nodes is readily apparent. If identified properly and students are guided in such a way as to encounter and overcome them, the quality and efficiency of their education may be significantly improved (Epstein 1995).

7.5.1.2 Lesson and Practice is Most Efficacious

For Epstein (1995), in her study of Hoyle, an artificial intelligence software designed to learn, 'lesson and practice training proved more reliable and powerful against all the challengers than most other kinds of instruction; it was never less reliable or less powerful at the 95% confidence level' (p. 302). Based on records generated by the program during gameplay, it was found that lesson and practice, in the form of software 'advisors' that guided gameplay, Hoyle was forced to visit more key nodes during learning. Based on this, Epstein (1995) stated that 'the ideal trainer would be aware of the key nodes appropriate [to the subject]… so that the learner would encounter each key node quickly' (p. 290). This recommends that key nodes in a variety of domains are identified, and then instructional materials are designed and teachers trained to deliver material that emphasises those key nodes and any associated threshold concepts.

   In this study, students had very little preparation for NURBS modelling, amounting to an understanding of the Maya interface and basic terminology. Within weeks, some students had acquired important spatial visualisation-related threshold concepts. Some students had years of experience with polygon modelling prior to the MD2 class, some had only the experience of a nine-week polygon modelling class. Regardless, some students in both groups attained proficiency. What this shows is that the timing of acquisition of the threshold concept was not dependent on prior experience and that it could be introduced earlier, provided the threshold concept was built into the curriculum and instructors understood it well enough to provide feedback. As with the example from Epstein, curriculum designed around threshold concepts has the potential to be more efficient than broad knowledge-based instruction.

7.5.2 Spatial Visualisation Taught Separately

Reconceiving the three types of spatial visualisation as threshold concepts, and keeping in mind that spatial ability can be trained (Arici and Aslan-Tutak 2013; Okagaki and Frensch 1994; Titus and Horsman 2009), this study suggests that the three types of spatial visualisation identified here can be extracted from the NURBS project and taught separately in a less-demanding learning environment, such as in industrial sketching or clay sculpting classes. One incentive to do this is that by de-coupling spatial visualisation from NURBS modelling tasks, proficiency in visualisation can be developed more quickly and then applied later to other types of projects. This could reduce the overall difficulty of the problem, making it easier for students to acquire the necessary skill. There is some support for this approach in the literature of spatial visualisation, where numerous studies show that spatial visualisation can be trained (Arici and Aslan-Tutak 2013; Prieto and Velasco 2010; Samsudin 2011) and in some studies it is trained passively, such as by playing video games (Dorval 1986; Okagaki and Frensch 1994). It would require further research to develop appropriate tests and instructional tools for this new type of spatial visualisation training, but this research indicates that such changes to testing and instruction for digital artists are possible and would be beneficial.

7.5.3 Industry Recommendations are Open to Interpretation

In addition to problematic curriculum at UK game art programmes, industry curriculum recommendations are not perfect either. The International Game Developer Association (IGDA) created their own list of recommended courses (IGDA 2008), as did Livingstone and Hope (2011), McCracken (2006) and Ip (2012). For any of these to work, however, consideration must first be given to how the recommendations are interpreted. This is because, in addition to sometimes conflicting recommendations, like putting an emphasis on art courses versus an emphasis on math, many are not detailed enough to be actionable by professional educators. For instance, Livingstone and Hope (2011) write the following

> If you want to make computerised water believable, it needs to look and move right. Which means you need to understand: the science behind the way light behaves as it passes through water, partially reflected on the surface to give bright highlights but also passing through the surface to illuminate what lies beneath; and the computational fluid dynamics that physicists use to model how liquids move. (p. 19)

What they have written is true, but it doesn't explain how these subjects are taught or if they are a complete list of what must be taught to solve this type of problem. It could be interpreted by educators in such a way that students are given rote-learning courses on physics or it could be used as the impetus for instructional design that forces students to deal with threshold concepts related to the artists' role in producing visual effects. It may require learning something about physics or how physics can be manipulated in existing software, but either way, if the students grow to understand how to visualise end-state goals for their project, they will be better off than if they learn limited use tool-related techniques that work today, but are outmoded and non-transferrable by the time they graduate (Ip 2012).

7.5.4 Avoidance of Troublesome Curricula

An issue for educators is the tendency at some universities to avoid troublesome curriculum in their curricula. An example of this is provided by Meyer and Land (2003) who report that at one school 'where students encountered severe conceptual difficulty such areas of the curriculum were quietly dropped. In this sense the conceptual thresholds served to trim the parameters of the curriculum' (p. 6). This has already happened at IGAD starting in the 2015–2016 academic year. At that time, several classes, including MD2 and the NURBS project were dropped in a curriculum adjustment that has resulted in higher grades and graduation rates for students overall, but at the cost of removing all of the most challenging projects from the curriculum.

Based on the research conducted for this study, classes that present threshold concepts to students are potentially the most valuable courses for students to take, regardless of difficulty. An alternative to dropping classes for the purpose of improving graduation rates would be to identify the most salient threshold concepts to each discipline and then to create teaching methods that support students in their efforts to overcome those threshold concepts and thus to acquire the tacit skills required in their domain of practice without resort to unnecessarily complex projects.

7.5.5 A Model of Proficiency Development

Complex or difficult subjects sometimes derive their difficulty from threshold concepts embedded within them. This is the case with NURBS modelling, and according to Meyer and Land (2003), other subjects as well. When these subjects are removed from university curricula, as has happened at IGAD and elsewhere, the result is a learning framework that shifts responsibility for threshold concepts to industry (Fig. 7.2). When that happens, students acquire rote knowledge at university, and then acquire tacit knowledge and threshold concepts in industry, either as an intern or junior employee. This is not optimal for industry because they are not receiving

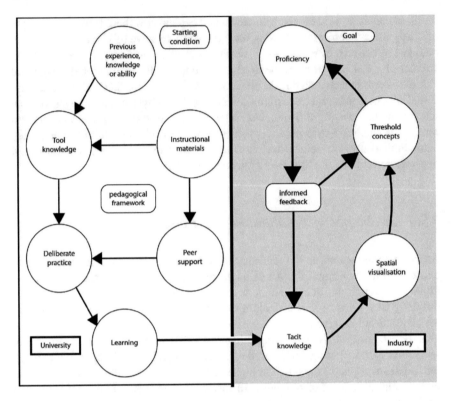

Fig. 7.2 Learning and proficiency development at university and industry

fully trained employees. It is also disadvantageous for students, who are spending more time than necessary on their education because it attempts to broadly cover subjects of interest while avoiding threshold concepts that would be useful in finding employment. A solution to this may be to put serious research effort into developing courses that focus entirely on threshold concepts, abstracted in such a way that they are easier to absorb, without diluting their efficacy.

7.6 Limitations and Future Research

The present study was designed to be exploratory. This does not inhibit the interpretation of collected data, but does prevent following up on some research opportunities. The present study design did not provide for following up on such things as: testing educational interventions designed to teach threshold concepts, follow-up research to test threshold concepts identified in this investigation, the development of new spatial visualisation tests to investigate the forms of spatial visualisation discovered here, and development of spatial visualisation training that incorporates the knowledge developed in this study.

A concern for this study was whether students would cross a skill threshold to proficiency, how it would happen if they did and when it would occur. The purpose of investigating these questions was to identify factors important to the development of proficiency. As an initial attempt to discover this information, this investigation did not allow for more detailed probing of whatever might be found. In this case, now that it is known that intersection and blend visualisation are threshold concepts for students and that their transition to proficient performance turned on overcoming them, a new study could be designed to focus on these aspects of the learning process. Such a study could incorporate new spatial visualisation tests designed for the purpose, take place in a new course or a research environment, to explore the transition to proficiency in greater depth.

The use of student participants as the primary frame of reference was useful because it provided a view of the earliest stages of the learning process for digital artists, but it did not allow for a comparison of, for instance, how professionals learn to overcome new problem types as technology changes or new problems are discovered. It would be useful to know if the findings of this study would be reflected in a study of the learning styles of professionals in a work environment. To compare proficiency and expertise, it would be useful to have expert and student participants engaged in the same or similar tasks to see what differences exist in their approach. Such a study might also allow for some insight on the subject of individual differences if any of the student participants outperformed expert performers. Based on many examples in the literature, it is not unlikely this would happen, and that would justify focussing the study on individual trait differences between participants.

The methodology used for this study did not allow any inferences to be drawn regarding how MD2 class performance might affect later performance in other classes or overall academic performance. This does not affect the findings of this study, which are focussed on proficiency. However, it would be useful to conduct a separate study that tries to determine the effect of visualisation skills on general academic performance by art students.

The impact of drawing skill on NURBS performance was interesting because the two students with the most drawing experience also had no prior CG experience but both were the strongest performers in their classes. This suggested the possibility of a link to drawing skill. The subject was addressed here, but only one student (Janet) provided an explanation that was relevant to the study. She said that she had studied industrial drawing, a type of drawing that mimics the design process of working with NURBS tools. It would be interesting to conduct a study where students are first taught industrial drawing and then NURBS modelling to see if that improves results. As it is, there is not enough data to make a claim that it definitely has this effect, though it is a reasonable explanation.

Maarten said that the choice of reference he used for his vehicle project was a decision that had strategic importance to the quality of the end product, and was a lesson that stayed with him. He felt that on its own, his knowledge of the importance of selecting the right reference for a job was a valuable outcome of the project and that it was not 'NURBS-related' even if it was NURBS-derived because it was generically useful to other problems he faced in the game development industry. This could be a threshold concept as well, though it was not a focus of this study, and would be worth investigating later in future research.

The three types of visualisation discussed in this chapter, projection, intersection and blend, are all pertinent to NURBS modelling. However, the degree to which existing tests measure these abilities is suspect. The PVRT likely overlaps significantly with projection visualisation, but it is also possible that none of the tests reviewed here capture either intersection or blend visualisation. The first step of new research would be to identify the tests most likely to correlate with NURBS performance and then to find out if they do. If not, new tests could be made that are custom designed to capture intersection and blend visualisation. If these are successful, then broader testing can take place to determine whether they correlate to skills in other domains.

The avenue suggested by this research is to begin with shape deformation as the principal visualisation factor in the tests. Unlike the McLeay and Piggins' (1996) knot topology test, shape deformations should require changes of scale in addition to shape, both of which are allowed and sometimes required by NURBS modelling.

Overall, the research conducted for this study indicates the importance of spatial visualisation to digital artists, but more research would be needed to design optimal methods for teaching spatial visualisation to students.

In the discussion chapter (p. 155), the link between spatial visualisation and the development of proficiency in NURBS modelling was strongly demonstrated. The three types of spatial visualisation discovered during the study modify our understanding of spatial visualisation as it relates to the literature of visualisation and possibly its application to other domains. These spatial visualisation types have demonstrated utility in domains other than NURBS modelling, such as drawing and improved adaptability to new technology. These findings lead to the conclusion that observation and spatial visualisation are more important than tool knowledge to the development of proficiency in this domain.

The previous chapter ends with the practical implications of the findings discussed in chapters four and five, particularly as they apply to the way computer graphics are taught to digital art students. If observation and visualisation are more important than software knowledge, schools that specialise in educating CG artists may want to provide students with classes that are designed to improve observation and visualisation. These classes could, by focussing narrowly on those subjects, prepare students for the projects that exploit those abilities. What form these classes take would have to be studied, but one option would be to introduce foundation level art classes, such as drawing, painting and sculpting classes, prior to introducing students to CAD software. This would have the effect of helping students develop crucial observation and visualisation skills on projects that are unencumbered by technology and that can be more quickly executed. This allows more iterations in the same amount of time and overall better preparedness for interacting with technology later, and at a level more appropriate to the goal of meeting an industry standard.

In addition to addressing the practical concerns that initially motivated this study, the results also provided some knowledge on the subjects of proficiency, expertise and threshold concepts. It has shown that proficiency and expertise can depend on a threshold concept or ability rather than domain knowledge. Indeed, the domain knowledge in the case of NURBS modelling appeared to be of scant importance relative to the value of spatial visualisation. The implication of this is that definitions of expertise that rely on broad knowledge will not apply to all domains of practice, such as NURBS modelling.

This research generally supports the view that expertise is a matter of efficient cognitive processes that can navigate problem space more effectively than others. This clearly leads to the acquisition of knowledge as well, and in so doing creates an opportunity to conflate expertise with knowledge among researchers who study expertise.

7.6.1   Mental Rotation Tests Unsuitable for Testing Intersection and Blend Visualisation

Beginning in the 1990s, design, engineering and animation domains have relied more heavily on software than traditional tools. This has created the possibility that practitioners in these domains improve their spatial ability as an incidental side effect of using CAD-related software. Many design-related software applications, even 2D applications like Photoshop, now allow users to view their designs in 3D, which may acclimatize them to visualizing objects in space. To do this, the software first defines a 3D environment into which 3D objects may be placed. To view the objects, users rotate a virtual 'camera' that allows the objects to be viewed from multiple angles. Working in any 3D software requires frequent adjustment of virtual cameras, an act that is similar to the mental rotation task presented in the PVRT and other spatial visualisation tests. Several studies report that this type of activity trains spatial skill as measured by mental rotation tests (Basham 2008; Feng et al. 2007; Kurtulus and Uygan 2010). The same effect has been observed among people who play video games, hence scores on mental rotation tests improve after playing 3D video games (Dorval 1986; Terlicki and Newcombe 2005).

If students are trained by their use of 3D software to perform mental rotations of virtual 3D objects, problems presented on mental rotation tests would no longer be novel. This is relevant to the present study because the validity of mental rotation tests is mediated by experience (Bodner and Guay 1997; Keehner et al. 2004). The more experience in a domain a person has, the more routine the problems are and the less reliable the test becomes. If this is applied to digital art, it could be that mental rotation is trained by repeated usage of 3D CAD-related software, causing all students to have an above-average mental rotation ability compared to people who do not regularly use such software. This is supported by the comparison made in this study between IGAD median PVRT scores and the median PVRT scores of students in multiple domains at Purdue University. To a statistically significant degree, IGAD visual art students scored higher than students in other domains. If mental rotation is not novel, this would negate the test's capacity to predict performance on novel spatial visualisation tasks. This leads to the following conclusions: (1) strong mental rotation ability is not a valid measure of visualisation types such as intersection and blend visualisation and (2) video game playing and CAD use improve mental rotation ability to the extent that mental rotation test results mask actual ability in other types of spatial visualisation and problem-solving.

Data from this study show that mental rotation is not a valid indicator of spatial visualisation ability in NURBS modelling. This conclusion is based on the following: (1) lack of correlation between PVRT tests and MD2 performance, (2) student reports and observations made during the MD2 class identifying intersection and blend visualisation as threshold concepts, (3) the plausibility of the explanation that correlation of PVRT results and MD1 grades is because polygon modelling is more similar to mental rotation than MD2, which is not as dependent on mental rotation.

Because mental rotation tests are ineffective at measuring spatial visualisation skills relevant to digital artists, an important contribution to the development of proficiency among digital artists may be overlooked by researchers who rely on those tests. Namely, that the relationship of visualisation to proficiency development would be misunderstood, causing a Type II error. Data from this study prove that intersection and blend visualisation are critical to the development of proficiency among student participants. This is the most challenging type of problem faced by students in this study, likely for the same reason that deformation problems in general are more difficult than isomorphs that do not require deformation (Clément and Richard 1997; Kotovsky and Simon 1990; McLeay and Piggins 1996). Findings from this research support the proposition that visualisation of surface deformation or topological awareness testing deserves a place alongside mental rotation tests as part of the spatial ability testing toolkit.

7.6.2 The Influence of Threshold Concepts on the Development of Proficiency

A problem encountered in the literature of proficiency and expertise is the small number of prospective studies. At least one researcher has proposed prospective longitudinal studies that would seek to identify significant features of the development of expertise as they happen (Ericsson and Williams 2007). The presumption that the development of expertise cannot be studied prospectively without great expense due to the amount of time thought to be required has led to inexact representations of factors that lead from a state of 'non-expert' to 'expert' or 'non-proficient' to 'proficient' status among study participants.

Retrospective study designs suffer from obfuscating any potential transition moments, making it difficult or impossible to determine whether threshold concepts play a role in the development of proficiency or expertise (Hambrick et al. 2014). Instead, development models are based on retrospectively identifying different levels of performance. Once identified, a theory is developed to explain how learners transitioned between performance levels, but the level of detail is coarse. This allows for greater generalisability but simultaneously blurs the boundaries between levels of performance, effectively making it impossible to observe any sudden changes such as might be expected if threshold concepts had played a role.

This research was designed to observe the transition from novice to proficient status by observing novices as they learned how to perform NURBS modelling tasks. Of the 20 student study participants, 8 succeeded in accomplishing this, and in doing so, provided an opportunity to determine when and how they crossed the proficiency threshold. More research with similar methodologies may allow for the identification of threshold concepts and a better understanding of the constituent elements of proficiency and expertise.

7.7 Conclusion

This study began with the recognition of a problem among visual art students at the IGAD academy of the NHTV university of applied sciences. The students who graduated were very good, but only a small number of students were graduating. At the time, the school hoped to deal with the problem by modifying their intake procedure, in the hopes that better students would be selected and that those students would improve the number of graduating students. This study was just one of many efforts to better understand the problem faced by the school. Here, I studied how students learned to overcome the most difficult problems faced by them in the visual art programme. Other attempts to deal with the problem involved changes to curriculum, grading and feedback methods and class structure.

As I write this, visual art students at IGAD are graduating in larger numbers than ever before, and the programme itself has changed considerably. However, although performance in NURBS modelling did improve somewhat year over year since this study began, the project remained extremely difficult for students and it was finally dropped from the curriculum in the 2015–2016 academic year. At the same time, many other 'difficult' classes were dropped and replaced with project-based learning. It is too early to know if this strategy will ultimately prove successful, but the results of this study indicate that students should be challenged if they are to learn about and overcome the threshold concepts valued in industry.

When hiring artists, one of the industry participants, Bas, said he was looking for 'artists that are pro-active in finding their own solutions to the problems that get presented to them, not necessarily always trying to get to do things the same way because every problem is different'. Stefano echoed this when he said he thought it was important to teach NURBS to students, because artists who were comfortable with NURBS were more flexible when it came to adopting new technology as it was introduced.

The profession of a digital artist can be summed up as a combination of observation skills, problem-solving and in both cases, challenge. Threshold concepts are challenging by definition, and it is useful to know what they are and where they are found so that students can be assisted in their attempts to overcome them. However, threshold concepts, and the challenges they present, should not be avoided because it is precisely the ability to overcome challenges that allows a student to become proficient.

References

Ackerman PL (2014a) Nonsense, common sense, and science of expert performance: talent and individual differences. Intelligence 45:6–17. https://doi.org/10.1016/j.intell.2013.04.009

Ackerman PL (2014b) Facts are stubborn things. Intelligence 45:104–106. https://doi.org/10.1016/j.intell.2014.01.002

Alexander PA (2003) The development of expertise: the journey from acclimation to proficiency. Educ Res 32(8):10–14

Arici S, Aslan-Tutak F (2013) The effect of origami-based instruction on spatial visualization, geometry achievement, and geometric reasoning. Int J Sci Mathe Educ 13(1):95–102. https://doi.org/10.1007/s10763-013-9487-8

Baillie C, Bowden JA, Meyer JHF (2013) Threshold capabilities: threshold concepts and knowledge capability linked through variation theory. High Educ 65(2):227–246. https://doi.org/10.1007/s10734-012-9540-5

Barradell S (2013) The identification of threshold concepts: a review of theoretical complexities and methodological challenges. High Educ 65(2):265–276. https://doi.org/10.1007/s10734-012-9542-3

Basham KLAK, Joe W (2008) The effects of 3-dimensional CADD modeling on the development of the spatial ability of technology education students. J Technol Educ 20(1):16

Bodner GM, Guay RB (1997) The purdue visualization of rotations test. The Chemical Educator 2(4):1–14

Bradley JH, Paul R, Seeman E (2006) Analyzing the structure of expert knowledge. Inf Manag 43(1):77–91

Bransford JD, Schwartz DL (1999) Rethinking transfer: a simple proposal with multiple implications. Rev Res Educ 24(1):61–100

Clément E, Richard J-F (1997) Knowledge of domain effects in problem representation: the case of Tower of Hanoi Isomorphs. Think Reason 3(2):133–157

Dorval M, Pépin M (1986) Effect of playing a video game on a measure of spatial visualization. Perceptual Motor Skills 62(1):159–162. https://doi.org/10.2466/pms.1986.62.1.159

Epstein SL (1995) Learning in the Right Places. J Learn Sci 4(3):281–319

Ericsson KA (2006) Protocol analysis and expert thought: concurrent verbalizations of thinking during experts' performance on representative tasks. In: Ericsson KA (ed) Cambridge handbook of expertise and expert performance. Cambridge University Press, Cambridge, UK, pp 223–242

Ericsson KA (2014) Why expert performance is special and cannot be extrapolated from studies of performance in the general population: a response to criticisms. Intelligence 45(1):81–103. https://doi.org/10.1016/j.intell.2013.12.001

Ericsson KA, Williams AM (2007) Capturing naturally occurring superior performance in the laboratory: translational research on expert performance. J Exp Psychol Appl 13(3):115–123

Feng J, Spence I, Pratt J (2007) Playing an action video game reduces gender differences in spatial cognition. Psychol Sci 18(10):850–855

Gao K, Park H, Rockwood A, Sowar D (2006). Attribute based interfaces for geometric modeling. Paper presented at the Sandbox Symposium 2006, Boston, Massachusetts

Hambrick DZ, Altmann EM, Oswald FL, Meinz EJ, Gobet F, Campitelli G (2014) Accounting for expert performance: the devil is in the details. Intelligence 45:112–114. https://doi.org/10.1016/j.intell.2014.01.007

IGDA (2008) IGDA Curriculum Framework. Retrieved from https://c.ymcdn.com/sites/www.igda.org/resource/collection/0DBC56DC-B7CB-4140-BF3A-22A9E92EC63A/igda_curriculum_framework_2008.pdf

Ip B (2012) Fitting the needs of an industry: an examination of games design, development, and art courses in the UK. ACM Trans Comput Educ 12(2):1–35

Keehner MM, Tendick F, Meng MV, Anwar HP, Hegarty M, Stoller ML, Quan-Yang D (2004) Spatial ability, experience, and skill in laparoscopic surgery. Am J Surgery 188(1):71–75

Kotovsky K, Simon HA (1990) What makes some problems really hard: explorations in the problem space of difficulty. Cogn Psychol 22(2):143–183

Kurtulus A, Uygan C (2010) The effects of Google Sketchup based geometry activities and projects on spatial visualization ability of student mathematics teachers. Procedia Soc Behav Sci 9:384–389. https://doi.org/10.1016/j.sbspro.2010.12.169

Livingstone I, Hope A (2011) Next generation transforming the UK into the world's leading talent hub for the video games and visual effects industries. Retrieved from http://www.nesta.org.uk/sites/default/files/next_gen.pdf

McCracken CR (2006) Issues in computer graphics education. Paper presented at the ACM SIGGRAPH 2006 Educators Program—International Conference on Computer Graphics and Interactive Techniques, Boston

McLeay H, Piggins D (1996) The Mental manipulation of 2-D representations of knots as deformable structures. Educ Stud Mathe 30(4):399–414

Meyer Jan H F, Land R (2003) Threshold concepts and troublesome Knowledge: linkages to ways of thinking and practising within the disciplines. In: Rust C (ed) Improving student learning—ten years on. Oxford, Oxford

Okagaki L, Frensch PA (1994) Effects of video game playing on measures of spatial performance: gender effects in late adolescence. J Appl Dev Psychol 15(1):33–58

Prieto G, Velasco AD (2010) Does spatial visualization ability improve after studying technical drawing? QualQuant 44(5):1015–1024

Rosalie SM, Müller S (2013) Expertise facilitates the transfer of anticipation skill across domains. Q J Exp Psychol 67(2):319–334. https://doi.org/10.1080/17470218.2013.807856

Samsudin KR, Hanif Ahmad, Samad Abd (2011) Training in mental rotation and spatial visualization and its impact on orthographic drawing performance. Educ Technol Soc 14(1):8

Simonton DK (2012) Foresight, insight, oversight, and hindsight in scientific discovery: how sighted were galileo's telescopic sightings? Psychol Aesthetics Creativity Arts 6(3):243–254. https://doi.org/10.1037/a0027058243

Sternberg RJ (1998) Abilities are forms of developing expertise. Educ Res 27(3):11–20

Terlicki MS, Newcombe NS (2005) How important is the digital divide? The relation of computer and videogame usage to gender differences in mental rotation ability. Sex Roles 53(5):433–441

Titus S, Horsman E (2009) Characterizing and improving spatial visualization skills. J Geosci Educ 57(4):242–254

Wai J (2014) What does it mean to be an expert? Intelligence 45:122–123. https://doi.org/10.1016/j.intell.2014.02.001

Chapter 8
Appendices

8.1 Appendix 1: Intake Assessment Drawings

8.1.1 Vehicle

Figures 8.1, 8.2, 8.3 and 8.4.

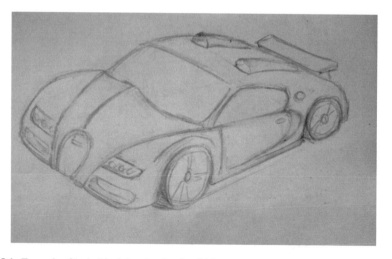

Fig. 8.1 Example of 'primitive' drawing level, vehicle

© Springer Nature Switzerland AG 2018
A. Paquette, *Spatial Visualization and Professional Competence*,
https://doi.org/10.1007/978-3-319-91289-9_8

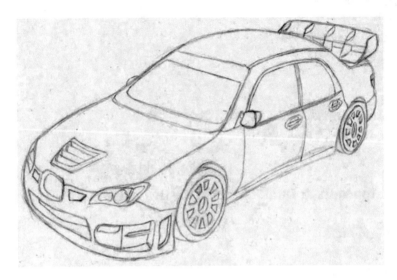

Fig. 8.2 Example of 'naïve' drawing level, vehicle

Fig. 8.3 Example of 'observed' drawing level, vehicle

Fig. 8.4 Example of 'excellent' drawing level, vehicle

8.1.2 Landscape

Figures 8.5, 8.6, 8.7 and 8.8.

8.2 Appendix 2: NURBS Project Instructions

MD2 Project: NURBS Automobile
Lecturers: Andrew Paquette and Luuk (pseudonym)
Project type: Homework and workshop
Time limit: Seven class periods + Study week + Exam week
Deadline: Friday of Exam week, 17:00

Fig. 8.5 Example of 'primitive' drawing level, landscape

Fig. 8.6 Example of 'naïve' drawing level, landscape

Grading: This project will be graded on a 0–10-point scale. A grade of 0 will be awarded if the project is not handed in on time. A grade of 6 or above is a passing grade. Any student receiving a grade below 6 must make an appointment with his or her mentor to discuss this class. A retake opportunity can be looked at as a deadline extension, so please do not ask for an extension.

Fig. 8.7 Example of 'observed' drawing level, landscape

Fig. 8.8 Example of 'excellent' drawing level, landscape

Percentage of final grade: 100%
Instructions:

1. Select your subject; this should have been done in Drawing Skills class
2. Create or acquire reference
3. Build NURBS model from reference

   a. Automobile may be of any kind, provided it is not built out of straight lines, such as a Mazda TR7, or has no blend curves, such as most cars built before 1980.
      i. Amount of detail will be a factor in grading. A perfect but low detail object will not be able to achieve a score of 8 or above.
      ii. Position the vehicle so that it is facing forward in positive Z and the centre of the front axle is at the global origin.

4. Convert body to polygons

   a. NOTE: For grading purposes, only the body is required. Wheels, interior and any other extras do not have to be converted to polys.
      i. If the full model is converted to polys, it may be counted towards extra credit if the NURBS model is complete. If the NURBS model is incomplete, no extra credit will be awarded for extra work on the poly conversion.

5. Optimise the polygonal model, body only

   a. Polygon limit.
      i. 3500 triangles.

6. Check model for errors against both polygon and NURBS checklists and fix all errors.
7. Deliver an archived file (RAR or .zip format) containing the following:

   a. Two orthographic reference images, jpg format, no bigger than 800 × 600
   b. Tape model
   c. NURBS model
   d. Polygon model

Criteria:
The finished model should resemble reference images closely, be free of obvious errors, be technically sound and be in agreement with optimisation goals.
Rough grading guide*
*Grades may vary, but this should give you a rough idea what to expect. Keep in mind that hand-in deductions will affect your grade strongly. This project will be used in at least two later classes.

0 = Not turned in
1 = Grossly incomplete
2 = Incomplete/technical errors irrelevant
4 = Incomplete/likeness irrelevant
5 = Complete/weak likeness, Incomplete/good likeness
6 = Low/average academic
7 = Good academic
8 = Low/average professional
9 = Good professional
10 = Excellent professional

8.3 Appendix 3: Questionnaire Questions

Note: answers that were not selected by any respondents are ignored

(1) Study participant ID number
(2) What is your age?

    a. 17
    b. 18–19
    c. 20–21
    d. 22–25

(3) What is your gender?

    a. Male
    b. Female

(4) Are you an international student?

    a. Yes
    b. No

(5) How long is your morning commute to school?

    a. 30 min or less
    b. 31–45 min
    c. 46–60 min
    d. 61–90 min
    e. 91–120 min

(6) What type of school did you attend prior to IGAD?

    a. MBO
    b. HAVO
    c. HBO
    d. VWO/Gymnasium

(7) What type of residence do you live in?

    a. At home
    b. Independent, alone
    c. Independent, roommates
    d. Independent, student housing

(8) Do you have a part-time job?

    a. No
    b. Yes

(9) How much prior experience with 3D did you have prior to enrolling at IGAD?

    a. None
    b. Assessment project was my first 3D project
    c. Less than 3 months
    d. 6 months to a year
    e. 2-3 years
    f. More than 3 years

(10) How much prior experience with traditional art did you have prior to enrolling at IGAD?

    a. None
    b. Less than 6 months
    c. 6 months to a year
    d. 1–2 years
    e. 4 years or more

(11) What type of traditional art skills had you practised prior to enrolling at IGAD?

    a. Drawing from life—landscapes
    b. Drawing from life—people
    c. Drawing from life—objects
    d. Drawing without reference—fan art
    e. Drawing without reference—fantasy
    f. Drawing in a software application
    g. Painting in a software application
    h. Painting—watercolour
    i. Painting—oil or acrylic
    j. Photography
    k. Technical drawing
    l. Architectural rendering
    m. None
    n. Other

(12) Did the MD2 class enhance your problem-solving skills? (Likert scale)

    a. $1 =$ No
    b. $5 =$ Yes, very much

(13) Did the MD2 class challenge you to solve problems on your own? (Likert scale)

    a. $1 =$ No
    b. $5 =$ Yes, very much

 14) Did you feel adequately supported by your lecturers and study materials during this class? (Likert scale)

    a. $1 =$ No, not at all
    b. $5 =$ Yes, very much

(15) Were your mental visualisation skills challenged during MD2? (Likert scale)

    a. $1 =$ No, not at all
    b. $5 =$ Yes, very much

(16) Are you satisfied with your vehicle project? (Likert scale)

    a. $1 =$ No, not at all
    b. $5 =$ Yes, very much

(17) Do you feel more confident in your modelling skills now than when you started the MD2 project? (Likert scale)

    a. $1 =$ No, not at all
    b. $5 =$ Yes, very much

(18) How would you rate your skill as a modeller? (Likert scale)

    a. $1 =$ Novice
    b. $5 =$ Expert

(19) If you had previous 3D experience before IGAD, do you feel it made the MD2 project easier to complete? (Likert scale)

    a. $1 =$ No, it made the project more difficult
    b. $5 =$ Yes, it made the project much easier

(20) Did you have difficulty visualising the original shapes of parts before trimming? (Likert scale)

    a. $1 =$ No
    b. $5 =$ Yes

(21) How do you rate your understanding of tangency and curvature continuity? (Likert scale)

    a.   1 = Poor
    b.   5 = Strong

(22) How did you feel about working with NURBS at the beginning of MD2? (Likert scale)

    a.   1 = Uncomfortable
    b.   5 = Comfortable

(23) How do you feel about working with NURBS now? (Likert scale)

    a.   1 = Uncomfortable
    b.   5 = Comfortable

(24) How do you rate the usefulness of the MD2 class? (Likert scale)

    a.   1 = Not useful
    b.   5 = Very useful

(25) What did you like the least about MD2? (open question)
(26) What did you like the most about MD2? (open question)
(27) Are there any MD2-related subjects you would like to address during the interview? (open question)

8.4   Appendix 4: NURBS Vision

8.4.1   Maike

'Well, I noticed that I actually look at cars and think of how to make NURBS patches out of them.'

    'Because I also had a look at some cars that friends drew for drawing skills class and because they asked me for feedback if their car looks correct, I immediately imagined the NURBS planes that were put here and there and everything, and that also helps for drawing already. Oh, yes, it does.'

8.4.2   Sebastian

'Well, this morning I walked over the street and looked at all the cars and I literally saw fillets in between some of the things.'

8.4.3 Wietse

'I had a hard time…We call it NURBS vision. Getting NURBS vision, as in how would something like that consist of shapes and how would I cut this out of that, and I had a really hard time getting used to that. It actually took me quite a while and [name deleted] had to help me, as in I had my rim, and he was like: Just imagine just a plain surface here, and imagine something else, a bread knife cutting it through like this, and how would it look if you did it like that. So, it took me quite a while to get used to seeing it like that.'

8.4.4 Pim

'I basically got a lot of respect for shapes around me because even if I look at a chair I'm now looking at how was that really built not in the polygon way like, you know, this in there, etc. but more like if I really go for it that works how would I really, and yes, that's what I really got out of it.'

8.4.5 Roel

'It's been hell of a fun ride to me and I feel confident in myself that I can fix most of the cars I see driving around in the street, and I turn them into patches. As you said, I would never have believed you if I didn't have this class, but it's actually true, you see patches.'

8.4.6 Timothy

Timothy: I see everything in NURBS now.

AP: So, let me ask you, is this something that's, kind of, automatic when you look at shapes, you just automatically start seeing it in patches or is it something you have to, kind of, mentally turn on?

Timothy: Sometimes it's automatic.

AP: Did you…do you remember when this happened the first time?

Timothy: Yes. Walking down the street and seeing cars.

AP: Okay. And how did…did you, like, make a mental note to yourself, oh my gosh, I'm looking at things in NURBS now?
Timothy: Yes.

8.4.7   Bart

Bart: A friend of mine, always when I walk to the, to the train station, we just constantly see NURBS in everything, just look at, we look at cars and he just, you know, he only says, just from there's a hard edge, that's a NURBS, that's… very annoying sometimes.

AP: So, let me get this straight, so is it, is it true that you are now involuntarily conducting shape analysis of everything you see?

Bart: Yes.

AP: Okay, and you do find that annoying?

Bart: Sometimes, I do find it annoying, yes.

8.4.8   Koen

AP: One of the other guys I was talking to said that after he felt like he suddenly understood NURBS, when he was walking around at the train station for instance, he is automatically analysing every shape he sees, and he has a pretty good idea of how things break down, but before that he wasn't doing that.

Koen: I have the exact same thing.

AP: So, if I tell you to look at that horse's head over there and imagine that it's patches, it pretty much automatically happens?

Koen: Well, not specifically with those kind of forms, but whenever I see a car yes, I think of this project.

AP: So that's a concrete difference, before and after that moment in the seventh week sometime?
Koen: Yes.

8.4.9   Ward

Ward: …when you're walking down the street and you're seeing a car coming by, and at some point, I couldn't help myself from thinking how to make that particular part of the car.

AP: Okay. So, when you're walking down the street now and you look at cars, you sometimes will think, okay, this is…

Ward: Yes, sometimes I do that and I can't…yes.

AP: Can't turn it off?

Ward: No, I can't turn it off. It's really hard and especially when I see a car that, kind of, looks like mine, I really start to think from a… how would I build that if I had to do that particular car.

8.4.10   Janet

Janet: …I was quite stressed out because of the thinking process. I just couldn't stop thinking of it. And actually, I see everything around me is kind of made of NURBS; all the shampoo bottles, everything. I just can't get it out of my mind. All the cars I see in the street, I just automatically analyse it; how can I cut it, how can I blend it, yes.

AP: Is this still happening, or was it just then?

Janet: No, now it has stopped. But yes, in Block C, the whole Block C.

8.4.11   Martin

Martin: …always when I'm walking towards school I always see cars and that is my car, and I see all my patches again.

AP: Okay, so how long did it take for that effect to wear off? Or did it wear off?

Martin: No, it did not wear off.

AP: So, you still do that?

Martin: Yes.

AP: You still break things down visually? And is it like an automatic thing you can't help it?

Martin: Yes, I can't stop it.

8.5   Appendix 5: Tower of Hanoi Isomorphs (Kotovsky et al. 1985)

8.5.1   A Monster Move Problem

Three five-handed extra-terrestrial monsters were holding three crystal globes. Because of the quantum-mechanical peculiarities of their neighbourhood. Both monsters and globes come in exactly three sizes with no others permitted, small, medium and large. The small monster was holding the large globe; the medium-sized monster was holding the small globe, and the large monster was holding the medium-sized globe. Since this situation offended their keenly developed sense of symmetry, they proceeded to transfer globes from one monster to another so that each monster would have a globe proportionate to its own size.

Monster etiquette complicated the solution of the problem since 11 requires that:

1.   Only one globe may be transferred at a time;
2.   If a monster IS holding two globes, only the larger of the two may be transferred; and,
3.   A globe may not be transferred to a monster who IS holding a larger globe.

By what sequence of transfers could the monsters have solved this problem?

Your first goal should be to take care of the small monster (i.e., to get him the right sized globe). This appeared in the hint condition only.

8.5.2   A Monster Change Problem

Three five-handed extra-terrestrial monsters were holding three crystal globes. Because of the quantum-mechanical peculiarities of their neighbourhood. Both monsters and globes come in exactly three sizes with no others permuted, small, medium and large. The small monster was holding the medium-sized globe, the medium-wed monster was holding the large globe; and the large monster was holding the small globe. Since this situation offended their keenly developed sense of symmetry, they proceeded to shrink and expand the globes so that each monster would have a globe proportionate to its own size.

Monster etiquette complicated the solution of the problem since it requires that:

1.   Only one globe may be changed at a time;
2.   If two globes have the same size, only the globe held by the larger monster may be changed; and
3.   A globe may not be changed to the same size as the globe of a larger monster.

By what sequence of changes could the monsters have solved this problem?

Your first goal should be to take care of the small monster (i.e., to get his globe to the right size.) This appeared in the hint condition only.

Reference

Kotovsky K, Hayes JR, Simon HA (1985) Why are some problems hard? Evidence from Tower of Hanoi. Cogn Psychol 17(2):248–294

Bibliography

British Educational Research Association (2011) Ethical guidelines for education research. Retrieved from http://www.bbk.ac.uk/sshp/research/sshp-ethics-committee-and-procedures/BERA-Ethical-Guidelines-2011.pdf

Printed in the United States
By Bookmasters